The Daily Telegraph
THIRD BOOK OF OBITUARIES

'The wondrous Hugh Massingberd ... As obituaries editor of *The Daily Telegraph* from 1986 to 1994 he did two important things: he encouraged vivid, sometimes outrageous pen-portraits rather than pious lists of achievements, and included delightful oddities who would never have found a place in the stuffy columns of former years.'
Jonathan Cecil, *The Spectator*

The Daily Telegraph
THIRD BOOK OF
OBITUARIES

Entertainers

Edited by
HUGH MASSINGBERD

PAN BOOKS

For Andrew
who had a go
and Eric
who saw them all

First published 1997 by Macmillan

This edition published 1998 by Pan Books
an imprint of Macmillan Publishers Ltd
25 Eccleston Place, London SW1W 9NF
and Basingstoke

Associated companies throughout the world

ISBN 0 330 36775 7

1 3 5 7 9 8 6 4 2

A CIP catalogue record for this book is available from
the British Library.

Typeset by SetSystems Ltd, Saffron Walden, Essex
Printed and bound in Great Britain by
Mackays of Chatham plc, Chatham, Kent

INTRODUCTION

ON REREADING the introductions to the two previous volumes in this trilogy of biographical short stories – *The Daily Telegraph Book of Obituaries: A Celebration of Eccentric Lives* and *The Daily Telegraph Second Book of Obituaries: Heroes and Adventurers* – I was mildly surprised to see that in both cases I had cited Damascene-style experiences in theatres as key inspirations for the approach I attempted as Obituaries Editor of the *Telegraph* from 1986 to 1994. Having thus already inadvertently touched on my fascination for "showbiz", I need hardly apologise for devoting this third volume to *Entertainers*.

In truth, having now abandoned any absurd pretensions as a "serious' commentator on the weightier events of the day, I am quite prepared to confess to a long-held obsession with the lower-brow elements of the entertainment industry. As an adolescent loitering by stage-doors or glued to the television screen for days (and nights) on end, I was admonished that such activity could only be adjudged an appalling waste of time. Yet, as it turned out, the material I had once eagerly tabulated in the flickering light – such as cast-lists of ostensibly "obscure" performers – came back to me vividly when I found myself, say, with a deadline of half an hour in which to cobble together an "obit" of a showiz figure whose face tended to be more familiar to the readers than his name. One of the joys of the job was a sense of vindication that the long years spent as a "couch potato" had not been wasted after all; far from being "useless information" such recondite knowledge suddenly came in remarkably useful.

Introduction

When I arrived at the obits desk of the *Telegraph*, the stock of showbiz material on file, such as it was, tended to concentrate on antediluvian performances in often long-since-demolished theatres. Yellowing galley proofs, which crumbled to the touch, faithfully recorded the estimation by the *Telegraph*'s "dramatic critic", the late, great W. A. Darlington, of a thespian's steady progress through classic parts at Stratford and the Old Vic. Then, in the last paragraph, one might, if one was lucky, come across a note to the effect that the player in question had also, apparently, appeared on the "kinematograph screen, and even on the television machine".

While yielding to few — other than Darlington's happily still extant deputy, Eric Shorter (long a favourite critic of mine) — in my love of the theatre, I was determined that the new obits column of the *Telegraph* would also reflect the less rarefied manifestations of what pompous sociologists call "popular culture". Part of the fun — indeed the defining element of the column's tone — was to contrast the often crass, crude and vulgar content with a slightly po-faced, formal "obit" style. Like a lugubrious Eeyorish comedian, we tried to play it deadpan. While eschewing any hint of patronage or editorialising, we sought to convey an objective non-partisan, "recording angel" approach.

On going through the mass of candidates for this personal selection, though, I couldn't help noticing the essential sympathy shining through the material. In many cases the nostalgia of the middle-aged telly addict, albeit tinged with affectionate irony, is the predominant mood — as in the obituaries for such "Soap" stalwarts as Margot Bryant ("Minnie Caldwell") and Lynne Carol ("Martha Longhurst") of *Coronation Street*, Ronald Allen (the debonair "David Hunter") of *Crossroads* and Arthur Pentelow (the gruff publican "Henry Wilks") of *Emmerdale Farm*. Popular programmes like *Minder* and *On the Buses* are lovingly hymned in the obits of Peter Childs (Detective Sergeant Ronnie Rycott, with his longing to nail "Arfur-bloody-*Daley*") and Michael Robbins (poor Olive's morose husband, "Arfur") respectively.

Partly inspired by my old school contemporary, Andrew Barrow (who went on the boards himself as a stand-up comedian and with whom I once memorably invaded the Palladium dressing-room of the great Ken Dodd), I was equally keen that comics should be given suitable send-offs. Unfortunately, as this selection reminds us, they made their exits at a depressingly brisk rate: Al Read, Harry Worth, Max Wall, Richard "Stinker" Murdoch, Cardew "the Cad" Robinson, Frankie Howerd, Benny Hill and Les Dawson – of whom, as Arthur Marshall said, "We could do with more like him."

Then there were the *Carry On* stars, such as the wonderfully epicene Kenneth ("Infamy, infamy! They've all got it *in-for-me*") Williams and Charles ("It fairly whistles up the Pass") Hawtrey. In this selection I have tended to leave out the obvious film stars – with the odd exception, such as the underrated Trevor Howard, who, as Robert Mitchum remarked, "you'll never catch acting" – and to celebrate instead a gallery of much-loved British character actors. These include Bill Fraser ("What I do is play stuffy, pot-bellied, pompous old sods. Thank God England is full of them"), Irene Handl, Roy Kinnear, Terry-Thomas, Gordon Jackson, Raymond Huntley, Wilfrid Hyde White, Joan Sanderson, Denholm Elliott and the ubiquitous "other rank", Victor Maddern – never to be forgotten for fluffing his lines in *Dixon of Dock Green*.

Given the words, "It's down at Dock Green nick", the redoubtable supporting player came out with: "It's down at Dick Green Dock." Trying to correct himself he then said: "It's down at Dock Green Dick." Finally, the exasperated Maddern cried out: "Who writes these bloody scripts? Can't I just say 'down at the nick'? F*** Dock Green!"

Connoisseurs of theatrical "camp" may prefer the more sophisticated wit of such *monstres sacrés* as Hermione Gingold ("But, my dear, you simply must come. It's Corset Week at Swan & Edgar"), "Bea" Lillie, Coral Browne and "Peggy" Ramsay, the legendary theatrical agent who is said to have remarked about *Lawrence of Arabia* to Robert Bolt on the telephone: "Lovely camels, dear. Bye-ee." Theatre buffs, too, find a place in the persons of Joe Mitchenson and Dr Eric Jones-Evans, the Irving fan who was "essentially modest – and with reason – about his own powers as a player".

Politically, or rather sexually, correct critics counting up the number of entries for women in the book may be somewhat confused by the factor of female impersonators – whether cabaret *artistes* such as "Duggie" Byng and pantomine dames like the Billys Dainty and Wells or more outrageous drag queens such as Craig Russell and Divine. There is also a pioneering transsexual, Christine (*né* George) Jorgensen.

Whereas the previous two volumes in this series have concentrated almost exclusively on British eccentrics, the *Entertainers* embrace an exotic American element. Apart from Divine (once voted "filthiest person alive"), there is, of course, the flamboyant Liberace, who, as the obit notes, once – "perhaps to lend himself an air of ruggedness with which nature had not chosen to endow him" – adopted the stage-name of "Walter Busterkeys".

Introduction

Hollywood adds its own tinsel to the proceedings in the sagas of such Silent sirens as the humourless Pola Negri ("I was the greatest film actress in the world") and the hypochondriacal Edwina Booth ("White Goddess" in *Trader Horn*). From Britain came the child star Freddie Bartholomew and the ill-fated Carol White. Among the American producers featured are the veteran Hal Roach, discoverer of Laurel and Hardy, and the car-smash junk merchant Toby Halicki, who was working on a scene in which a tractor-trailer was to ram through a series of parked cars when a telephone pole fell on his head, with fatal consqeuences.

The musicians range from celebrated names in jazz such as Slim Gaillard, Miles Davis and Dizzy Gillespie to Joe Loss, Yana and Donald Swann; from Serge Gainsbourg (who used a 1928 Rolls-Royce, occasionally, "as an ashtray") to "Aunt Jennie" Wilson, the Appalachian banjo-player. Nico, of the Velvet Underground, it is noted, "gave up heroin for bicycling, which was to turn out the more dangerous amusement – she died when she fell off a bicycle while on holiday".

Circus performers, such as the lion-tamer Togare and the "Queen of the Elephants", Victoria Sanger Freeman, contribute extra colour, as do the larger-than-life broadcasters Jack de Manio, Ray Moore, Barbara Woodhouse, Bill Grundy, Kenneth Robinson and Jess "The Bishop" Yates, unctuous host of *Stars on Sunday*.

Pursuing a liberal policy of interpreting the concept of "Entertainers", I have included, to boot, various popular authors (Jean Plaidy, Leslie Charteris, Jack Trevor Story) journalists (Jean Rook, Patience Strong, the Reverend Norman Vincent Peale, Debbie Raymond) and chefs. Room has also been found for the world's fattest man,

Walter ("Food, *Food*, FOOD!") Hudson and an assortment of idiosyncratic figures including the dancers Arthur Murray and Olga Spessivtseva (whose quest for perfection drove her out of her mind), the dubious prophets Bhagwan Shree Rajneesh, Frederick von Mierers and Sun Bear, the naughty-knicker merchant Frederick Mellinger, the battling boxer Rocky Graziano and the buffoonish Billy Carter.

The credits following the cast-list are no less varied. Apart from Andrew Barrow and the indefatigable Eric Shorter (the co-dedicatees of this book), I would also like to thank such greatly valued contributors as the late David Holloway, Robert Chalmers, Craig Brown, Daniel Farson, Dame Barbara Cartland, Jeremy Sandford, Don Stacy, Dean Godson, Jim Godbolt, Nicholas Dromgoole, Stanley Reynolds, Tim Heald, Peter Paterson, James Delingpole, Kenneth Buddell, Hugh Fearnley-Whittingstall, and – from the fevered world of showbiz itself – Sandy Wilson, Ron Moody, the late Willam Douglas Home, and Cyril Fletcher. Special acknowledgement is due, above all, to my deputy editor and successor, (David) Lewis Jones, who did more than anyone to fashion the particular style of the column and who wrote many of the most striking examples in this collection. Heartfelt thanks, too, to my other colleagues on the desk over the years – notably my original deputy (from 1986 to 1987), David Twiston Davies, my successive assistant editors Claudia Fitz-Herbert, Aurea Carpenter and Kate Summerscale (who subsequently succeeded David Jones in the chair), Robert Gray, Will Cohu (whose own theatrical experience was a considerable boon), Diana Heffer, Martine Onoh, Dorothy Brown and, of course, our editorial assistant, Teresa Moore.

Teresa tirelessly assembled the material for the book

with her inimitable determination and good humour. I am also grateful to the current obituaries editor of *The Daily Telegraph*, Christopher Howse, for his continued indulgence of these forays into the back files, and to many other old colleagues and friends for all their help and support. We can only hope that one or two readers may be tempted to emulate the elderly *Emmerdale* fan who tugged the sleeve of Arthur Pentelow in a Leeds shopping mall and said: "I'd like thee to know, tha's given me an hour or two of *real* pleasure."

HUGH MASSINGBERD
London, February 1997

BILLY DAINTY

BILLY DAINTY, who has died aged 59, was a song and dance man of genius who became one of Britain's greatest pantomime dames.

He represented the authentic and exuberant spirit of the old music halls, far more at ease alone on a large variety stage than in the crowded and artificial confines of a television studio. He scored notable successes in three Royal Variety Shows and was said to have been a particular favourite of Queen Elizabeth the Queen Mother. Cocky, hearty, toothy, rather on the stout side and looking more like a plumber's mate than the extraordinarily skilled dancer that he was, Dainty's nimble footwork and bursts of physical agility always came as a delightful surprise to the audience.

After some 20 distinguished but unfulfilling roles in pantomime, Billy Dainty was finally persuaded in 1964 to play dame opposite Harry Worth's Old King Cole at the Bristol Hippodrome. Here, his interpretation of the dame's traditional strip-tease was judged a supreme comic achievement, bearing comparison with Mr Pastry's hilarious solo performance of the "Lancers". He went on to play dame at the London Palladium opposite Tommy Steele's Dick Whittington and was proclaimed as "one of the last of the genuine music-hall performers" and as "one of the outstanding artists of his generation".

Dainty was his real name. He was born at Dudley on February 22 1927 and made his stage debut as the only boy dancer in a troupe of girls. The family later moved to London where Billy received lessons in tap-dancing from the American-born hoofer Buddy Bradley and won a scholarship to the Royal Academy of Dramatic Art. Doing his stripper routine years later, he muttered to a friend in the wings, "Two years at RADA for this!"

He made his West End debut in December 1942 playing the hind legs or "full bottom" of a dancing donkey in a Norman Evans pantomine, *Mother Goose*, at the London Coliseum. The following year he landed a part as a chorus boy in *Strike A New Note* at the Prince of Wales Theatre, starring the comedian Sid Field, with Jerry Desmonde and the newly formed duo Morecambe and Wise in the cast.

After serving in the Second World War with the Army in the Far East, Dainty resolved to become a solo song and dance man with a strong slant towards comedy. His first engagement was in a show called *Gaytime* at Newquay's Cosy Nook Theatre. Dainty was later to acquire a seaside home renamed "Gaytime" in Torquay's Thatcher Avenue.

By 1954, Dainty had become billed as "an eccentric dancing comedian", appearing in October that year at the Ipswich Hippodrome in a show starring the crooner Jimmy Young.

Dainty's repertoire of silly walks was unrivalled. Trained in the tradition of raffish physical diversity stretching back to the days of Dan Leno and Little Titch, he could traverse the stage on his right foot, his left leg raised throughout. At the height of his career, he also provided notable impersonations of a narcissistic and emasculated tennis star – "More balls, please!" – and vivid parodies of Shirley Bassey, Fred Astaire and a ballet dancer he chose to name Rudolf Nearenough, whose insinuating gyrations and winks at the front row of the stalls were said to have reduced the Queen Mother to tears of laughter.

Dainty's appearances in Royal Variety Shows and on ITV's *Sunday Night at the London Palladium* led to further television opportunities and his own series, *Billy Dainty Esquire*, but like many great comedians, including Tommy Cooper, he was not a natural on the box and his broadcasts never had the impact of his live shows, where he could exploit the stage and his audience to its full advantage.

Fellow comics regarded Dainty as a lousy rehearser, not good at learning lines and even worse at remembering gags, but once on stage "the butterfly emerged".

In the 1980s he became particularly associated with another stalwart survivor of the music-hall days, Roy Hudd. Together they appeared in a rumbustious show called *Just a Verse and Chorus* at the Greenwich Theatre, which featured the work of Bob Weston (Hudd) and Bert Lee (Dainty), authors of such staples as "Hello, Hello, Who's Your Lady Friend?" and "I'm 'Enery the Heigth I Ham."

A small and bumptious man, who never lost his Black Country accent, Billy Dainty's career ended on a sudden note in January 1986 when a tumour in the groin forced him to withdraw from a pantomime at the Theatre Royal, Nottingham, where he was playing Widow Twankey.

Dainty, who was married with a son (Laurence), lived latterly at a house called High Hopes at Ruislip, Middlesex, and finally at a house called Cobblers at Shackleford in Surrey. Off-stage he was said to be a complex man, extremely sentimental but also a "financial wizard" who enjoyed telling people how stingy he was.

Defining his approach to pantomime, Dainty once confessed that he played the dame as "a tough old bird" and added, "You can be a bit vulgar with the dame, show your knickers, even take your knickers off. But there's got to be some point to it; you can't do things just for the sake of it."

November 20 1986

LIBERACE

LIBERACE, the flamboyant American popular pianist who has died aged 67, was the world's single highest paid performer throughout the 1960s and 1970s.

He appeared in concert halls, theatres, ballrooms, nightclubs and also in several films, notably as the deaf pianist in the spectacular flop *Sincerely Yours* (1955) and as an unctuous "casket" salesman in an otherwise unmemorable film of Evelyn Waugh's *The Loved One* (1965).

Liberace's extraordinary success as an entertainer can be credited to his peculiarly American synthesis of sentimentality, bravado and showmanship.

For one devoted to extravagance in an age of puritanical austerity, there was bound to be a backlash. It came in peculiarly venomous form from the journalist William Connor writing as "Cassandra" in the *Daily Mirror* in 1956 when Liberace appeared at the London Palladium.

"He reeks with emetic language that can only make grown men long for a quiet corner, an aspidistra, a handkerchief and the old heave-ho" was one of the milder passages from this celebrated tirade. Cassandra also described the performer as "this deadly, winking, sniggering, snuggling, chromium-plated, scent-impregnated, luminous, quivering, giggling, fruit-flavoured, mincing, ice-covered heap of mother-love."

However, the passage that caused most offence both to the star and his mother read: "He is the summit of sex, the pinnacle of masculine, feminine and neuter, everything that he, she and it can ever want."

After denying his homosexuality in the High Court in London in 1959, Liberace won libel damages of £8,000 and an apology.

Wladizu Valentine Liberace (known to his besotted public as "Lee") was born in Milwaukee on May 16 1919. His Italian father had enjoyed some small success as a French horn player, and as a bit-part actor in silent movies before concentrating on his career as a grocer.

His Polish mother, Frances, had been a concert pianist before her marriage, and throughout her life maintained her interest in showbusiness, calling Liberace's younger brother Rudolph Valentino Liberace after the screen idol of the time.

A child prodigy, Liberace performed before Paderewski at the age of seven and a half. "Some day that boy may take my place", commented the celebrated pianist.

His career began on more formal lines than those along which it would progress. After one tour as a soloist with the Chicago Symphony Orchestra, Liberace found himself attracted to a less-restrained form of music and dress, much to the chagrin of his father, a musical purist.

He found much sympathy though, from his mother, to whom he always remained devoted, later exhibiting many of her personal effects, including her knitting basket, in his own Liberace museum in Las Vegas.

This attachment to his mother was to form an important part of his stage persona: invariably in attendance at his concerts, she would happily wear furs and jewellery identical to her performing son's, and the audience would applaud both of them for their pride in their mutual devotion.

Perhaps to lend himself an air of ruggedness with which nature had not chosen to endow him, he adopted the stage name "Walter Busterkeys" when he embarked on his early career in a dance band, but swiftly changed hats, calling himself simply "Liberace" and playing up his already bizarre character.

"I began to disarm my audience and say what people were thinking before they could say it. I heckled myself," he once said.

The first sign that Liberace had embarked upon a road along which reticence would never ride came when he placed a candelabra on his piano when playing for the dance band. At this, the dam of discretion appeared to burst: first came a white tail suit, followed by stage patter about his mother and his philosophy of life, then a gold lamé jacket and a diamond-studded tailcoat.

His piano playing, though unfaltering, was never rigid in its adherence to tradition: of the 153 pages of Tchaikovsky's First Piano Concerto, he would perform only the first 12 and the last four, adding four bars in the middle of his own creation.

As success grew, so too did flamboyance: in 1984, he was spotted wearing a $300,000 (£200,000) rhinestone-studded Norwegian blue fox cape with a 16 foot train; and last year (1986), stepping on stage out of a Rolls-Royce painted with Stars and Stipes, he was witnessed in red, white and blue hotpants.

Liberace's private tastes were similarly steeped in an

absence of sobriety. His master bedroom was painted with a re-creation of the Sistine Chapel ceiling, his lawn was centrally heated, his swimming pool was piano-shaped and among his possessions – or "happy-happies" as he liked to call them – was a piano made out of 10,000 toothpicks.

He is also credited with having invented a lavatory that could disappear into a bathroom floor at the flick of a switch. "There's no reason why you should walk into a bathroom and see a toilet. It's unglamorous," he explained.

His adoring audience – he averaged 27,000 Valentine cards and 150 marriage proposals a year – admired him for converting the sophistication of classical music into something a little more catchy and plush, for his love of luxury, his self-deprecating sense of humour and his seemingly innocuous flirtatiousness.

In 1982 his formerly resident secretary-cum-chauffeur, Scott Thorson, brought a "palimony" suit against Liberace. The case was eventually settled out of court last year whereby, in return for $95,000 in cash, a Rolls-Royce, two other motor cars and a couple of dogs, Thorson agreed to drop the action.

"Nobody loves me but the public," he said time and time again.

He was unmarried.

February 5 1987

BARONESS MARIA
VON TRAPP

BARONESS MARIA AUGUSTA VON TRAPP, who has died in Vermont aged 82, was the inspiration for the popular musical play and film *The Sound of Music*.

She said that she was much wilder as a girl than Julie Andrews's film portrayal – "not so goody-goody" – and preferred Petula Clark's more tomboyish version in the 1981 revival of the Rodgers and Hammerstein musical.

As an unruly 20-year-old novice nun in the Tyrolean Alps she was temporarily assigned as governess to the family of a local nobleman, Baron Georg von Trapp. She fell in love first with the seven children and then with their father. They were married a year later, in 1927, and had three more children.

The Baron, who his wife said was by no means the martinet portrayed in the film, was a fierce opponent of the Nazis, and his feelings were shared by his wife. She once called Hitler "someone you would not want to have in your living room".

The von Trapps fled when the Germans invaded their country. They crossed the Alps on foot and travelled to the United States on visitors' visas, arriving with $4 between them.

At home in Austria, the family had sung in concerts for friends around Salzburg. They decided to turn professional in America, where they soon became famous.

Dressed in Tyrolean costume and armed with flutes, recorders, cellos and a spinet, they performed Austrian folk songs, old English madrigals, operatic arias, Gregorian chant and hymns on tours throughout the United States and South America.

After three years' touring, the family bought a ramshackle house near Stowe in Vermont, where the scenery reminded them of the Tyrol. They continued to tour as the Trapp Family Singers until 1957, by which time their ramshackle house had become the Trapp Family Lodge – a skiing hotel and musical centre.

The Baroness wrote five books, one of which, *The Trapp Family Singers*, was the source for Rodgers and Hammerstein's 1959 musical (which grossed about £18 million) and the Oscar-winning film in 1965 (which made about £100 million).

Having sold the film rights to a Germany company for £1,500, the Baroness made very little from the phenomenal success of her story – about £250,000 in all. "But I have never felt sorry. I have seen how destructive riches can be to the human character," she said.

In 1980 the Trapp Family Lodge was destroyed by fire, but the Baroness began anew with a good humour and built a rather grander hotel in its place. She retired from active life in 1985, after two strokes.

She is survived by 3 children, 5 stepchildren, 12 grandchildren, 8 great-grandchildren and 50 great-great-grandchildren.

March 30 1987

DOROTHY WARD

DOROTHY WARD, who has died aged 96, was one of the greatest "principal boys" in the history of pantomime.

Even after her retirement in 1957, Miss Ward's name remained synonymous with "panto": its doublet and hose, sheer silk stockings, chorus numbers and the inevitable duets between "Boy" and "Girl". But she was equally at home in variety, musical comedy, revue and the occasional operetta.

With her striking orange-coloured hair, expansive smile and exquisitely shaped legs, Miss Ward would make superb "star" entrances. Audiences rejoiced at the way she merrily slapped her thigh and at her instructions to stand up and sing.

Among her legion of admirers were such celebrities as Lloyd George, "Bend Or" Duke of Westminster and Winston Churchill. The Crazy Gang paid tribute to "the lovely Dorothy Ward" in their "walk-down" number "Principal Boys".

During the Second World War, she toured for ENSA and was known to the adoring soldiery as "Mademoiselle from the Maginot Line" (the title of one of her best-known numbers).

Born in 1890 and brought up in Birmingham, Dorothy Ward made her first appearance at the age of 15 as Zeobia in *Bluebird* at the Alexandra, Birmingham. The following year, she made her debut in the West End as Betty in *The Dairymaids* at the Apollo and soon there was no stopping her.

Perhaps her most spectacular triumph was as Jack in

Jack and the Beanstalk at the London Hippodrome in 1922. She took over from Clarice Mayne at short notice in a role that contained all the best ingredients of panto: handsome hero, adventure, melodrama, heroine in distress and comic pathos.

The comic pathos was particularly to the fore as she was playing opposite the legendary George Robey as Dame Trot. In his autobiography, Robey recalled that Dorothy Ward "not only looked the part finely, but showed an infectious jollity and, where necessary, quite a pretty gift of emotional acting."

Out of pantomine, Miss Ward's best-known musical performance was when she played opposite Carl Brisson in *The Apache* at the London Palladium in 1926.

In her heyday as a "headliner" between the wars, Dorothy Ward was constantly touring in variety both in Britain and abroad. She would crown the end of each performance by bringing on a troupe of diminutive, prettily dressed young children known as "Dorothy Ward's Tiny Tots". The Tots would aid and abet the star as the chorus in song and dance numbers, enjoying enormous success.

Dorothy Ward made recordings of such popular numbers as "Take Me Back to Dear Old Blighty", "The Sheik of Araby", "A Shanty in Old Shanty Town", "Let the Rest of the World Go By" and several with her husband, Shaun Glenville.

She and Glenville would often act in pantomine together as "Boy" and "Dame" respectively. Their son, Peter Glenville, became a distinguished stage and film director.

When Miss Ward made her last stage appearance shortly before her 70th birthday, it was fitting that the farewell should have been at a provincial theatre (the Old Pavilion, Liverpool) and in the role of a pantomine principal boy.

April 1 1987

HERMIONE GINGOLD

HERMIONE GINGOLD, the British character actress who has died in New York aged 89, was a theatrical legend, celebrated for her "high camp" mannerisms, flamboyant eccentricity and outrageously funny remarks, delivered in her extraordinary gurgling tones.

To modern cinema and television audiences Miss Gingold was best known for her comparatively restrained performances in *Gigi* (in which she sang "I remember it well" with Maurice Chevalier) and as Mme Armfeldt in *A Little Night Music*, which she also played on stage on Broadway and in London in the 1970s. But an older generation of theatregoers will principally recall the Gingold genius in "intimate revue", where she projected an immensely forceful stage presence.

The kind of satirical revue in which she made her special reputation has long since ceased to exist; and as the late W. A. Darlington, the dramatic critic of *The Daily Telegraph*, wrote: "For those who never had the experience of watching her at work, she must remain beyond imagination."

In Miss Gingold's heyday the prohibitive power of the Lord Chamberlain was still absolute and the limits within which he could be persuaded to permit any personal satire of public figures were narrow. Consequently, the theatre took the way of safety and confined its more barbed attacks to its own world; Miss Gingold's intimate revues were full of wicked "in-jokes".

Thus, when it was said that a performance by Larry Olivier had been a *tour de force*, Miss Gingold observed in her most lugubrious tones that Donald Wolfit in the same role had been "forced to tour".

Hermione Gingold was one of those rare performers who are capable of spontaneous witty repartee off the stage as well as on. At a Foyles' literary luncheon a fellow guest explained that she was engaged in public relations. Miss Gingold looked startled, murmuring, "I prefer to keep mine private."

A playwright who had asked the actress's opinion of his script was told, "My dear boy, in future I advise you never to write anything more ambitious than a grocery list."

Attempting to persuade a friend to visit London from the depths of the country, she said, "But my dear you simply *must* come. It's Corset Week at Swan & Edgar."

Miss Gingold had an endearingly individual approach to life. In New York she was regularly seen rummaging through other people's dustbins. On one occasion she found a complete set of *Encyclopaedia Britannica*, on another an antique table. Characteristically she was quite unrepentant: "A lot of millionaires started in the junk business."

Hermione Ferdinanda Gingold was born in London on "December 9" (as she wrote in her *Who's Who* entry – the omitted year was 1897) and trained for the stage with Rosina Filippi. She made her first appearance on the stage at His Majesty's Theatre shortly after her 11th birthday in 1908, as the herald in *Pinkie and the Fairies* with Sir Herbert Tree.

It was not, however, until 1932 that she made any real mark. That season she played a series of parts at the old Gate Theatre. In 1936 her peculiar talent for revue was recognised when she appeared in *Spread it Abroad* at the old Saville, and two years later she scored a notable success in *The Gate Revue*.

This show transferred in 1939 to the Ambassadors, where she enjoyed a phenomenal series of personal triumphs in intimate revue during the war years. *Sweet and Low*, *Sweeter and Lower* and *Sweetest and Lowest* firmly established Miss Gingold as a star.

Her name was frequently linked with that of another revue star, the late Hermione Baddeley; inevitably they were known as "The Two Hermiones", even if they were not always on the most harmonious terms. In 1949 the Hermiones appeared together in a spectacularly undisciplined revival of Noël Coward's drunken farce *Fallen Angels* at the Ambassadors. While Miss Baddeley spat bread pellets at the audience, Miss Gingold did suggestive things with a table napkin.

The two actresses' behaviour incurred the Master's severe displeasure, but the nightly outrages packed in the audiences. By the end of the hugely successful run, the two leading ladies (or "Gorgeous Gargoyles" as Frank Marcus described them) were reputedly no longer on speaking terms.

In 1951 Miss Gingold made her first appearance on the American stage in the revue *It's About Time*. From then on she spent most of her career in the United States, appearing in films, television and "legitimate" plays as well as revue. Her films included *Around the World in 80 Days*, *Bell, Book and Candle* and *The Music Man*.

In 1965 she was back in London playing the part of

Mrs Roepettle in *Oh Dad, Poor Dad, Mama's Hung You in the Closet, and I'm Feelin' So Sad*, which she had earlier taken over on Broadway. In 1969 she was Agnes Derrindo in *Highly Confidential* at the Cambridge.

When Harold Prince was holding auditions for Stephen Sondheim's *A Little Night Music* in 1972, Miss Gingold turned up uninvited. The director told her that she should not bother to play a woman of 74. "But Mr Prince," she replied, "I *am* 74."

Later she enjoyed another success in *Side by Side by Sondheim*. Her versatility was reflected in her touring one woman show and her recordings of *Façade* and *Lysistrata* even if her character parts on American television tended to the grotesque.

She was the author of an hilarious autobiography, *The World is Square: My Own Unaided Work* and *Sirens Should Be Seen Not Heard*.

Miss Gingold also had a remarkable flair for interior decoration, and collected china as well as objects from dustbins.

Both her marriages, to Michael Joseph and the lyric writer Eric Maschwitz, ended in divorce. She had two sons by the first marriage, one of whom survives.

May 25 1987

POLA NEGRI

POLA NEGRI, who has died at San Antonio, Texas, aged 92, was the legendary silent-screen siren whose career ranged from the 1914 Polish film *Love and Passion* to Walt Disney's *The Moonspinners*, made in England in 1964.

Essentially an actress of strong personality, she exuded an aura of slink and mink, of vamping heroes that stayed vamped. Although her three husbands were styled baron, count and prince, she was more famous for her liaisons with Rudolph Valentino and Charlie Chaplin as well as a bitter row with her rival Gloria Swanson.

As an actress she had distinct limitations, being almost devoid of humour and incapable of suggesting light and shade. After being smitten with her blonde hair, smouldering eyes and usually black clothes, American audiences began to go off her offbeat pseudo-culture and, with the advent of sound, found her thick Polish accent almost incomprehensible.

Yet she was Queen of Hollywood in the transition period between the decline of the earlier vamps such as Theda Bara, and the great stars of the 1930s, Greta Garbo and Marlene Dietrich.

Born Barbara Apollonia Chalupiec in 1894 at Janowa, Poland, she was supposedly the child of a gypsy violinist who died in exile in Siberia. His daughter, who abbreviated her second forename to Pola and took a surname from the Italian poet Ada Negri, worked as a dancer and violinist before making her stage debut in Warsaw in 1913.

Negri made three films with Aleksandr Hertz before being brought to Berlin for a play by Max Reinhardt. She rapidly became a star of the German cinema, but it was the series of costume films she made with the young director Ernst Lubitsch, particularly *Carmen* (1918) and *Madame du Barry* (1919), which became an immense success in America under the title *Passion*, that led Paramount to invite her to the United States in 1922.

Her first American films fell far short of her German work until she made *Forbidden Passion* with Lubitsch in 1924. Raoul Walsh's *East of Suez* (1925) and Malcolm St Clair's *Good and Naughty* were among her other films, but while her star began to dim Negri started to attract widespread attention with her private life.

She had married first Baron Popper, a Polish Army officer; then, in Berlin, the Polish Count Eugene Domski after a tempestuous affair which involved an escape from his castle. He was granted a divorce, but when she told the world of her devotion to Charlie Chaplin the Count turned up to challenge the comedian to a duel. Later, there were several well-publicised engagements until she met Rudolph Valentino. "Our souls", she proclaimed "met upon our lips, and we were one. Two aching hearts, tired of the battle."

A year later Valentino died, and Negri made a dramatic appearance at his funeral, clad all in black, with a doctor and a nurse, dressed entirely in white, supporting her on either side. "All joy has fled from my life for ever," she cried, fainting over his coffin.

Six months afterwards, she married the *soi-disant* Prince Serge Mdivani, a Georgian. "I did love my husband; I adored Valentino; and I grew very fond of Charlie Chaplin," she said. "But Serge means more to me than them all."

"I have no doubt that at the time she was sincere," observed Campbell Dixon, *The Daily Telegraph* film critic, in the advance obituary he wrote on her in 1931. "But her temperament was something she could not control if she would, and soon she was announcing that yet another romance was broken. 'Pola', she said, 'is cursed with an unlucky star of love' – one of the many pronouncements which revealed both her habit of dramatising herself and her complete lack of humour."

Negri left Hollywood to make a film in England, *The Woman He Scorned*, which was not a success, and began to make another in Paris – only to tear up her contract and pay £4,000 compensation because there was no bathroom in the studio. It was later claimed that she sacrificed the £1,000 a week contract because the script required her to strip to the waist and undergo ordeal by fire.

Her name continued to be linked with supposed fiancés, including an unnamed former British MP and Adolf Hitler. Hitler was said to have considered her his favourite actress, and she made a supposedly brilliant comeback in the 1935 German film, *Mazurka*, directed by Willi Forst, though its real sensation was a 16-year-old Garbo-lookalike. There were even stories that the dictator had sent special agents to Poland to check her Aryan blood.

But she settled in Nice, and shortly before the Second World War successfully sued a French newspaper which had described her as one of the three great rivals for the dictator's love, winning £56 damages.

By the time Miss Negri returned to America in 1941, she wanted to forget her romantic past. "Ah no, ah no. I've had no romances," she told reporters who met her at the New York dockside. "I now think only of my work. I belong to the public." Immigration officers were less sure about this: she had arrived without an entry permit.

Another film, *Hi Diddle Diddle*, followed in 1943. For her last 30 years she settled in Texas, attracting brief attention in London when she appeared, dressed in black as always, with a cheetah which went with her cameo part in *The Moonspinners*.

Only an autobiography, *Memoirs of a Star*, describing her love affairs with Chaplin and Valentino, brought her to any public notice again in America. But she never forgot her past glory. Even when in hospital during her last illness she continued to put on her false eyelashes, and she rose in her bed to tell a young doctor who did not know who she was: "I was the greatest film actress in the world."

August 4 1987

DOUGLAS BYNG

DOUGLAS BYNG, who has died aged 94, was one of the most redoubtable entertainers of the present century, celebrated especially for his outrageous comedy songs and risqué female "characters", most of which he wrote himself.

His achievements as an *artiste* in revue, variety, cabaret and indeed as a pantomine dame were legendary. He was accorded the sobriquet of "High Priest of Camp" long before the theatrical word "camp" became part of common usage.

"Duggie" Byng's skill in performance vanquished prudery. His material – a trifle rude but never crude – was to range from such numbers as "Sex Appeal Sarah", "Milly the Messy Old Mermaid" and "The Lass who Leaned against the Tower of Pisa" to "The Girl Who Made Them Pay in Peyton Place" and "Playboy Club Bunny".

Without sacrificing style and subtlety – Byng's "class" was never in doubt – he was able at times to make his allusions explicit without causing offence. Before his day, if the borderline was reached and suggestion became no longer implicit, then the performer courted disaster, but no member of Duggie Byng's audience felt any worse for being presented with fact properly told – better that than fancy improperly told or bluntly hinted at.

He held the floor during the Blitz at the old Café de Paris in London's West End, where his billing was "Byng: Bawdy but British". After the place was bombed he continued to render his own favourite romantic ballad (as he called it), "Blackout Bella", to the troops throughout Britain and in the Far East.

Douglas Byng was born at Nottingham in 1893. His mother's maiden name was Coy.

Educated at Waverley School, Nottingham, Stanley House, Cliftonville, and in Germany, he worked initially as a designer of theatrical costumes and was never to lose his love of dressing up.

He made his professional debut as a performer in concert party at Hastings on the eve of the First World War. After a spell on tour in such shows as *The Girl in the Taxi* and *The Cinema Star*, he arrived in the West End as an understudy in *Theodore and Co* in 1916, eventually getting on to the stage the following year.

A crop of comedies and farces followed before he tasted twice-nightly variety on tour with Harry Day's revue *Crystal* from 1922 to 1924. He scored a signal success as Eliza the Cook in *Dick Whittington* with his own number "Oriental Emma of the Harem".

After that there was no going back. Byng's singular

talent for observing and creating characters on the distaff side soon proved to be his greatest asset as a comedian.

His unmistakable presence was a feature in most of the Cochran revues at the London Pavilion in the 1920s, including *On with the Dance* – in which he portrayed a *passé* spinster preparing for bed in the sketch *Oranges and Lemons – One Damn Thing after Another* and *This Year of Grace*.

It was also in the hectic 1920s that Byng found his feet in cabaret. After the shows at the Pavilion he would go on to the Chez Henri Club where together with Laurier Lister he would send up the sister acts of the period like the Trix Sisters, Bettie and Babs and Lorna and Toots Pounds. "The Cabaret Boys", as they were known, pioneered this sort of transvestite comedy turn. Recalling this period of his career, Byng said it was "the first slightly *queer* number of the lot".

When he made his cabaret debut in New York in 1931 Byng was billed as "London's most important cabaret star". In Monte Carlo shortly afterwards he was announced as "*l'acteur extraordinaire anglais*".

Although appearing in his heyday in some of the most outstanding revues between the two world wars, Byng's appeal transcended typecasting. Thus at the Alhambra in the 1930s he presented a one-man pantomine *Hop O' My Thumb*, when he made his first appearance on a trapeze bar, warbling, as he descended just above the footlights: "I'm Doris, the Goddess of Wind."

He followed this burlesque with others in the same mould: offbeat monologues which were gems of their kind. His arboraceous interpretation of "I'm a Tree" vied with such curiosities as "Whistler's Mother's Mum" and

"The Girl Who Went and Found It at the Astor." Then there was that never to be forgotten policewoman, a well-known "sight" of Piccadilly, whom Byng wickedly impersonated to the life in *Hi Diddle-Diddle* at the Comedy in 1934.

During the Second World War Byng was busy in musicals and variety, as well as cabaret and entertaining the troops. Afterwards he appeared in some more comedies and farces, the best remembered being Feydeau's *Hotel Paradiso* with Alec Guinness. He also turned up spasmodically on television, notably in the series *Before the Fringe* in the 1960s when he sang, or rather recited, some of the old revue songs.

It is thought that faint echoes of Douglas Byng may have contributed to the character of Max Pilgrim, the cabaret performer in Anthony Powell's great novel sequence *A Dance to the Music of Time*.

Even in semi-retirement, during the last years, Byng could not resist "getting back into harness" when he would occasionally team up with another veteran Billy Milton in a double act that delighted their old fans. Until finally moving to Denville Hall, the Actors' Charitable Trust Home, he lived at Brighton, a town he found "both breezy and salty".

Characteristically he composed his own epitaph:

> So here you are, old Douglas, a derelict at last.
> Before your eyes what visions rise of your vermilion past.
> Mad revelry beneath the stars, hot clasping by the lake.
> You need not sigh, you can't deny, you've had your bit of cake.

August 26 1987

BILL FRASER

BILL FRASER, the robust comedy actor who has died aged 79, was best known for his performance as the spluttering Sergeant-Major Snudge in the long-running television comedy series *The Army Game* and *Bootsie and Snudge*.

Together with the put-upon character of the diminutive Bootsie, played by Alfie Bass, "Snudge" became one of the most familiar faces on television in the late 1950s and early 1960s. But Fraser also had a stage career of remarkable versatility covering more than 55 years which ranged from variety and revue to parts in Ibsen, Shaw and Chekhov as well as Shakespeare.

Only last year he won a Laurence Olivier Award for his role as the inebriated photographer in the revival of J. B. Priestley's *When We Are Married* at the Whitehall Theatre. He had been the Dame in pantomime and Sir Toby Belch in Shakespeare's *Twelfth Night* and earlier he played "straight man" to numerous comedians including Ted Ray, Arthur Askey, Tommy Cooper, Tony Hancock, Charlie Drake and Jack Benny.

Burly and florid, with bulging expressive eyes, and exploiting a slightly worried look, Fraser was a brilliant character known for his hearty geniality, trim moustache, pouting lips and stately walk. "What I do," he once said, "is play stuffy, pot-bellied, pompous old sods. Thank God England is full of them."

Born in 1908 at Perth and educated at Strathallan School, Fraser was first employed as a bank clerk but hankered after the stage. He went in search of work in London, sometimes sleeping on the Embankment.

After making his first stage appearance with a Broadstairs repertory theatre in 1931, he then toured India. He founded a repertory company of his own at Worthing in 1933, directing and acting in it for six years. He first entered films in 1938.

After the Worthing rep disbanded at the outbreak of the Second World War he made his first London appearance in 1940 in the revue *New Faces* at the Comedy Theatre. He joined the RAF as a signals officer and was involved from 1942 to 1945 in preparing and producing troop shows.

The war over, Fraser appeared in the revue *Between Ourselves* at the Playhouse and went on to other West End revues, appearing with stars such as Bobbie Howes and Binnie Hale. In the 1950s he played John Mallory in *The Schoolmistress* at the Saville and directed *Between Ourselves* at various coastal resorts.

When the television boom began he established himself as one of its best-known character actors. Apart from *The Army Game* and the two spin-off series *Bootsie and Snudge* and *Foreign Affairs*, he appeared in such popular programmes as *That's Your Funeral* and *Rumpole of the Bailey*.

In the mid-1960s there was a remarkable renaissance in Fraser's stage career. At the Chichester Festival his parts included Mr Sterling in *The Clandestine Marriage*, Pischik in *The Cherry Orchard* and Gibbet in *The Beaux' Stratagem*. In 1969 he joined the Royal Shakespeare Company at Stratford. At the Old Vic in 1970 he was Sir George Crofts in *Mrs Warren's Profession*; in 1971 John Tarleton, the underwear king, in Shaw's *Misalliance* at the Mermaid, showing much comic resourcefulness.

In 1976 he starred with Googie Withers in Somerset

Maugham's *The Circle* at the Haymarket, playing the sullen Lord Porteous.

Among numerous supporting parts, Fraser made a small gem of the impoverished landowner Telegin in *Uncle Vanya* at the Haymarket in 1982.

His memorable wireless roles included Max, the father, in Pinter's dark play *The Homecoming* in 1977.

Thirty-two films included *Doctor at Large*, *All the Way Up*, *The Corn is Green* and *Last Tribute*. His leering performance as the bewigged butler Groping in the Frankie Howerd film *Up the Front* was seen on television the weekend of his death.

He is survived by his wife, the actress Pamela Cundell, whom he married in 1981.

September 7 1987

AL READ

AL READ, who has died aged 78, was a Salford sausage-maker whose wry observations of ripe Northern characters made him a great comic, familiar for such catch-phrases as "right monkey" and "you'll be lucky".

In the eyes of many he was the principal exponent of wireless comedy to be ranked alongside only such other stars of sound as Tommy Handley, the Goons, Sandy Powell, Arthur Askey, Elsie and Doris Waters and "The Squire of Hogsnorton", Gillie Potter.

Read was discovered in the late 1940s when a BBC producer was struck by the Lancashire businessman's golf-club turn, an impression of a building decorator uttering the most gloomy prognostications. Within 18 months,

Read had become one of the household names of radio, establishing himself as resident comedian on the BBC's *Variety Bandbox*.

He went on to have his own series on wireless and television, including *Such is Life* and *What a Life*, starred for several seasons in music-hall revue at the Adelphi Theatre in London's West End and appeared in several Royal Variety Shows.

On stage he would stand with little facial make-up and even less "costume" worn than any other radio comedian, looking, as one theatre critic put it, "like any stranger one might meet in a crowded tube train going home to the suburbs any night of the week". Read's highly individual humour depended on his scrutiny of people around him and what they said. He was emphatically not a wisecrack merchant with a gang of gag-writers; indeed he did not tell jokes as such, nor did he have a scriptwriter.

"All I do," he used to say, "is tell the truth." He would present a beautifully observed gallery of all-too-familiar everyday people: an awkward customer in a pub, an unco-operative car park attendant, a loud-mouthed spectator at a football match and tiresome know-alls of every type.

Among his best-loved sketches were the study of the stages of a motorist's humiliation by a garage mechanic and the undermining of a householder's confidence by a plumber ("I suppose you know . . .").

Read represented the man in the street, the chap who could tell you quite confidentially about the lady who was trying to park her car, the garage proprietor of doubtful temper and the Mancunian housewife who hinted conspiratorially at dark secrets when she confided to her friends that "there was enough said at our Billy's wedding". Appreciation of Read's humour depended a good deal on how frequently his audiences travelled north of Watford; no doubt there was a large section of the viewing and listening public who failed to see anything funny in him at all. "He does nothing but grumble," one puzzled foreigner said of Read's act.

But Al Read was undoubtedly an original personality. His solid roots in the real world of Mancunian meat-packaging gave him a welcome detachment from the incestuous backslapping of showbiz.

He was born in 1909 into a prosperous dynasty of meat-pie and sausage manufacturers. His family firm was the first to can meat in the north of England.

Away from the stage and the factory, Read relished the Turf, owning You'll be Lucky and other similarly named racehorses.

Largely forgotten in the early 1980s, Read enjoyed a revival of interest in his wireless sketches earlier this year through repeated broadcasts on BBC's Radio 2.

He is survived by his second wife, Elizabeth, and by two sons and daughter from a previous marriage.

September 11 1987

RAYMOND FRANCIS

RAYMOND FRANCIS, the actor, who has died aged 76, became one of the most familiar faces on television in the 1950s and 1960s through his crisp portrayal of the unflappable Detective-Inspector (later Chief Superintendent) Tom Lockhart in various crime series – *Crime Sheet*, *Murder Bag* and, above all, *No Hiding Place*.

The Lockhart of the Yard *persona* – beady eyes, trim moustache, trilby, snuff and somewhat over-precise diction – was so pervasive that it became difficult for viewers to accept the dapper Francis in any other part once *No Hiding Place* finally ended its long run in 1967. When he did crop up, generally in crusty character parts, the audience's reaction tended to be along the lines of, "What's old Lockhart doing pretending to be an admiral?"

In their heyday – somewhere between the cosy beat of *Dixon of Dock Green* and the robust realism of *Z Cars* and *The Sweeney* – the fairly one-dimensional Lockhart adventures were immensely popular, and regarded as wholesome enough to go out before children were sent to bed. "We could have one bloody and two damns in a programme, but that was all," Francis recalled. "I always got my man and I never lost a case," he said. "I used to plead: why can't the villain get away this week, just this once – I'll nick a couple next time to make up for it."

Born at Finchley in 1911, Raymond Francis described himself as "35 per cent Irish, 25 per cent Scots and 40 per cent Cockney", and his education as "nil". He acquired a taste for performing as an adolescent conjuror.

After early experience in the West End as a comic footman in *Cinderella*, and a disastrous production of *Lord Byron*, he worked his way up through years of provincial repertory work. During the Second World War Francis served in the Royal Armoured Corps. He first made his mark on television as Dr Watson in an early *Sherlock Holmes* series for the BBC in 1950.

But he was still a comparative unknown when he landed the part of Lockhart for what was initially intended to be a six-part series. His starting salary was £75 for each episode; by the time the last series ended he was reputed to be receiving £1,000 a time.

Francis's other parts on television included Southern's lunchtime soap opera *Together*, set in a housing association block of flats, and the dotty general who chaired the prep school governors in *Drummonds*.

Among his many appearances on the stage were in Somerset Maugham's *Lady Frederick*, with Margaret Lockwood; as the ulcerous father in the Francis Durbridge thriller *The Gentle Hook*; and as the dribbling old bore of a husband in Simon Gray's play, *Molly*, based on the Rattenbury murder case of the 1930s.

. In his numerous films, which included *Reach for the Sky* and *Carrington VC*, his best role was the tweedy, MG-driving squire in James Herriot's *It Shouldn't Happen to a Vet* (1976).

The genial Francis, who enjoyed cooking, watching cricket, gardening and – like his *alter ego* – taking snuff, was never resentful about the decline in his career after Lockhart: "That's the fascinating thing about this business, you're up and you're down; it can happen to anybody."

He is survived by his wife, the actress Margaret Towner, two daughters and a son, the actor and caricaturist Clive Francis.

October 26 1987

IRENE HANDL

IRENE HANDL, who has died aged 85, was one of Britain's most popular comic actresses, celebrated for her performances in such films as *I'm All Right Jack* and in the television comedy series, *Never Say Die*.

Although her extraordinary and endearing Cockney whine, on which she superimposed an ineffable veneer of refinement, seemed to the manner born, Handl was in fact from an affluent Viennese background and based her accent and stage persona on the conversation she had overheard between staff at her parents' house in Maida Vale. She could not have been less like the gormless charladies she played with such verve – ample bosom, rolling gait and cocked head – as she was an accomplished literary as well as dramatic performer, the author of such highly original novels as *The Sioux* (1965) and *The Gold Tipped Phitzer* (1966).

Miss Handl was a relative latecomer to the stage, making her name at Wyndham's in her mid-30s with the prototype role of Beer, the maid in *George and Margaret*. Calling on her childhood memories she created an uproariously funny character who made almost every word she spoke inaudible and punctuated her mysterious remarks with an odd little curtsey. Film companies clamoured for her services, but the theatre's management would not release her until the end of the play's run two years later.

She first became known on television in *Hancock's Half Hour*, though she later confessed that she did not relish her connection with Hancock, whom she found moody and aloof. Her favourite associate was Peter Sellers, with whom she first appeared in the Boulting Brothers' satirical farce *I'm All Right Jack* (1959), as the mumsy Mrs Kite, who finally turns on her Hitlerian trade union official husband. The next year she appeared again with Sellers in

Two Way Stretch. They became firm friends, and she was greatly affected by his death.

Irene Handl was born at Maida Vale, London, in 1901, the daughter of an Austrian banker and an aristocratic Frenchwoman. She liked to tell the story of her sorry appearance as a newborn baby, covered in thick simian hair: "It's a beautiful boy," the doctor announced. "No, sorry, it's a beautiful girl."

When her mother died she took over the running of the house; but her father, who worked such odd hours that she had always imagined him to be a burglar, insisted she have some more intellectually stretching occupation and suggested she go on the stage.

She enrolled at the Embassy School of Acting in Swiss Cottage and from there made her debut at the Embassy Theatre as the Stout Woman in *Night Alone*. Within three weeks she was on the West End stage at Wyndham's.

During the Second World War Miss Handl played a number of character parts and began her film career with the British mystery *The Girl in the News* (1940) with Margaret Lockwood and Emlyn Williams.

These were followed by parts in *Pimpernel Smith* (1941), *Temptation Harbour* (1946), *Silent Dust* (1948) and *One Wild Oat* (1951), before she entered the most popular period of her career with *The Belles of St Trinian's* (1954). From then on she went from strength to strength in such roles as Mrs Cravatte, the awful landlady in Hancock's *The Rebel* (1961), and such varied productions as *Morgan – a Suitable Case for Treatment* (1966) and *The Private Life of Sherlock Holmes* (1971), in which she reached the apogee of her servant roles as Mrs Hudson, the great detective's housekeeper.

Throughout that period she continued to appear in the West End – notably as a wonderful Madame Arcati in Noël Coward's *Blithe Spirit* – and on television, starring in *For the Love of Ada*, *Maggie and Her* and *A Legacy*.

Miss Handl was a much better cook than the characters she so often played, and she also loved gardening. Her other main interests – aside from literature and art – are indicated by her quondam presidencies of the British Chihuahua Club and of the Lewisham Elvis Presley Club – "Rock appeals to me because of the beat – I'm mad about the beat."

She was also a rival to Sir John Gielgud in tactlessness: "Who's that actor with all the acne? Oh, I know, dear – David Warner!"

Her regrets were few: that she had not gone on the stage when younger, and so been able to play classical roles; and that her novels did not enjoy greater popular success. The admiration of Noël Coward, as recorded in his diaries, went some way towards making up for the latter disappointment: "I am at the moment reading an extraordinarily original novel by – of all people – Irene Handl. It really is quite brilliantly written. She has an authentic touch of genius."

Looking back on her life in a recent interview she said, "Fulfilled? 'Course I'm fulfilled dear. I'd hate to die starvin' . . ."

She was unmarried.

November 30 1987

MARGOT BRYANT

MARGOT BRYANT, the actress who has died aged 90,
became one of the most familiar faces on television in the
late 1960s and 1970s through her portrayal of the
simpering, cat-loving Minnie Caldwell in 560 episodes of
Granada TV's interminable serial, *Coronation Street*.

The diminutive old dear, who always had a faintly
flyblown look and a distracted manner, was the put-upon
member of that formidable coven which held sway in the
snug of the Rovers Return. Delicately supping her milk
stout, Minnie would be subjected to acid tongue-lashings
by the other occupants of this moral crow's nest, Ena
Sharples and Martha Longhurst, for her vague incompre-
hension of the finer points of the latest gossip.

The verbal interplay between the three yielded some
of the Street's richest moments, delighting John Betjeman
and all other fans of the serial's earthy Northern humanity.
The triptych in the snug was affectionately caricatured in
Victoria Wood's television show.

Harry Kershaw, the veteran producer and scriptwriter
of the Street, said that it was "a privilege to write for one
of the most rewarding triumvirate of women in the history
of drama – let alone TV".

Minnie Caldwell's life tended to revolve around her
ginger tom-cat, Bobby (once a permanent fixture on the
rooftops in the programme's opening sequence), and his
various vicissitudes. At one stage in the early 1960s she
had a lodger, the cheeky Jed Stone (played by Kenneth
Cope), with whom she enjoyed a maternal relationship; he
called her "Ma", she called him "Sunny Jim".

Later she toyed with the affections of the miserable old codger, Albert Tatlock; marriage was in the offing, but when Minnie discovered that their union would have a deleterious effect on her pension she cancelled the match.

Having appeared in the third episode of Coronation Street in 1960, Moaning Minnie stayed on until 1976. According to the storyline, the character left the Street to keep house for her old schoolfriend, Handel Gartside, in Derbyshire.

Margot Bryant, a doctor's daughter, was born at Hull in 1897 and began her career as a chorus girl in pantomime. She went on to dance in the Fred Astaire show, *Stop Flirting*, in the 1920s, and her other West End roles included Lucy in *Gay's the Word* at the old Saville.

Miss Bryant toured in *My Mother Said* and appeared in the show's television production. She was also seen on the small screen in *The Bell Family*, while among her films were *I Get Myself Arrested* and *The Larger Rope*.

A dedicated trouper, who insisted on high standards of professionalism and good manners, Miss Bryant was much distressed by her declining ability to learn her lines as her health deteriorated.

Quite unlike Minnie Caldwell in real life – the only thing they had in common was a preference for the feline species to the human – Miss Bryant was outspoken, caustic and sophisticated with a love of travel.

"She always had a twinkle in her eye," recalled the Street's only survivor from the original cast, William Roache (who plays Ken Barlow), "and liked to shock people."

She never married.

January 5 1988

34

TREVOR HOWARD

TREVOR HOWARD, who has died aged 71, was celebrated as a film star and a hard-drinking hell-raiser, his
craggy features being particularly associated with such
roles as Lord Cardigan, Captain Bligh and other larger
than life characters which he attacked with memorable
relish. But he was also a fine and perceptive actor whose
genius tended to be underrated.

He revealed a rare subtlety in his portrayals of the
anguished Scobie in the film of Graham Greene's novel,
The Heart of the Matter, and the lovelorn doctor in *Brief
Encounter*, the film for which he will be most affectionately
remembered.

Although he was nominated for an Oscar for his
moving performance as the father in *Sons and Lovers* (1960),
Howard never received the honours he deserved in his own
country. But his strongly masculine individuality left an
indelible stamp on some 75 films, including *Cockleshell
Heroes*, *Odette*, *The Battle of Britain*, *Von Ryan's Express*, *The
Long Duel*, *Stevie,* and *Ryan's Daughter*.

One of his co-stars in *Ryan's Daughter*, Robert Mitchum, observed: "You'll never catch Trevor Howard
acting" – an approach which blazed the trail for younger
actors like Albert Finney and Alan Bates.

From the start of his career he shunned the use of
heavy make-up and props – "they would get in the way"
– and developed a deceptively casual style which concealed
a hard professionalism. When they saw Howard's name on
the billing, people knew that he would make it worth-
while. Few screen stars commanded such sympathy, or

conveyed more feeling by use of the eyes. Even in the tiny role of a judge in *Gandhi*, his impact was considerable.

Howard's image as a "hell-raiser" (he preferred the term eccentric) grew from his insatiable appetite for life and an equal thirst for drink – "it makes the world a nicer place," he said. Sometimes this landed him in difficulty, as when he was arrested in Vienna for conducting the band in a restaurant late at night, dressed in the uniform of a British major for his part in *The Third Man*. Errol Flynn, who also suffered from the hell-raising label, became a friend when they starred together in *Roots of Heaven*.

Howard seldom talked about his work once he left the set, but on it he was thoroughly disciplined; he only abandoned his usual discretion when he spoke of Marlon Brando's behaviour during the filming of *Mutiny on the Bounty* – a bitter experience, aggravated when Sir Carol Reed was replaced as director. Exasperated by Brando's mumbling his lines or forgetting them, he later dismissed the American as "unprofessional and utterly ridiculous".

The son of an English insurance agent who worked for Lloyd's in Ceylon, and a Canadian mother, Trevor Wallace Howard-Smith was born in 1916 and educated at Clifton, where he nurtured his life-long passion for cricket.

The loneliness of his early years accounted for a certain shyness, which he masked with bravado. Destined for the Army, Howard startled his family by insisting on going to RADA.

His first stage success came with Terence Rattigan's *French Without Tears* in 1936. He had a small role compared to Rex Harrison's, but the play ran triumphantly for two years in the West End.

This caused an aversion to long runs, leading him to

reject the part of Professor Higgins in *My Fair Lady* – which was taken by Harrison instead – a decision which Howard "never regretted".

A season at Stratford-upon-Avon was interrupted by the Second World War. Having been rejected by the RAF, he joined the Royal Corps of Signals, but was invalided out three years later.

The widely credited story that he had won the Military Cross was perhaps begun by a well-meaning publicist. The legend grew until it could no longer be denied, reinforced by Howard's impeccable portrayals of gallant British officers. If this was a deception it was of little consequence; but he was none the less troubled by it in recent years.

In 1943 Howard starred with Helen Cherry in the Arts Theatre production of *The Recruiting Officer*, and fell in love with that gifted and humorous actress. "Marrying Helen was the best thing I ever did in my entire life," he said.

Throughout their close though turbulent marriage she was the constant factor he depended on, and a clause was inserted in subsequent film contracts that she could join him on location anywhere in the world.

A small but vital film part in *A Way to the Stars* (1944) provided a boost to his career and led to his being cast opposite Celia Johnson in *Brief Encounter*. He was paid a mere £500 for the film, was not invited to the press show and was ignored at the première by Noël Coward – who failed to recognise his leading man – but it established him as one of those actors beloved by the camera.

His special gift was to make the audience see him thinking; and his voice – which ultimately became a roar – was redolent of warmth and promise. Though far from the conventional heart-throb, Howard helped make the film a classic.

From then on his versatility enriched a series of major films, though at times he chose parts hastily and rejected several in which he might have proved magnificent. Often typecast as a crusty old soldier, he nobly sent himself up in the acclaimed surrealistic comedy film, *Sir Henry at Rawlinson End*.

Howard once declared: "I think staying in a film studio for ever is the coward's way out – you have to venture out and do some real work from time to time." He returned to the theatre in 1953 in *The Devil's General*, appearing, at his insistence, with his friend and drinking companion Wilfrid Lawson,

One night the audience was baffled by their antics, especially as Lawson seemed to die in one act and reappear in the next. But, as Richard Attenborough remarked in a different context: "If it was necessary for two people to get pissed in order to give the performance that emanated from Trevor Howard and Wilfrid Lawson, I'm all for getting pissed." It was Lawson's performance in *The Father* which inspired Howard to take the same part in 1964, which he tackled with similar bravura.

Ten years later Howard enjoyed another success as General St Pé in *Waltz of the Toreadors* at the Haymarket. With his conviction that Shakespeare was the basis for all acting, it is a cause for regret that he never attempted Lear.

More recently he appeared on television in cameo parts such as Sir Isaac Newton in *Peter the Great*. Thirty-six years after *Brief Encounter* he was reunited with Celia Johnson in the adaptation of Paul Scott's last Raj novel, *Staying On*. His last film performance was as the voyeuristic Jack

Soames in *White Mischief* (1988), the story of the notorious Kenyan *crime-passionnel* in 1941.

For the last 38 years of his life Howard and his wife lived at their home in Arkley, Herts, preferring a visit to their local pub to the parties of the "jet set", which he detested. He leaves no children: looking after him was a full-time occupation for Helen Cherry, and the further responsibility of a family might well have jeopardised their long and devoted partnership.

When asked on his 70th birthday what he considered was his finest work, he roared back: "Nothing at all!" Fortunately, the rich legacy of his filmed performances will prove otherwise.

January 8 1988

LESLIE THOMPSON

LESLIE THOMPSON, the Jamaican trumpeter who has died aged 86, was one of the pioneers of jazz in Britain where in the 1930s he worked not only with "Spike" Hughes and Ken "Snake Hips" Johnson but also with C. B. Cochran, Noël Coward and William Walton.

However, in the mid-1950s he underwent a Pauline conversion and forsook the fleshpots of Soho for good works, eventually becoming a welfare officer at Pentonville Prison where the governor would sometimes prevail on him to play for the inmates.

Leslie Thompson was born in Jamaica in 1901 and educated at the Alpha Boys' School – an institution attended by Bertie King and Joe Harriot, two saxophone players active in Britain.

He first came to Britain aged 18, when he was already a proficient musician, to study at the Military Music Academy, Kneller Hall, where he won a silver medal. Among friends at his tiny flat in Gower Street he would recall that "people were surprised that someone straight from the jungle could play an instrument" – his gently derisive way of noting the racial prejudice and misunderstanding he was to meet in various guises for the rest of his life.

Thompson applied to be a bandmaster at Kneller, but the military establishment debarred commissions to entrants of non-European descent, so he went home to Jamaica and played at dances and for silent films. The advent of the talkies put him out of a job, however, so in 1919 he returned to Britain for good, determined not to be beaten by prejudice. One of his first engagements was at a Jewish wedding at Dalston in the East End.

From 1930 to 1932 he embarked on a series of recordings with Spike Hughes and his Dance Orchestra (originally called the Decca Dents) at the Chenil Galleries in Chelsea – the first regular jazz recordings by a British band. Thompson was no soloist, but proved himself as a good and reliable technician.

Hughes wrote material for C. B. Cochran's 1931 Revue and played bass in the band when the show opened at the Palace Theatre, Manchester. Thompson was also in the band, and the two of them lodged at a boarding house in the suburb of Chorlton-cum-Hardy. In his memoirs, *Second Movement*, Hughes recalled his anger when their landlady asked him to tell Thompson to find alternative accommodation because the other guests were worried about sharing a bathroom with a black man.

In 1934 Thompson played – and recorded – with

Louis Armstrong's Paris Band. He then lost contact with "Satchmo" for more than 20 years. In 1956, when Armstrong appeared at the Empress Hall, Earl's Court, his dressing room was besieged with musicians, fans and reporters, and Thompson was refused admission. But Armstrong overheard his voice and cried out: "My lead trumpeter! Let him in!"

The same year he was in the pit band of the *Black Birds*, a show starring the trumpeter and vocalist Valaida Snow; and then worked in various West End club and restaurant bands. In 1936 he formed an all-black band which was eventually taken over by the dancer "Snake Hips" Johnson; and the next year he recorded with the multi-instrumentalist Benny Carter before going on to play with Edmundo Ross.

During the Second World War he served in the Royal Artillery and later transferred to the "Stars in Battle Dress" unit. After the war he returned to his old life in the clubs, but in 1954 he gave it up to become warden of the Alliance Club, a London hostel for overseas and British students. In his early 60s he started another career, working with the North London magistrates court; and in 1963 was appointed a welfare officer at Pentonville Prison where he started up a jazz band and continued to give concerts in his 70s.

Thompson was an immensely courteous and dignified person, and a deeply religious one. He preached at churches of all denominations and could usually be persuaded to give an impromptu trumpet performance as well.

January 25 1988

DIVINE

DIVINE, who has died at Los Angeles aged 42, was an obese female impersonator who achieved cult status for his outrageous performances in such "underground" films as *Lust in the Dust*.

At the time of his death he was about to break into mainstream cinema with *Hairspray*, a nostalgic look at Baltimore, *circa* 1962, in which he has two starring roles – as a housewife and as a racist television station owner. The film was released recently in America where it received generally excellent reviews and is likely to be an international hit.

Divine also made some records – "You May Think You're a Man" and "Walk Like a Man" among them – and so helped pioneer a style of pop music known as "hi-energy", which has a wide following among homosexuals.

Though he was once voted "filthiest person alive" Divine was a shy and pleasant character when he took off his female costume and make-up. He said recently that his sluttish persona was just a mask. "I hate that, when they call me a transvestite," he said of his cha-cha heels and thigh-splitting spandex dresses. "Those are my work clothes. That's how I make people laugh."

Harris Glen Milstead, to give him his real name, was born in 1945 and began his career as a hairdresser in Baltimore, Maryland. He was renamed by the film director John Waters, who made a series of films about Divine and his seedy cronies. Waters' black and white productions, made in the 1960s and 1970s, are essentially a suburban, and rather wilder version of Andy Warhol's New York films of that period.

Waters, who had been at school with Divine, filmed the hideous brown streets of downtown Baltimore, strewn with rubbish and lined with junk shops, in a style which borrowed the bad taste of B-grade horror movies in much the same way as Warhol borrowed his style from "porn flicks".

Among the freakish cast of such films as *Pink Flamingos*, *Female Trouble* and *Desperate Living*, Divine stole the show with the amusing flair of an amateur actor, as he engaged in such grotesque activities as eating dog excrement (apparently to make a satirical point about America's gross consumerism). And as the star grew ever fatter, so his husky voice and gigantic *embonpoint* became underground trademarks. Nightclub acts, disco records and ubiquitous "public appearances" added to his *louche* glamour.

Divine made a great splash at the Cannes Festival three years ago in the film *Polyester*, in which he played a housewife victimised by a swindling Casanova. After his previous film, *Lust in the Dust*, he had become an acknowledged character-actor star, with a New York apartment and a Florida home to show for it.

At the time of his death Divine was in Hollywood to film an episode of the television show *Married . . . With Children* in which he was to play the role of Uncle Otto.

He was unmarried.

March 9 1988

KENNETH WILLIAMS

KENNETH WILLIAMS, the actor who has died aged 62, was an extraordinarily original and inventive entertainer, whose range of hilariously exaggerated voices and expressive face, with its famous flared nostrils, gave pleasure to millions.

Although best known for his outraged double-takes amid the bawdy *double entendres* in the *Carry On* films and his contributions to such radio series as *Around the Horne* and *Just a Minute* – not to mention innumerable TV chat shows – Williams was also a talented stage actor. He excelled not only in revue but also in the "legitimate" theatre, where his roles included the Dauphin in *St Joan*, Elijah in Orson Welles's production of *Moby Dick* and the title role in *Gentle Jack* opposite Edith Evans – the subject of many a Williams anecdote.

On learning that the Dame had remarked on Williams's "peculiar voice", he replied, "I think that's a bit much coming from her!"

Probably his best stage performance was as the private detective in the Peter Shaffer play *The Public Eye*, together with his old friend from revue, Maggie Smith, at the Queen's in 1963.

A slight, diminutive figure, away from the limelight Williams had little in common with his camp public image. Shy and serious, he acquired the intense erudition of the autodidact, immersing himself in music, philosophy and literature.

"If they think our comedy is all tits and bums," he once wrote in the *Telegraph Sunday Magazine* about the prospect of being interviewed for a French documentary about the British cinema, "I'll point out the precedents set by Aristophanes as well as Plautus. And I'll bring in that bit about Alberoni embracing the posterior of the Duke of Vendome when the latter rose from the *chaise percée* . . ."

Like most genuinely funny people, Williams was a melancholic. He lived alone in a small obsessively tidy flat in Marylebone and, so the story went, never invited anybody in, in case they might wish to use his lavatory: "I can't stand the idea of another bottom on my loo."

Though he was friendly with flamboyant homosexuals – notably Joe Orton the playwright – and played such characters with panache, Williams had a horror of sex. "I'm basically guilty about being a homosexual you see," he once confided to Orton, who noted in his diaries: "Kenneth W. isn't able to have sex properly with man or woman. His only outlet is exhibiting his extremely funny personality in front of an audience and when he isn't doing this he's a very sad man indeed."

Supremely disciplined, Williams appeared to be frightened by the spectre of self-indulgence and dined most days with his mother, to whom he was especially close. His father, a strict Methodist, had managed a hairdressing shop.

Kenneth Williams was born in the Caledonian Road, North London, in 1926 and educated at Lyulph Stanley School in Mornington Crescent. He remembered his school days in the familiar manner of comedians: "I was vulnerable and weak, so the only way I could protect myself was by play-acting. The bigger boys liked my jokes and impressions of teachers."

At the age of 14 he left school to study lithography at

Bolt Court, off Fleet Street, and then found employment as a draughtsman. During the Second World War he served in the Royal Engineers survey section in Bombay and at the end of hostilities was posted to the map reproduction section at Kurunegala, Ceylon.

In 1946 he managed to obtain a posting to Combined Services Entertainments based at Singapore, only to fail the audition. His effeminate patter act – "Are you one of Wingate's men?" "No, I'm one of Colgate's girls!" – was ill-received and resulted in an "RTU" (Returned to Unit).

He persuaded them to let him stay and produce posters, however. On one occasion when an actor failed to turn up, he found himself on stage.

Soon he was appearing with his great friend and mentor Stanley Baxter in the sort of revues which were guyed so lovingly in *Privates of Parade* – written by another CSE alumnus, Peter Nichols. One of Williams's routines out East went: "My Granny's got a nose like the Malayan peninsula, with a wart at Singapore." He also specialised in impersonations of Nellie Wallace.

Demobbed with the rank of Sergeant, Williams returned disconsolately to the drawing board. But Baxter urged him to become a professional actor and in 1948 Williams made his first appearance on the English stage as Ninian in *The First Mrs Fraser* at the Newquay Repertory Theatre.

Several years' experience in rep followed before he achieved a London engagement. But his West End debut as Slightly in *Peter Pan* was a disaster. As the Dauphin in Shaw's *St Joan* at the Arts in 1954, he seemed like just a good, sound, serious and vocally incisive player.

He confirmed that impression in Orson Welles's idea of *Moby Dick* at the Duke of York's. But he began to show hints of what was to come in Sandy Wilson's *The Buccaneer* at the Apollo, which was all about classical boys' magazines and brought out Williams's eternal boyishness (some said puerility) with special force.

He held his own as Maxime in *Hotel Paradiso*, London's first English experience of Feydeau at the Winter Garden in 1956, with Alec Guinness and Irene Worth romping about. But he seemed immediately in his peculiar, gnome-like element with Maggie Smith, then unknown, in Bamber Gascoigne's revue *Share My Lettuce*.

Revue was then still in fashion, having its last gasp before *Beyond the Fringe*, and Williams became a striking example of its value in developing a technique of direct, incisive, split-second timing. The genre developed personality faster in a player than any other form of theatre, and Williams was among the quickest.

The personality in his case was to become that of a friendly, leering and highly comical mimic with no particular satirical power or character which he could call his own but with a warmth and wit which sprang directly from his vocal and physical attributes: the assorted voices, the deadpan stares and the way he addressed most people down his nose.

Williams went next to lead two Peter Cook revues in succession – *Pieces of Eight* and *One Over the Eight* (1959 and 1961). After these his campness was to resist restraint for the rest of his career. It was seldom more fascinatingly exhibited than as Julian in Peter Shaffer's double bill at the Globe, *The Private Ear and the Public Eye*.

As a stage actor Williams's talent could be said to have gone to seed by exploiting its tricks to the point (for some people) of nausea. His Inspector Truscott in the first and unsuccessful pre-London tour of *Loot* by his friend Joe

Orton, was probably too much of a caricature. The character could not hold the stage with authority while daft doings were going on all round him if the actor playing him knew that he was being funny.

Williams was to appear intermittently in several other light West End comedies; but perhaps he needed the discipline of a basically serious text if his "legitimate" acting was not to look tongue-in-cheek. He kept it more or less invisible at the Cambridge in 1971 for Shaw's *Captain Brassbound's Conversion* – mainly out of respect, one imagines, for the grace and beauty of Ingrid Bergman, who was at the helm of the revival.

Towards the end of his career he directed two of Joe Orton's plays at Hammersmith, *Loot* (which had never reached London when he was in it) and *Entertaining Mr Sloane*.

But more than for his stage work, it is for his joyfully broad characterisations in the *Carry On* series that Kenneth Williams will be most fondly remembered – as an effete Caesar, for example, in *Carry On, Cleo* ("Infamy! Infamy! They've all got it *in-for-me*!"), as the preposterously exotic Khazi in *Carry On Up the Khyber*, or the NCO with ludricrous pretensions to gentility in *Carry On, Sergeant*.

"I like smutty old jokes," he said. "Honest vulgarity is the central tradition of English humour, and uninhibitedness the essence of comedy."

Williams's catch-phrase of "Stop messing about," delivered in a glutinous Cockney whine, became a celebrated feature of the two Kenneth Horne radio series, *Beyond Our Ken* and *Round the Horne*. Here Williams's repertoire of accents was given full rein, from the agricultural burr of "The answer lies in the soil" to the strangulated tones of choleric colonels.

Together with Hugh Paddick on the Horne shows, he created a double act featuring the adventures of two outrageously camp chorus boys, Julian ("Jules to *you*, ducky") and his friend Sandy.

His brilliant, self-parodying improvisations in *Just a Minute* provided some of the most inspired moments on radio in recent times. Williams had first come to prominence on that medium in *Hancock's Half-Hour* but Tony Hancock grew jealous of his partner's following. "It's a gimmick, a funny voice, it's cartoon stuff, I don't want it in the show," he said when he sacked him.

But the public delighted in the bizarre and stylised comic *persona* Williams was fashioning for himself: a somewhat soiled garden pixie, exultantly queer, adenoidal and insolent. Children, in particular, revelled in Williams's idiosyncratic delivery and he became a popular presenter of *Jackanory*. His readings of the *Just William* stories were especially relished by admirers of Richmal Crompton.

He launched a new television career as the compère of *International Cabaret*, where his anecdotal patter between acts led to a constant round of chat show appearances. Recently Williams was thrilled when asked to sit in for Terry Wogan as host of the thrice-weekly BBC1 programme.

Few comedians, even those who write their own material, have a capacity for producing good prose at anywhere near book length. Williams did, and could speak from the page in his own unmistakable voice. His first book, *Acid Drops* (1980), a collection of "put downs", included much first-rate material, welded together with characteristic comments. One of his favourite anecdotes concerned the occasion when a drunken male bigot in the audience kept complaining loudly about the preponderance of "pansies" on the stage. "Here's another one!" he snorted on Williams's entrance. "Do be quiet, *Madam*!" snapped back the actor.

Perhaps it was the success of this book that led Williams to the more self-indulgent *Back Drops* (1983), supposedly a diary of his year, which showed every sign of heavy rewriting. Although remarkably well presented and showing to good effect his remarkable knowledge of English literature (particularly poetry, for which he had an amazing capacity for quotation from memory), it suffered from his conviction that anything he said or wrote was "a little gem".

When he came to produce *Just Williams* (1985), his autobiography dealing mainly with his childhood and war service in India and South-East Asia, his natural skill as a storyteller overcame his tendency to be funny at all costs. Williams's own account of his CSE days served to give verisimilitude to the otherwise unlikely story of Peter Nichols's *Privates on Parade*.

Obviously, when engagements as a performer were coming thick and fast, Williams had little time to settle down to serious writing. This is a pity because he had considerable natural gifts, which an editor not too dazzled by the incessant flow of spoken words, could have harnessed most effectively.

Williams claimed to be unworried by the passing years and the prospect of death: "The shorter the better. I think to go at 65 or 70 is fine. Why hang about?"

April 10 1988

BARBARA WOODHOUSE

BARBARA WOODHOUSE, who has died aged 78, became famous with the BBC series, *Training Dogs the Woodhouse Way*, in the 1970s, sweeping the nation with her ringing catchphrase: "Walkies!"

A real life Dr Doolittle in a tweed skirt, Woodhouse enjoyed a magical ability to communicate with animals, using love, enthusiasm, will-power and "the telepathic communication without which I could never talk to animals at all".

Her personality had a seemingly miraculous effect, as she demonstrated when one nervous dog, terrified of entering Tube trains, jumped straight aboard at her stentorian command. She could train any dog in basic obedience in less than six minutes; one of her own dogs was taught to answer the telephone.

Woodhouse had such rapport with animals that when she kept a boarding school for dogs her charges kept running away from their owners and coming back to her. Altogether she trained more than 17,000 dogs – a world record.

The daughter of a clerical headmaster, Barbara Blackburn was born near Dublin in 1910. Her father died when she was nine, and she was brought up in Brighton and Oxford by her mother and assorted nannies. She once overheard her mother say: "Why can't Barbara be beautiful, like the other children?" From that moment she decided that she preferred animals, because they did not care what she looked like.

After school at Headington and in Switzerland, she

boldly went to Harper Adams Agricultural College in Newport, Shropshire, where she was the only woman among 60 men. She studied veterinary science, building construction and engineering, and gained the second highest marks in the college: she became an expert motor mechanic, and could lay bricks as fast as a professional.

After a time running a riding school, the redoubtable Miss Blackburn set off, aged 24, on a cargo boat to seek adventure in Argentina. During her time there she contracted foot and mouth disease, and suffered from diabetes. She spent four years on great estates on the pampas, and earned a wide reputation for her skill in breaking wild horses, which was considered an exclusively masculine occupation.

Back in England in 1940, she married Dr Michael Woodhouse, and during the Second World War kept cows, discovering that milk production improved if the animals wore rugs in winter.

In 1954 she published her enduring bestseller, *Talking to Animals*, which she had dashed off in only five days. She later wrote more than 20 books, including an autobiography, *Just Barbara* (published in 1981).

Her television career began in the early 1950s, when she demonstrated her animal-training skills on Scottish television. After appearances on *Pebble Mill at One*, she was finally given the series which made her a celebrity.

Among her most successful pupils were her two Great Danes, which made more than 100 screen appearances, and the famous Old English Sheepdog trained to carry a can of paint for Dulux advertisements.

After suffering a stroke in 1984, she was scarcely able to walk, and could only speak very slowly. She none the less took 30 to 40 telephone enquiries a day from dog owners and wrote a book advising stroke sufferers how to come to terms with their condition.

In 1987 she used her teaching skills as part of a personal battle against unemployment, training backward jobless youths to read and write. Before her recent second stroke she had been due to appear in a television documentary, *Where There's Life*, in which she defended the right of stroke patients to refuse, as she had done, the painful process of rehabilitation through physiotherapy.

She is survived by her husband, a son and two daughters.

July 11 1988

NICO

NICO, who has died in Ibiza aged 49, was the Dietrich of the 1960s: an exquisite blonde, melancholy and amused, she sang about the mysteries of sorrow and sin, and radiated sex and angst in roughly equal measures. She obviously knew too much about men and took too many drugs.

Nico's style was throwaway, cool, essentially urban. Her allure owed much to Berlin, where she passed her infancy in the postwar rubble; and her apotheosis occurred in New York, as one of Andy Warhol's "superstars", a product of his Factory of the Arts.

Between Berlin and New York came Rome, where she caught the eye of Federico Fellini, the film director; Paris (Alain Delon, the actor, by whom she later had a child); and London (Brian Jones of the Rolling Stones).

She pursued careers as underwear salesgirl, model, actress and singer.

Nico was born Christa Pavloski, at Cologne in 1938. Her father died in a concentration camp when she was two, and her mother took her to live with her grandfather, a railwayman, near Berlin.

In 1950 she and her mother moved to Ibiza. After a protracted idyll on that island and a brief period in Rome, appearing in Fellini's *La dolce vita*, Nico moved to Paris, where she entered the bohemian world she was later to reign over. Five years later she moved, via London, to New York, where she studied at the Lee Strasberg school of acting – in the same class as Marilyn Monroe.

Nico was soon taken up by Warhol, and adopted her definitive role of *femme fatale*.

When Warhol was introduced to her by Bob Dylan in 1965 she was singing "intimate songs" at the Blue Angel Lounge on East 55th Street.

Warhol had recently taken control of the Velvet Underground – a rock group which opposed the prevailing cult of Californian "peace and love" with raucous songs about sado-masochism, homosexuality and heroin – and decided that Nico should become a member.

The Velvets bowed to their patron, but were unenthusiastic about the new recruit, particularly as she expected to take over the singing from Lou Reed. They played tricks on her, sabotaging her microphone and so on, and the songs Reed wrote for Nico tended to mock their singer.

None the less, the Velvet Underground and Nico were for a time a potent combination: her deadpan, eerie voice contrasted well with their amphetamine-fuelled guitar playing and street-gang choruses.

The two styles are at their most pointed in "Femme Fatale", in which Nico sings mournfully about a character not unlike her own, and the band delivers the one-line chorus in a bored, sneering tone:

> *Everybody sees*
> *(She's a femme fatale)*
> *The things she does to please*
> *(She's a femme fatale)*
> *She's just a little tease . . .*
> *She's going to smile to*
> *make you frown*
> *What a clown . . .*

It was her finest hour. Towards the end of 1967 Reed took full control of the band and dispensed with the services of Nico, Warhol and Cale.

Nico resumed her solo career, recording a collection of cover versions on an LP called *Chelsea Girl* (she had starred in Warhol's film of the same name). She made a new friend in the singer Jim Morrison, who urged her to write and perform her own material. Borrowing an idea from the poet Allen Ginsberg, Nico acquired an Indian pump organ to accompany her depraved Germanic lullabies.

Cale proved an abiding influence, and she produced four LPs in collaboration with him: *Marble Index*, *Desert Shore*, *The End* and *Camera Obscura*.

She also appeared in 10 avante-garde films directed by her lover, the French film director Philippe Carelle.

In recent years Nico dyed her hair jet black, moved to Manchester and became a pillar of the "punk" movement, of which the Velvets had been the forerunners. She also gave up heroin for bicycling, which was to turn out the more dangerous amusement – she died when she fell off a bicycle while on holiday.

July 25 1988

ROY KINNEAR

ROY KINNEAR, the popular character actor who has died aged 54, was as broad a comedian as the British theatre has produced this century, both in his girth and style.

He put his physique to work on all occasions with a blubbery face, rubbery jowls, a spherical figure, and a sweaty grin, with all things combining to present fatness as funny. In rumbustious plays at Stratford East for Joan Littlewood; or more orderly productions at Stratford-upon-Avon for Peter Hall; in films of the simple-hearted *Carry On* tendency and above all, in the television series *That Was The Week That Was*, Kinnear rose in the 1960s to be a reliably comical supporting actor.

He huffed and puffed, wheezed and spluttered his way through any part that came his way – and he was almost constantly in work. Sometimes he would appear on the point of literally exploding with mirth, weeping with laughter at a joke nobody else had seen; his chuckles could shake the whole of his heaving body until he resembled a vast blancmange.

Kinnear suffered, inevitably, from typecasting, though he would have made an interesting Falstaff, by the look of him, had he been put upon, and he did make an interesting Baptista in the *Taming of the Shrew* for the Royal Shakespeare Company, and his Touchstone in *As You Like It* won approval.

And at Chichester last year he finally achieved a role which might have brought a change of direction to his career. He played the Common Man in Robert Bolt's *A Man For All Seasons*, and proved himself a first-rate actor with his button-holing, casual-seeming, throwaway manner, charming in its unforced friendliness, bridging the centuries with a hospitable grin.

Roy Mitchell Kinnear was born at Wigan in 1934 and educated at George Heriot's School, Edinburgh. He trained for the stage at the Royal Academy of Dramatic Art and made his first appearance at Newquay in 1955.

Four years later he made his London debut in Wolf Mankowitz's musical, *Make Me An Offer*, for Joan Littlewood's Theatre Workshop in the East End of London, whence many of the shows moved west. Amid the motley crowd of cockney rogues and vagabonds with which her stage was often cluttered the fat boy from Wigan stood out.

He became a national celebrity through BBC Television's pioneering Saturday night satirical revue *That Was The Week That Was* in which his comic talents outshone everything else on the screen. He endowed such sketches as the squaddie delivering a party political broadcast ("Get your knees brown, Lord Home!"), or the henpecked man suffering from gaping fly-buttons, with a memorable zest.

One of his most brilliant turns was as the "Safe Comedian", a wickedly observed study of an oleaginous stand-up comic qualifying his digs at politicians with painfully sincere disclaimers ("but seriously he's doing a grand job . . .") before launching into a sentimental song.

He graduated to the Palladium pantomime and then to the Royal Shakespeare Company for Bolt's charming Christmas play *The Thwarting of Baron Bolligrew* in which Kinnear played the baron imperiously. He was kept on for the Stratford season and next made his mark in the classics as Sancho Panza at the National.

Kinnear was now proving himself a subtler actor than his looks might suggest. But having made his name within a small area of clowning he seemed to be stuck with the same role in films, plays and on television: that of the fat man who must be funny just because he is fat.

His television shows included *A World of His Own* and *Inside George Webley* and among his numerous films were *Help!*, *The Three Musketeers*, *Hammett* (playing a Sidney Greenstreet-style villain) and *The Zany Adventures of Robin Hood* (cast, of course, as Friar Tuck).

He is survived by his wife, the actress Carmel Cryan, their son and two daughters.

September 22 1988

BILLY CARTER

BILLY CARTER, who has died aged 51, was President Jimmy Carter's hard-drinking roly-poly brother whose bibulous verandah chair comments from the peanut township of Plains, Georgia, caused periodic embarrassment at the White House.

Unabashed by his much-publicised reputation as a buffoon, he often made matters worse by joking at his own expense. A favourite story was that one night he had been drinking heavily and took two cups to bed – one contained bourbon, the other minnows he needed for fishing. Feeling thirsty, he stretched out for the bourbon, only to discover in the morning that he had swallowed the minnows.

It was one of many such anecdotes which confirmed the Anarchist party of Canada's description of him as "a preacher of gross consumerism".

At a time when Colonel Gaddafi was on the State Department's list of public enemies Billy Carter headed a trade delegation from Georgia to Tripoli, but President Carter stepped in and ordered government agencies and officials to rebuff any member of his family who might seek dealings with them. The affair became known as "Billygate".

On another occasion he advertised mementoes of his brother's inauguration for sale at outrageous prices, and flogged inauguration postal covers from the Plains post office. Less successful was his introduction of "Billy Beer", a brand which lasted less than a year.

Describing himself as a "beer-drinking good ol' boy", he held court to a ring of reporters and columnists who syndicated his expletive-punctuated observations at times of crisis when the White House could well have done without them.

Even so, his long-suffering brother made patient allowances, furrowing his brow as he ticked him off, but always forgiving him. During Billy's illness he took him into his home.

William Alton Carter II, who was born near Plains in 1937, was the youngest of four children of James Earl Carter, a prominent businessman, and his wife Lillian – Jimmy Carter's other family cross, the opinionated "Miz Lillian".

He married his high-school sweetheart, Sybil Spires, and joined the Marines. After serving in Japan and the Philippines he drove a truck for the peanut business and attended Emory University, Atlanta, but was expelled after submitting an examination paper written by someone else.

He later ran a petrol-filling station from which he also dispensed beer and soft drinks. But on encountering difficulties with federal tax collectors and other inquisitive government agencies he dropped out, living largely off personal appearance fees.

Carter died of pancreatic cancer, the same disease which killed his father and a sister. "I always said what I thought and I didn't hold anything back," he said in a recent interview after he was diagnosed as suffering from the illness.

He is survived by his wife and their six children.

September 26 1988

CHARLES HAWTREY

CHARLES HAWTREY, who has died aged 74, was an endearingly eccentric comedy actor whose bespectacled, spindle-shanked figure and dotty, weedy, often outrageously "camp" characterisations tended to be more familiar than his name.

The name had, in fact, been cheekily borrowed from the celebrated Edwardian actor-manager Sir Charles Hawtrey, who died in 1923, a couple of years before the young Hawtrey (*né* Hartree) began his career as a boy soprano.

He made his mark as Slightly in *Peter Pan*, and then in revue before becoming a regular member of the ageing schoolboy troupe in the Will Hay films; but it was in another series of even broader comedies, the *Carry Ons*, that he achieved his apotheosis. Resembling a mischievous stick insect, with a face curiously reminiscent of an elderly maiden aunt topped by an incongruous toupée, and with a distinctive high-pitched voice verging on the hysterical, Hawtrey cropped up in one absurdly unlikely role after another as the *Carry On* series established itself as a great British institution.

Carry On Sergeant led to *Carry On Nurse*, *Carry On At Your Convenience* to *Carry On Camping* – though Hawtrey needed little encouragement in that direction. He had an insouciant way with a double entendre which was all his own; somehow he retained an innocently spinsterish persona amid all the tired innuendoes and remorseless allusions to bodily functions. Indeed Hawtrey frequently managed to steal scenes from fellow stalwarts of the series such as Sid James, Kenneth Williams and Kenneth Connor and became one of the most hilarious "turns" in the cinema.

Many will cherish the memory of Hawtrey as the skittish Seer in *Carry On Cleo* popping his head out of an Egyptian urn, with the lid worn like a beret at a jaunty angle, and prefacing his latest vision with a breezy "Stop me if you've heard this before". Or as the fastidious Red Indian Chief, Big Heap, in *Carry On Cowboy*; or as the kilted Private Widdle in *Carry On Up the Khyber* complaining that "the wind fairly whistles *up the Pass*".

George Frederick Joffre Hartree came from a theatrical family, though his father was a motor mechanic. Born at Hounslow, Middlesex, in 1914, he studied for the stage at the Italia Conti School and made his first appearance at Boscombe in 1925 as a street arab in *The Windmill Man*. His London debut as a boy actor was at the Scala Theatre on Boxing Day 1927 as the White Cat and Bootblack in *Bluebell in Fairyland* and the next year he appeared in *Where the Rainbow Ends* at the Holborn Empire.

In 1929 he began his long wireless career which was to include roles in the Will Hay series, the Norman and Henry Bones children's hour comedy and *Just William* – in which he played the snooty Hubert Lane. In 1931 Hawtrey was seen at the Palladium as the First Twin in *Peter Pan* and five years later he played Slightly in another production of Barrie's classic fantasy at the same theatre. He was commended by W. A. Darlington, dramatic critic of *The Daily Telegraph*, for showing "a comedy sense not unworthy of his famous name".

Hawtrey's many other stage appearances included the Shakespearean role of Gremio in *The Taming of the Shrew* at the Old Vic (1939) and the following year he earned rave notices for the Eric Maschwitz revue *New Faces*, particularly for his "chic and finished study of an alluring woman spy".

During and after the Second World War he appeared in the West End in such shows as *Scoop*, *Old Chelsea*, *Merrie England*, *Frou-Frou* and *Husbands Don't Count*, as well as directing several plays at the Q theatre. But it was in the cinema that he was best known.

He resumed his partnership with Will Hay in *Good Morning Boys* (1937), *Where's That Fire?* (1939), *The Ghost of St Michael's* (1941) and *The Goose Steps Out* (1942). Other film credits included *A Canterbury Tale* (1948), *The Gallop-ing Major* (1950), *Brandy for the Parson* (1952) and *You're Only Young Twice* (1953).

In 1957 he appeared in the popular TV comedy series *The Army Game* as one of the scruffy lead-swinging squaddies stationed at the forgotten transit camp of Nether Hopping. Hawtrey's character found it restful to indulge in the unmilitary pastime of knitting.

The following year he was cast in what seemed a fairly indifferent film comedy, *Carry On Sergeant*, but it turned out to be the precursor of the phenomenally successful series of *Carry On* films. Bawdy, unsubtle and stuffed with atrocious puns, these basic farces were churned out at production-line speed – roughly two a year for almost two decades – and kept to a notoriously low budget.

Laurence Olivier, arriving at the film studios in a limousine, was surprised to see Hawtrey, one of the best-loved stars of the British cinema, proceeding to work on foot in an old mackintosh, carrying a plastic bag.

Hawtrey's preferred mode of parlance was a weird nonsense language, a sort of telegraphese, which few apart from his *Carry On* co-star Joan Sims were able to fathom.

His mother, to whom he remained very close, was equally eccentric. On one occasion at the film studios, during a break from the *Carry On* action, Hawtrey and the other actors were listening enthralled to one of her spirited monologues when he noticed that her open handbag was on fire. He drew this to the attention of his mother who, with the minimum of effort, poured the contents of a cup of tea that she was holding into the reticule, snapped it shut and continued with her anecdote as if nothing had happened – while steam billowed out of the bag.

Hawtrey lived in an old smuggler's cottage near the seafront at Deal, from which he was rescued during a fire in 1984, emerging as a pathetically dishevelled figure, *sans* toupée, but characteristically refusing hospital treatment.

His recreations included playing the piano and collecting antiques. He was unmarried.

October 28 1988

JACK DE MANIO

JACK DE MANIO, who has died aged 74, was a popular broadcaster on BBC radio, notably on Radio 4's early morning *Today* programme which he hosted for 13 years.

His cheery manner won him a large following and set a new fashion for banter and fun on the radio. But his lightness of touch and cavalier disregard of the Corporation's *mores* carried their own perils.

Executives were not amused, for example, when they discovered that the lion he had invited into Broadcasting House for an interview had not been insured. Nor did they appreciate his tendency to scratch his chest while addressing the microphone.

De Manio was also given to verbal gaffes, blundering over his cues – "Now we've got two little boys on the programme . . . No . . . Here! I've got the wrong story! It's one little boy" – or missing them altogether, explaining his failure to his audience with such excuses as, "I was locked in the loo."

He was also notorious for getting the time wrong: a motorist once tried to sue him for damages because he heard de Manio give the time incorrectly, looked at his watch and drove into the car in front. He once warned a broadcasting colleague to be careful if he drove down Park Lane, "because there's a little grey car hanging round there and it's full of coppers".

Blunt and outspoken, de Manio had an impressive collection of *bêtes noires*, including badly driven dustcarts, nodding dogs in the rear windows of cars and garden gnomes. And he read out so many jokes from *The Daily Telegraph* that the Corporation deemed it necessary to warn him against political bias.

He was an enterprising journalist, however, and in 1969 achieved a broadcasting coup when he obtained the first radio interview with the Prince of Wales. In 1975 his favour with the Palace was confirmed by an invitation to one of the Queen's luncheons.

The qualities which made him successful were summed up by a *Daily Telegraph* radio critic: "He sounds the sort of man you would like to talk to you, and when he does you feel at ease. It's the essence of good broadcasting and worth far more than technical perfection."

A *Sunday Telegraph* critic once compared de Manio's "purring voice" to the sound of a "pre-war Bentley ticking over". A portly man, similar in build to Sir Winston Churchill, he was considered the most English of Englishmen; yet his father was an Italian and his mother Polish.

Giovanni Batista de Manio was born in London in 1914. He once said: "I don't feel anything but English. If I go to Italy I don't feel Italian. I went to Poland in 1928 and hated it."

His father was a pioneer aviator who once crashed on to a roof in Palmers Green. He was killed during an air race to Lisbon just before Jack was born.

De Manio was brought up by his mother and educated at Aldenham, where he loathed school discipline and did "frightfully badly". The chief consolation of his schooldays was the perpetration of practical jokes – on one occasion he put treacle on the organ pedals in church.

His first job at 18 was as a junior invoice clerk in a brewery, but he was dismissed because, as he put it, "I was absolutely hopeless." He then worked as a waiter at the Ritz, in the kitchens of Grosvenor House, at the Miramar in Cannes and the Congress in Chicago. He retained his love of cooking and came to regard himself as a spaghetti specialist, creating a tripe bolognese for home consumption.

After failing an audition for a post as a BBC announcer in 1938 de Manio was commissioned into the Royal Sussex Regiment from the City of London Yeomanry and fought in France and North Africa. Twice wounded, he was awarded the Military Cross and Bar and promoted major.

The Second World War did not diminish his broadcasting ambitions, and in 1944 he was taken on by Forces Radio in Palestine; impressed by this experience, the BBC gave him a job as an announcer on the Overseas Service. He joined the Home Service in 1955, leaving the staff to become a freelance in 1964.

De Manio made gaffes over the air from the start, and felt that he was only saved from dismissal by regard for his war service and rank. Shortly before the *Today* appointment, for example, he had been dismissed after calling an important radio talk, "Land of the *Nigger*" instead of "Land of the Niger."

He landed the *Today* job soon after its inauguration in 1958 and remained with the programme until 1971; he always insisted that he was given the job only because no one else would want to begin work at such an early hour, and that the BBC was "scraping the absolute bottom of the barrel". Such a self-deprecating and throwaway remark gives the clue to de Manio's enduring popularity with listeners.

After leaving *Today* in 1971 he was given his own

programme, *Jack de Manio Precisely*, which ran until 1978, when the BBC dropped him to make way for the broadcasting of Parliament. He returned briefly – and unhappily – to the BBC in 1979 as a contributor to *Woman's Hour*.

His former extravagance left him with little money; as he told one interviewer: "Being out of a real job is the most frustrating thing in the world. I'm hard up and I want to work." But he avoided bitterness and found use for his time in helping the Friends of Queen Charlotte's and Chelsea Hospital for Women.

De Manio published two books – *To Auntie with Love* and *Life Begins Too Early* – and was a frequent contributor to *Punch*. He was voted Radio Personality of the Year by the Variety Club of Great Britain in 1964 and by the Radio Industries Club in 1971.

He was twice married: to Juliet Gravaeret Kaufmann, an American (the marriage was dissolved in 1946); and to Loveday Elizabeth Matthews, a widow, who survives him with a son by the first marriage.

October 29 1988

RAY MOORE

RAY MOORE, the disc jockey and announcer who has died aged 47, was a popular radio broadcaster, famous for his early morning show on BBC Radio 2.

Moore faced the programme's 5.30 start with a mixture of deadpan humour and deliberately low-key bravado, and he faced his death the same way. After learning in the summer of 1987 that he had cancer, Moore continued to work until forced to retire at the beginning of last year.

He won much admiration for his courageous and characteristically cheerful refusal to be bowed by "that blue devil".

His large regular audience found Moore's distinctive yet modest manner a refreshing contrast to the tone of counterfeit bonhomie favoured by many of his fellow broadcasters. The intimate style of his presentation gave the programme a conspiratorial feel which flattered the listener. Moore worked without a script and often said that he imagined himself to be broadcasting to an audience of one. An important part of his radio repertoire consisted of in-jokes and quirky approximations of regional accents.

Although he contributed voice-overs and introductions to such varied television programmes as the *Miss World* contest, *QED*, *All Our Yesterdays* and *Come Dancing*, Moore remained a radio man at heart and described radio broadcasting as his vocation.

A Liverpudlian, Ray Moore was born in 1942 and was still a child when he decided to work for the BBC. As a schoolboy he took elocution lessons in an attempt to alter his Scouse accent — a decision he later regretted, as the Beatles' rise to prominence encouraged disc jockeys to shift their speech patterns in the opposite direction.

Moore left Waterloo Grammar School academically unqualified to take up a place at the London School of Economics, as he had hoped. Instead he went to work, first as a cotton sampler on Liverpool Docks, then as a clerk with the Mersey Docks and Harbour Board, sometimes delivering wages to the Birkenhead Chain Works. He later compared the atmosphere of the factory to that created by Fritz Lang in *Metropolis*.

Through an advertisement in the *Stage*, Moore secured a position as assistant stage manager at Oldham Rep, where he is affectionarely remembered for having glued Jessie Matthews to a grand piano. Moore had covered the instrument with multiple coats of gloss white paint and unsuccessfully attempted to harden the paint with a hairdryer.

In 1962 he moved to repertory in Devon, in a touring production by the Mercury players. The trip gave him, as he recalled in his autobiography, *Tomorrow is Too Late*, welcome opportunities for further study of Southern vowel sounds and mixed naked bathing.

Later in the same year Moore called at the Granada Studios in Manchester and was offered a job as an announcer – aged 20, the youngest on the ITV network. He was an immediate success and had a seemingly insatiable appetite for broadcasting, even volunteering for unpaid overtime.

In 1965 Moore was hired by the BBC to write and shoot promotional films for BBC2 and worked from Broadcasting House in Manchester as an announcer. After two years he moved to London to help launch Radio 2, where he impressed producers with the relaxed and capable style of his announcements and his flair at coping with items about Sir Abu Bakar Tafewabalewa.

In the late 1960s he went on to present *Ray Moore's Saturday Night*, a live two-hour show, broadcast from a dance hall; and in 1973 he went freelance, doing voice-overs, promotional videos and commentaries at events like the Ideal Home Exhibition.

Moore's mischievous sense of humour occasionally landed him in trouble: at one Eurovision song contest there was an official protest from a Turkish harmony ensemble. His parody of his own voice-overs during a dress rehearsal for Miss World – a joke for the benefit of the sound engineers, but accidentally transmitted over the public address system – provoked heated remarks from Miss Sweden and Miss Nigeria.

Such gaffes were exceptional. For the most part his humour and good works – he raised £250,000 for Children in Need with his "Bog-eyed Jog" – made Moore one of the most popular broadcasters of his generation.

He is survived by his wife, Alma.

January 13 1989

BEATRICE LILLIE

BEATRICE LILLIE, otherwise Lady Peel, who has died aged 94, was a theatrical entertainer of genius.

Her credits stretched from revue in the 1920s, when she sang Noël Coward's "Poor Little Rich Girl", to the musicals *Auntie Mame* and *High Spirits* in the 1950s and 1960s, when she also scored a success as a villainous Chinese madam in the film *Thoroughly Modern Millie* opposite Julie Andrews and Carol Channing. Along the way she toured the world with her brilliant one-woman show, *An Evening With Beatrice Lillie*.

Like the accepted wit who has only to say: "Pass the mustard, please," to set the table guffawing, Miss Lillie was never anything but funny on or off stage. She had a reputation as a prankster and in 1951 ordered a live alligator from Harrods and sent it to Noël Coward with the message: "So what else is new?"

But Miss Lillie was no actress. Nature did not intend her to create any character except her eccentric own. If she tried her hand at legitimate drama or indeed any show where the lines were presumed to be sacrosanct, she only caused chaos.

Whatever success she had in such circumstances was usually won at the expense of the play and her fellow-players (not to mention the director). Yet her kind of chaos was apt to be more enjoyable than anybody else's order, and was relished for its wrecking effect in musicals.

It was in revue or as a solo turn that "Bea" Lillie won the affection of theatregoers the world over, to the extent of becoming a cult with her ability to demolish social pretence. An inflected eyebrow, a furtive sniff, a *sotto voce* growl or a steely grimace (her repertoire of grimaces was limitless) were her favourite weapons.

Words hardly mattered as she chattered incoherently because the pulling of faces, shooting of glances, the under-the-breath murmurs and the disdainful corners of the mouth expressed all she had to say. And because she seemed incapable of taking anything or anyone seriously, least of all herself, she enjoyed adulation on both sides of the Atlantic for over half a century, though it was in America where her scatty and spontaneous comedy was most appreciated.

From being one of André Charlot's discoveries in the 1920s, and sharing the limelight with Gertrude Lawrence, she veered into variety and musical comedy, but it was not for acting, singing or dancing that she was revered. It was for clowning, and this she brought to a peak in the 1950s with her much-travelled one-woman show.

She had the gift of making everything she did look fresh, however often she had done it. Her impishness revelled in being inexplicable.

The cropped hair tightly hidden by a pink fez, the long cigarette holder as something to toy with, the tendency to bang her head inexplicably but repeatedly against the proscenium arch: these were beyond rational explanation, like much of her humour.

Her art, though elusive, had something of the amiable air of a game of charades. She had a trick of seeming to ignore the audience so that her private fantasies might be indulged as if unperceived.

It was, however, the unexpected and impromptu-seeming side of her fooling which made it so different, summed up perhaps by the story of a pigeon which flew by chance into her apartment. "Any messages?" she asked blandly.

Miss Lillie made many film appearances (including *Around the World in 80 Days*) and something of her garbled, mimic's joking came through, as it did in her work on television. But her off-the-cuff, buttonholing fun required a playhouse or cabaret in which to flourish.

Rarely did she need to drag topical events into the spray of light, larky satire. To set the house on a roar she had merely to come up with a warbled complaint about the "wind round my heart", or to muse upon a hostess who had ordered a dozen double-damask dinner table napkins, or to attack the proscenium arch with her head, or to moralise on a friend called Maud whom she accused of being "rotten to the core".

The daughter of a schoolmaster from Co Down, Beatrice Gladys Lillie was born in Toronto in 1894. Reputedly expelled aged eight from the church choir for making faces while singing hymns, she left school at 15 to move to England with her mother and sister.

At 16 she sang in the bill at Chatham music hall and later that year appeared at the London Pavilion in *The Daring of Diane* and at the Alhambra in the revue *Not*

Likely. It was the celebrated Anglo-French producer Charlot who perceived and encouraged the Canadian girl's unusual style. She worked in shows with titles like: *Now's The Time*, *Samples*, *Cheep*, *Tabs*, *Oh Joy*, *Bran-Pie*, *Now and Then*, *Pot Luck* and (her first legitimate role) *Up In Mabel's Room*.

In 1920 Miss Lillie married Robert Peel, great-grandson of the famous Victorian statesman Sir Robert Peel. He was a Guards officer who resigned and became a sheep farmer and racehorse owner.

In 1925 when her father-in-law died and her husband succeeded to the baronetcy, Bea Lillie became Lady Peel. "Get me", which was one of her catchwords, was applied on more occasions than that when social posturing needed puncturing. Sometimes, however, the title landed her in difficulties as when her routine about a suburban snob down on her luck ("I always had my own 'orses") was taken literally by an embarrassed Mid-Western audience. Unbeknown to Miss Lillie she had been billed as "Lady Peel".

In 1928 she appeared in Coward's revue *This Year of Grace* in New York and four years later played the nurse in Shaw's *Too True To Be Good*, but she never looked at home off the light musical stage. Nor was she ever off it for long.

During the Second World War she toured the world, entertaining the troops for ENSA. Her husband had died in 1934, and in 1942 their only child, the 6th Baronet and an Ordinary Seaman, lost his life when the destroyer *Tenedos* in which he was serving was attacked by Japanese dive bombers.

After the war she returned to the West End in the revue *Better Late* (Garrick, 1946). Then came summer shows, and tours, in America. In the 1950s *An Evening With Beatrice Lillie* set the seal on her popular but subtle art.

She appeared in the *Ziegfeld Follies* of 1957 on Broadway, and in 1958 took over the title role in Patrick Dennis's *Auntie Mame* from Greer Garson in New York before playing the same part in London.

At the Edinburgh Festival in 1960 she returned to her revue form in *A Late Evening With Beatrice-Lillie*.

In the mid-1970s she suffered a stroke and became bedridden. In 1977 she was brought back to England from New York to be nursed. She died at her home in Henley-on Thames.

January 21 1989

MICHAEL SMITH

MICHAEL SMITH, who has died aged 61, was a cookery writer, broadcaster, restaurateur and champion of English cookery in the Mrs Beeton tradition.

That tradition, Smith felt, had suffered because of two world wars, recession, unemployment and the public school system. As the instigator, designer and guiding light of three of the best English restaurants in London – the English Garden, the English House and Waltons – he did much to revive it.

Not for him the fastidious austerity of *nouvelle cuisine*, which he regarded as a French confidence trick to charge more for less: "When you've eaten one pigeon breast fanned out and decorated with three redcurrants and three mangetout facing north-north-east, where do you go for lunch?"

One of the key adjectives to be found in Smith's cookery books and columns was "lusty", and he was constantly extolling to his readers the merits of "a goodly knob of butter", "a cushion of rich soft fat" or of "cream – thick, rich, yellow double cream". "Life without pudding," he once wrote, "is unbearable."

Michael Smith was born in Yorkshire in 1927, the seventh and youngest child of a textile family. He recalled of his childhood that there "was always plenty of bread and butter in the kitchen".

His father was surprised at young Michael's ambition to become a caterer, but as he was a liberal man he sent him to hotel courses at Lausanne, which he liked, and Paris, which he hated. Smith's first job was to have been at an hotel in Cairo; but it burnt down – "just as well: much too far east and hot and foreign" – so he went instead to one at Copenhagen.

On his return to Britain he met his wife, Elisabeth, at King's Cross railway station, and together they opened a restaurant outside Leeds. The enterprise was not a success, as Smith insisted on serving such dishes as quiche to Yorkshire businessmen who wanted only steak.

A shop in Leeds selling kitchen utensils was also a failure – "after my friends had bought six balloon whisks, that was it" – but he attracted the attention of the Earl of Harewood and began preparing banquets at Harewood House. Initially he cooked French food, as he had been taught.

Smith's life was changed, however, by the chance purchase of a 1776 edition of *The Experienced English House-*

keeper by Elizabeth Raffald: he had found his vocation. He started to cook English food at Harewood, and it was such a success that he moved to London to proselytise his cause.

He did so with a passion, publishing a string of books (*Fine English Cookery*, *The Posh Nosh Book*, *New English Cookery*, *A Cook's Tour of Britain*, *Afternoon Tea* and *Michael Smith Entertains*); writing for *Homes and Gardens*, *A La Carte* and *The Daily Telegraph*; lecturing women up and down the country (he once addressed 6,000 at the Royal Albert Hall); and winning audiences with his enthusiasm and bow-tie on BBC Television's *Pebble Mill at One*.

Called in to advise Hudson the butler on how to open a bottle of vintage port, he became "montage-creator" and cook for the television series *Upstairs Downstairs*, and went on to do the same for *The Duchess of Duke Street* and *By the Sword Divided*.

At times Smith could be almost messianic in his fervour, as when he heckled Sir Keith Joseph at the opening of a new branch of Prue Leith's cookery school. Sir Keith boasted that Britain now had 500 catering schools. "Better 50 schools turning out decent cooks," yelled Smith, "than 500 turning out managers!" But he never lost his sense of humour.

Aside from cooking he was passionate about music: he was a capable pianist and for many years a keen chorister. His marriage was dissolved in 1968; he is survived by a son and a daughter.

January 25 1989

TOGARE

TOGARE, one of the most colourful and romantic figures of the circus world, who has died at Krefeld in Germany aged 88, wore a picturesque Oriental costume – turban, baggy trousers, Turkish pointed shoes, with heavy earrings, arm bangles and a jewelled 13th-century Arabian knife – copied from the 1924 film *The Thief of Baghdad*, starring Douglas Fairbanks.

Togare had a magnificent physique and a striking personality, which led Lady Eleanor Smith (F. E. Smith's elder daughter and a great fan of the circus) to dub him the "Valentino of the Circus Ring".

The *Evening Standard* dilated on his theme. Togare had "all the characteristics of Valentino," it said: "You see them in his eyes, his lithe, easy bearing, his swarthy complexion and his muscular frame. There surely has never been a more wonderful double, and because of it, Togare has fascinated women of every country he has visited."

One of his most cherished possessions was a ring given to him by the Mayor of Birmingham after he had saved eight lions from a fire which broke out when Carmo's Circus was there in 1930. Despite the efforts of firemen to prevent him, Togare smashed through the smouldering roof of the animals' wagon with his bare hands, making a hole through which he could drop among the beasts.

Calling them by their names and stroking their singed fur, he calmed them down and drove them to the safety of another cage. Afterwards, armed with a number of raw eggs and a bottle of olive oil, Togare entered the cage of the three lions most injured and anointed their burns; they all made a full recovery.

That episode was typical of his kindness to animals. One of his favourite lions, named Paris, ended his days at the Berlin Zoo. Though Paris was responsible for some of the 80 or so maulings he suffered during his career in the big cage, Togare would often visit him in Berlin, sitting inside his cage and petting and kissing him; Paris would grow excited long before Togare's arrival, sensing his approach.

Born Georg Kulovits in Hungary in 1900, he joined Germany's Circus Krone in 1921 as a "beast-boy", working as assistant to the bear trainer, Lola Tex. Before long he was training lions and tigers, and he went on to work in various countries, including Russia, under the name of Helios.

In 1925 he took the name Togare, and from 1928 he worked in Ireland and England – first with the ill-fated Great Carmo Circus and later with Bertram Mills. He began with a group of nine lions and then developed his own tiger act, which was featured in many leading European circuses.

Having lost his animals during the Second World War, Togare returned to Bertram Mills in 1946 to present the lions. But three years later he quarrelled with the management, quit without notice and went back to the continent, where he worked with Germany's Circus Sarrasani until his retirement in 1958.

Togare was twice married. He met his second wife, Taranda, in a Dresden hospital in 1943; she tended his wounds and nursed him back to health after a particularly severe clawing, and he later taught her to present a lion act herself.

February 27 1989

LOCKWOOD WEST

LOCKWOOD WEST, who has died aged 83, was one of the most engaging and experienced charactor actors of his time.

Recently he created a gem of characterisation as the eccentric and sexually obsessed old chaplain in the television adaptation of Tom Sharpe's novel *Porterhouse Blue*. Many will cherish the memory of his dialogue with Zipser (played by John Sessions) when, in order to facilitate the deaf confessor's hearing, the undergraduates's intimate problems are discussed by means of a loud hailer.

"*Is it SELF-ABUSE?*" enquires the chaplain, his amplified tones reverberating round the college court, before proceeding to issue his standard recommendation about female foreign language students.

He made another touching contribution as the old actor playing the Fool in the play and film of Ronald Harwood's *The Dresser*, and he was a stately Edward VII (a part subsequently defined by his actor son, Timothy) in London Weekend Television's *Upstairs, Downstairs*. West also played the title role in the popular series, *After Henry*, opposite his daughter-in-law, Prunella Scales.

A most sensitive player, West proved a splendid asset in the margins of many comedies and farces. His most affecting quality was his reticence in roles which other players might be tempted to overdo.

He could dither delightfully as ancient priests or other spiritual advisers and invest butlers with an absurd dignity. Seemingly incapable of acting insincerely, his elderly manner, baldness, modesty and apparent absence of humour enriched his acting because he never allowed his own enjoyment to be signalled to the spectator.

West looked back on Geoffrey Thornton in *The Dresser* and Reggie in another play by Ronald Harwood, *The Ordeal of Gilbert Pinfold* (after the novel by Evelyn Waugh), as among his favourite roles along with William Howard in Graham Greene's *The Complaisant Lover*; Oscar Nelson in *Mary, Mary*; and Jones in *Half-Life*, the only role he played at the National Theatre.

He was also much praised for his extremely funny study of a vicar coping with a homosexual "marriage" in William Douglas Home's play, *And As For Jonathan*.

Behind such mastery lay 60 years of stagecraft. Following exhaustive experience in pre-war rep, he went on to give stalwart support to such stars as Ralph Richardson (in *The White Carnation*, 1953, and *The Complaisant Lover*, 1959) and John Gielgud (in *A Day by the Sea*, 1953, and *The Potting Shed*, 1958).

Henry ("Harry" to his friends) Lockwood West, son of an insurance broker, was born at Birkenhead in 1905 and educated at St Paul's. He worked for a spell with the Doncaster Collieries Association before making his debut in 1926 at the Margate Hippodrome in *Alf's Button*, the first success of W. A. Darlington (dramatic critic of *The Daily Telegraph*).

He then immersed himself in the provinces, though he did have a fortnight at London's Queen's Theatre in 1931 in *The Barretts of Wimpole Street*. On the outbreak of the Second World War he was playing in Bristol and remained there, serving in the city's police war reserve for the duration.

In 1948 he made his first film, *Dandy in Aspic*, and was later seen in *Life at the Top*, *Bedazzled*, and *Jane Eyre*. On the stage West played Major Swindon in an all-star revival of Shaw's *The Devil's Disciple* at The Winter Garden in 1956, and had a particular success as Monsieur Damiens in Anouilh's *The Rehearsal* which moved from Bristol in 1961 to a succession of West End theatres.

In 1974 he played Councillor Duxbury in the musical version of *Billy Liar*, starring Michael Crawford, at Drury Lane. Television, however, brought West his widest fame in such productions as *The Power Game*, *The Newcomers*, *Brett*, *No Hiding Place*, *Big Brother* and *The Pallisers*.

On radio his voice was heard in a record-breaking total of 4,000 programmes – notably as the finicky Mr Tyson in *Waggoner's Walk* – and the BBC organised a jubilee party for him on the 50th anniversary of his first broadcast in 1937.

One of West's radio series was called *Legal, Decent, Honest and Truthful*, and these words could easily have applied to the actor himself. He made his last broadcast in November while stricken with cancer, but only a handful of people were aware of the pain and the courage he displayed.

West's hobby was paddle-steamers. His wife, the actress Olive Carleton-Crowe (whom he met on a tour of *The Ghost Train*), died in 1985 and he is survived by a son and a daughter.

March 29 1989

CHRISTINE JORGENSEN

CHRISTINE JORGENSEN, who has died at San Clemente, California, aged 62, became a woman in 1952 as a result of the world's first legal sex change operation.

The operation was performed in Denmark under the supervision of Professor Christian Hamburger, with permission from the Danish Ministry of Justice. Jorgensen was given an award by a learned Scandinavian society for her "contribution to science". Hamburger, however, was forbidden by the Danish government to perform any more such operations.

She never regretted her decision to change sex, lamenting only the colour of her eyes, which were hazel: "I only wish they were either green or blue, instead of neither one thing nor the other."

Christine Jorgensen was born George Jorgensen in the Bronx, New York, in 1926. His childhood was troubled by envy of his elder sister's pursuits and by his male peers shouting such epithets as "sissy" at him.

Jorgensen studied photography before being called up by the American Army, and after an unhappy year as a GI he returned to his *métier*. A passion for an older man convinced him that he had "the yearning heart and mind of a woman" and was merely "masquerading in men's clothing".

Acting on a tip-off, Jorgensen left for Denmark in 1950 "when life as George was no longer tolerable". He interrupted Professor Hamburger on holiday at his country retreat outside Copenhagen, and the professor agreed to treat him free of charge. In return Jorgensen agreed to be a guinea pig in various hormone experiments.

Two years later George rose up from his hospital bed as Christine, a willowy blonde. An initial unwillingness to sell her story was melted by the fan mail she received from around the world from men who felt as she had. In 1953 Jorgensen returned to America and was in immediate demand on the nightclub circuit, singing such songs as "I Enjoy Being a Girl" – though she drew the line at striptease.

In 1954 Jorgensen made a brief appearance at the Manchester Hippodrome, where the show was a great success. Her autobiography, *The Christine Jorgensen Story* (1967), was made into a film, though she herself refused many offers to appear on the screen.

She was much in demand at colleges in California for her lectures on "gender identity" and was a passionate advocate of the sexual revolution. She never married, despite "dozens of offers". She confessed: "Men are wary of me – and I'm wary of the ones who aren't."

May 5 1989

HARRY WORTH

HARRY WORTH, the stage, radio and television comedian who has died aged 71, turned the traditionally vulgar art of stand-up comedy into something tasteful, genteel and respectable.

He was best known for the opening scene of his BBC television series, *Here's Harry*, in which he stood at the corner of a shop window and lifted an arm and a leg in the air – a gesture much imitated by schoolboys in the

1960s; but his roots were firmly in the old music halls where he perfected his act.

As a stand-up comedian Worth was more in the tradition of Sandy Powell or Robb Wilton than Max Miller or Tommy Trinder: he was not at all the "cheeky chappy". With his soft Yorkshire voice, fat friendly face, thick grin, thin lips, furtive glances, Homburg hat and rolled umbrella, he epitomised correctness and dithering charm.

Worth's promotion of his own timid, fallible and far from pushy character took shape before some highly critical and responsive audiences, and when he moved to broadcasting he missed them: studio audiences, who applauded to order and had not paid, were not an adequate substitute.

But his move from the theatre did not greatly damage the quality of his humour, because Worth's homespun and confessional style was essentially intimate. His domesticated persona was better suited to the small screen than those of broader, more boisterous comics.

He had a good run from 1955 to 1974 and made himself comfortably independent from his earnings, and his BBC television series ran for 104 episodes. In 1971 he was badly miscast as William Boot in a BBC adaptation of Evelyn Waugh's novel *Scoop*.

In 1974 Worth played a comedy series for ITV and toured in the lead of *Harvey*, a play about an amiable misfit and a giant rabbit. The next year he appeared briefly in *Norman, Where Are you?* at the Phoenix. But such "vehicles" were ill-judged.

In 1976 he led a Radio 4 comedy series, *Things Could Be Worse*; three years later he played a likeable old-fashioned widower in *How's Your Father?* for ITV; and in

1980 he was on BBC television in *O Happy Band*! about a well-meaning villager striving to stop plans for an airport.

Worth was also among the artists featured in the revived *Workers' Playtime* on Radio 2 to mark the BBC's 60th anniversary in 1982. *Thirty Minutes' Worth* on Radio 2 last year featured him again as the confused individual buffeting against circumstances.

Worth stood firmly for the ordinary man, for law and order, and as much of what you fancied on the side if you could get away with it; if there was something sly about his humour, as about his grin, it was never less than human.

The youngest of 11 children, he was born Harry Burlon Illingsworth at Hoyland Common, near Barnsley, on January 13 1920. His father, a miner, was fatally injured when Harry was an infant, and he grew up in extreme penury, going down the local pit himself at the age of 14 and remaining there for eight years.

He was first attracted to comedy by the films at his local picture palace, and then inspired by a ventriloquist who gave a show at the village school. He was taught the art by a local girl, and won a talent competition for his efforts.

During the Second World War he served with the RAF in India and Burma as a fitter, although he displayed little aptitude. His NCO told him: "As a fitter Illingsworth, you're a very good ventriloquist."

Soon after leaving the service he decided to become a full-time entertainer and gave turns as ventriloquist, with his dummies Fotheringay and Clarence, on Southport beach, in working men's clubs and pantomimes.

Worth was persuaded to become a comedian by

Stanley Laurel and Oliver Hardy, whom he met on tour. Without his ventriloquist's doll he felt so nervous that he bumbled and mixed up his words – "That was how I stumbled on my diffident style."

He made his London debut in 1947 at the Windmill Theatre where the all-day non-stop variety allowed the newcomers their chance between the singers and dancers and the immobile nudes. It was a hard training, as the all-male audience was not looking for laughs. While a comic like Worth was trying to catch attention, spectators would clamber over the unreserved seats towards the front row whenever anyone left to obtain a closer view of "gorgeous girls".

He then went into full-scale variety at the London Hippodrome, toured South Africa with the singer Johnnie Ray and returned to play what was left of the British variety circuits.

In the 1950s they were still a twice-nightly matter in such places as Manchester, Leeds and Liverpool, and even in smaller towns like Peterborough, Blackburn and Doncaster. The symbol of their decline, John Osborne's Archie Rice, still had plenty of work; and Worth's quiet and gentle tones seemed refreshing, if risky, in an art form which had run to seed.

When the music hall died it left no real artistic alternative for its performers. In any medium, though, Worth inspired affection, with his puzzled view of life and his resignation to its rigours.

He is survived by his wife Katy, whom he met in a pantomime and married in 1947, and their daughter.

July 22 1989

DOMINIC BEHAN

DOMINIC BEHAN, who has died aged 61, was variously a house-painter, labourer, roustabout and author. In the last two roles he was overshadowed by his brother Brendan, who once observed of him: "Somewhere inside Dom there's a little me trying to get out."

Like his brother, Dominic Behan had an ambivalent attitude towards the Irish Republican Army. In America he recorded a collection of Fenian folk songs and went on fund-raising tours "to buy guns" for the Republican cause.

In Britain, on the other hand, he wrote a number of plays satirising the sentimentality and violence of the Irish "patriots" – notably *Posterity Be Damned*, which was performed at London's Metropolitan Theatre in 1960. "I wrote it," Behan explained, "attacking the IRA and the Establishment while I was living on £6 5s a week National Assistance. I reckon it is very democratic of the British Government to have paid me while I attack it."

Brother Brendan attended the dress rehearsal of the play and snored ostentatiously for 45 minutes. He woke up, however, at a reference to "IRA murderers". "It's a lot of nonsense," he exclaimed, "there was no murderers in the IRA!"

From the stage the author berated his brother. "What are you saying, man? 'Tis you who was the worst of the lot." When Brendan walked out Dominic said: "'Tis the needle Brendan gets when he has a few jars on him. I takes no notice of it."

He also wrote a number of plays for the BBC and ITV; a guardedly affectionate biography of his brother, *My*

Brother Brendan (1965); *The Life and Times of Spike Milligan* (1988); and last month he published his first novel, a sub-Joycean tour of Dublin's pubs, *The Public World of Parable Jones*.

Pubs were his natural habitat, and he was occasionally arrested in disturbances in and around them. A typical episode occurred in 1962, when he was found guilty of assaulting a taxi driver called Mr Mousley, whose cab he had hailed with a friend in Soho. Behan made some unflattering remarks about Sir Oswald Mosley; Mr Mousley took offence and refused to take them any further, whereupon violence broke out.

Dominic Behan was born in 1928 in a working-class suburb of Dublin and received an elementary education there before coming to Britain to work in various menial capacities.

In 1953 he was sentenced in London to two weeks' imprisonment for what the magistrate called "a brutal, cowardly and entirely unprovoked" assault on a fellow house-painter who did not wish to join his union.

In 1958 Behan made his recording debut as a folk singer, and the same year contrived for BBC Radio a programme of songs called *The Cantata of Christ the Worker*, set in an espresso coffee bar.

A fitful literary career ensued, interspersed with such employment as he could find. In 1960, for example, he worked on the erection of Billy Smart's Big Top on Clapham Common.

The next year he mislaid the 100,000-word manuscript of his autobiography, "somewhere between the pubs of Leicester Square and my home in Balham ... If any young woman finds it she should hand it to her mother without reading it." It was recovered, however, and published as *Teems of Times and Happy Returns*. Full of Dublin pub talk, it was fitfully brilliant but of little consequence; it was later seized by the Irish Customs.

In 1963 he was taken on by Nicholas Luard as a cabaret performer at the Establishment Club, on condition that he did not drink. The stipulation was vigorously disputed. "I'll not be bowed down by it," Behan said, "when I want a drink I shall have one."

The same year he performed a revue at the Edinburgh Festival and the Prince Charles Theatre in London, excruciatingly entitled *Behan Bein' Behan*. *The Daily Telegraph*, dismissing it as "dead horses savagely flogged", suggested that "Has-Behan" would have been a more appropriate title.

Brendan Behan died in 1964, and his brother is survived by a wife and two sons.

August 15 1989

TOBY HALICKI

TOBY HALICKI, who has died at Buffalo, New York, aged 48, once described himself as "chief executive of the fanciest junkyards in the world"; he was also the director and star of *Gone in 60 Seconds* (1974), a cult film about car crashes.

The proprietor of the Hawk House Motor Car and H. B. Halicki Mercantile Co & Junkyard, of Gardena, California, he was inspired by his surroundings to write a film script, which took him four hours. When Halicki took his script to Hollywood, though, the studios simply laughed at him. He was unimpressed by the directors he met – "they lived in little houses, drove Mustangs with bald tyres and were only $40,000-a-year men" – so he decided to make the film himself. Actors he thought were no good at playing ordinary people, and stunt men were too stupid, so he took on the starring role as well, with his cocktail waitress girlfriend as the female lead. The real stars of the film, however, were the cars, 93 of which were written off in the course of the action.

The film made millions of dollars, and at the time of his death Halicki was directing a sequel, *Gone in 60 Seconds II*. He was working on a scene in which a tractor-trailer was to ram through a series of parked cars before crashing into a tower; but a telephone pole fell on his head, with fatal consequences.

One of 13 children of a second-hand car dealer of Polish extraction, Toby Halicki was born in New York in 1941 and left home at the age of 15 to seek his fortune in California.

To begin with he worked at a petrol station, washing the cars of successful gamblers. He went on to become a "customiser" – one who modifies production-line cars to make them look like originals – before moving into the junkyard business and then into films.

August 22 1989

DR ERIC JONES-EVANS

DR ERIC JONES-EVANS, the physician, actor and author who has died aged 90, was one of the last and most eloquent links with Sir Henry Irving.

Historians depended on his memories of the great Victorian actor and theatre manager, especially for details of Irving's performance in *The Bells*, which Jones-Evans saw as a boy at the Grand Theatre, Boscombe, in 1905. After it, alone in his bedroom, young Eric re-enacted the play every night, illuminating his face with a torch. Irving died a few months later, but Jones-Evans's imagination had been fired for ever.

He became not only a much-interrogated theatregoer but also an actor devoted to Victorian melodrama and its techniques, though he pursued at the same time a successful career in medicine.

Jones-Evans himself was essentially modest – and with reason – about his own powers as a player. But in his manner, both on and off the stage – and even, it was said, in his surgery – he remained unflinchingly flamboyant all his days.

Eric Jones-Evans was born at West Coker, Somerset, on October 2 1898. His parents, the Reverend and Mrs John Llewellyn Jones-Evans, were both committed Irvingites and had spent their month's honeymoon in London visiting Irving's theatre, the Lyceum, every night.

Educated at Sherborne and St Thomas's Hospital, Jones-Evans qualified as a doctor, and served as a medical officer in the First World War. He had started professional acting as a medical student – in *The Trumpet Call*, with a touring company short of an actor. After the war he joined a repertory company run by the actor-manager John Soden.

Jones-Evans also found time to establish a medical practice at Fawley, near Southampton, while acting at the Grand at night – he closed the practice on matinee days. In 1928 he formed his own company, for which he wrote and acted in melodramas adapted from Dickens or George Eliot.

He kept in touch with other old-style actor-managers and acquired a notable collection of playscripts and theatrical memorabilia, now at the Russell-Cotes Art Gallery and Museum in Bournemouth.

In 1928, with his own troupe, Jones-Evans had himself played Mathias – "the fulfilment of an actor's dream". In 1954 he appeared as the Public Prosecutor opposite Bransby Williams's Mathias for the BBC.

Although he had to disband his company in 1939, Jones-Evans continued to give now and then a one-man, quick-change Dickensian entertainment which included, inevitably, the dream scene from *The Bells*.

He was predeceased by both his wife and their son.

August 22 1989

R. G. G. PRICE

R. G. G. PRICE, the author and journalist who has died aged 79, was a stalwart contributor to *Punch*, whose history he wrote and whose "Table" he adorned for many years.

He used to say that he had "wanted to write for *Punch* since the age of eight", an ambition which he first achieved in 1935.

Besides his humorous pieces, Price was a particularly valued book reviewer and was praised by the former literary editor, Anthony Powell, for his sure touch in the elusive art of the short notice. He had the enviable ability, Powell writes in his memoirs, of conveying "a word of warning to the potential reader without egregiously insulting the author".

R. G. G. Price

Richard Geoffrey George Price was born in Streatham Hill, London, in 1910 and educated at Dulwich and Jesus College, Oxford. He went on to study at the Institute of Education in London as a preliminary to becoming a schoolmaster.

Teaching, however, was a profession to which he was not by nature well suited and he abandoned it when opportunity served to follow his true vocation as a writer. None the less, the pedagogical training left a certain mark on Price's prose: as John Betjeman pointed out in his *Daily Telegraph* review of Price's *History of Punch* (1957), the descriptions of contributors past and present "read like a housemaster's shrewd reports on his boys".

Among Price's other publications were *How To Become Headmaster*, and *Betty Hope's Survive With Me*, in which monstrous events are survived by pure stupidity as a bingo-playing, telly-watching, budgie-loving suburban housewife tells how to cope with the H-bomb.

His wife, Susan, predeceased him.

Stanley Reynolds writes: Dick Price was one of the nicest of *Punch*'s rather splendid collection of pre-war buffers – at least he was one of the only ones who did not want to see P. G. Wodehouse hang, which endeared him to Malcolm Muggeridge, when the latter came to edit *Punch* in 1953. He also, and perhaps alone among the bufferdom, never openly lost his temper over the many changes he had seen since he first contributed to the magazine.

Dick wore an old-fashioned rather out-sized hearing aid with wires that were attached to a contraption resting somewhere just below his chest. He had a ragged, Mr Pastry-like moustache, schoolmasterly tweeds and walked with a limp. The limp was the result of spinal tuberculosis which kept him on his back in a brace for a number of his boyhood years. He acquired a love of light literature and comic poetry in those years of confinement.

Dick was a very good talker, but limited by deafness. He used to detach his hearing aid at luncheon not, he said, to banish bores but because the ancient contraption made horrible noises when wine was being poured into his glass. He said he was going to purchase a new device, but never did.

He had a somewhat old-fashioned turn of speech, always acknowledging a word's Latin or Greek roots in a most eccentric fashion. He would, for example, refer to "oikonomics" and one could see a certain puzzlement on the face of the guest seated beside him at *Punch*'s old weekly luncheons.

This inspired much affection among the young forgeys at *Punch*, as did his use of the word sport only for such pastimes as hunting, fishing, shooting and racing. Many times luncheon guests would find themselves at cross purposes with him about "sport", with Dick suddenly saying, "Oh, you mean games!"

He was, however, interested in neither sport nor games. Parody was his great love. He wrote many short amusing literary parodies up until three years ago, when he suffered a serious stroke.

Dick was exceedingly modest about his own work and generous with praise about the work and the character of colleagues. This lack of any regrets or bitterness made him much-loved, especially by the younger members of the staff.

September 20 1989

MILTON GOLDMAN

MILTON GOLDMAN, who has died in New York aged
75, was a leading American theatre agent whose gregari-
ousness and munificent hospitality was the stuff of "showbiz" legend.

Together with his close friend and partner, the late
Arnold Weissberger, Goldman gave valuable support
to at least three generations of actors and playwrights.
Besides representing American clients they made it their
business to look after numerous British stars in New
York.

Unlike the tall and elegant Weissberger, Goldman
was a short, stout figure but bursting with bonhomie. An
unstoppable raconteur, Goldman often described himself
as a man who could not say "no" – his mother used to say
she was glad he was not a girl.

When he said, "Give me a ring if you're in town," he
meant it. Nearly every night of the week, it seemed,
Goldman and Weissberger would be having a drinks
party. The cast list was usually better than any to be found
on Broadway, ranging from Lilian Gish to Alger Hiss,
plus any visiting "Brits" who happened to be in town,
from Olivier down.

But no one ever felt unimportant or left out at
Goldman's, since it was his art to make sure that everyone
in the room was introduced to everyone else – at least
twice. The new arrival would be propelled round by the
elbow, firmly held.

On one occasion at his annual summer party at
London's Savoy Hotel he persisted in introducing Robert

Morley to his son Sheridan, ignoring the latter's protestation: "We know each other – he's my father."

"If he could," observed Nicol Williamson, "he would introduce you to yourself."

Goldman concluded his parties with equal expertise, pushing people out into the cold New York night at precisely 7.45 p.m. so they would not be late for the theatre.

The son of a shoemaker, Milton Norman Goldman was born at New Brunswick, New Jersey, on August 11 1914 and educated at Rutgers University. He graduated during the Depression and had difficulty finding a job, so he worked in his brother's gas station.

But he adored the theatre and read widely. It was after meeting Arnold Weissberger, a theatrical lawyer who introduced him to the stars, that Goldman became an agent in the 1940s, later joining International Creative Management.

When Weissberger died in 1981, Goldman arranged memorial services for him in New York, Los Angeles and London. He was delighted by the joke that circulated in the West End: "He's taking him on tour."

Ron Moody writes: At the sight of you a great beam would spread across his face, with a warm shake of the hand, assurances that you looked great, questions about the family. If the show was a hit you were a genius; if it was a flop – "What do the critics know?"

"Ron Moody, meet Joan Bennett, this is Jose Ferrer. Have you met Barbara Cartland? This is Arthur Miller, you all know Claire Trevor . . ."

Through his New York office on West 57th Street,

his luxurious apartment in Sutton Place, his English home from home in Eaton Square, passed the world's showbusiness greats, the lesser greats, the once-greats, the promising greats – all great in his eyes.

A courteous man, a kind man, a man who made you feel you were not only in showbusiness, but an important part of it. No put-downs, no fish-eyed stares, no inflated egos, not for Milton Goldman.

This all-powerful theatrical agent, a legend in his own time, always made you feel you were somebody. Whether you were up, down, in or out, hit or miss, he made you feel good.

He was a unique man, and I shall miss him. I shall miss knowing he's around somewhere, introducing his "greats", bouncing creative talents off each other to start up new ball games, stirring up his own unique mess of patronage, subtly arranging, as good agents do, that the right people are always kept in touch with the right people.

On the other hand, do I really doubt that his gregarious, outgoing, party-loving spirit would take more than the briefest of brief pauses before he is at it again: "Leonardo, meet Karl Marx. This is D. W. Griffith. Have you met Moses? This is Irving Berlin, George Bernard Shaw. You all know Larry . . ."

October 10 1989

PETER CHILDS

PETER CHILDS, the actor who has died aged 50, was best known as the chirpy Cockney Detective Sergeant

Rycott in *Minder*, the brilliantly stylised television series about London low life.

Childs brought a rare manic zest and breezy – if often dented – self-confidence to his portrayal of "Ronnie" Rycott in six series of the hugely popular programme. He was consumed by a burning desire to nail "Arfur-bloody-*Daley*", the shifty second-hand car dealer (played by George Cole) and his amiable accomplice "with form", Terry McCann (played by Dennis Waterman). The story-lines were given added spice by Rycott's running feud with his dourly ambitious colleague, Sergeant "Charlie" Chisholm (played by Patrick Malahide). The scenes between them as they blamed each other for being constantly sidestepped by Daley and McCann provided some of *Minder's* most richly comic moments.

The part of a frustrated copper who cannot feel a collar was not new to Childs as he had made his name on television as Detective Inspector Ron Gash in *Public Eye*. This nattily dressed and menacingly cheerful officer kept a wary eye on the seedy private detective Frank Marker (played by Alfred Burke) in another long-running cult series.

A chunky, fair-haired man with a cleft chin and clipped diction, Childs had an angelic smile which sat oddly with the aggressive characters he tended to play. Indeed he made something of a speciality of playing policemen – another notable characterisation was Detective Sergeant Grant in *Softly, Softly* – though he was equally plausibly cast as villains on the wrong side of the law.

Peter Childs was born at Eastbourne on August 31 1939, and educated at the local grammar school before training for the stage at the Birmingham Theatre School. He toiled for 10 years in repertory before breaking into television playing a small part in the Anton Rodgers crime series, *Zodiac*.

Childs gained valuable experience with the Manchester 59 Company, appearing in *Erb* which transferred to the West End and contributing a richly comic undertaker to Joe Orton's *Loot*.

He was also a regular at the Theatre Royal, in London's Stratford East and gave an outstanding performance in Joan Littlewood's last production there, *So You Want To Be In Pictures*. He demonstrated considerable gifts for comedy and improvisation in the role of a perpetually humiliated duff screenwriter.

Childs was seen at the Royal Court (and later in the West End) in David Storey's play, *The Changing Room*, directed by Lindsay Anderson, who also cast him in the film, *O Lucky Man*. His most recent West End Theatre appearance was as Froggy, the bomb disposal expert in *The Foreigner*, opposite Nicholas Lyndhurst, in 1987.

Childs's long list of television credits reads like a contemporary history of the medium. His familiar features cropped up in such programmes as *Coronation Street* (where he had the painful task of informing Emily Bishop that her husband was a bigamist), *The Sweeney, The Onedin Line, Rumpole of the Bailey, Bergerac, Juliet Bravo, Foxy Lady, Give Us A Break, Out* and *Ever Decreasing Circles*.

Among his films were *Ellis Island, Kim, An Officer and A Car Salesman* and, most memorably, *Minder on the Orient Express*, when he gave a bravura reprise of the Rycott character.

Away from stage and screen Childs was an assiduous

attender of racecourses and greyhound stadiums. His untimely death from leukaemia has deprived television of one of its most dependable and engaging character actors.

November 3 1989

PHILIP CORE

PHILIP CORE, the American-born artist and writer who has died aged 38, was both an historian and an ornament of the 20th-century *demi-monde*.

A flamboyantly "camp" figure, he used to sashay about London in motor-cycle boots, bomber jacket and cropped dyed hair. He once attended a Surrealist Ball in an exact reproduction of Salvador Dali's *Aphrodisiac Waistcoat*, with half-full glasses of *crème de menthe* attached.

Core lived and worked in his black-painted studio in south London, surrounded by an enviable collection of first editions. There he produced dark, expressive portraits of figures ranging from Richard Hell, the punk musician, to Sir John Betjeman, and large, often overtly homo-erotic compositions set in changing rooms or *louche* bars.

He also published two books. *The Original Eye*, a survey of "arbiters of 20th-century taste", was a series of turgidly baroque essays on the influence of the Comte de Montesquiou, Diaghilev, Cecil Beaton, Malcolm McLaren and others. More successful was his compendium, *Camp: The Lie That Tells The Truth*, in which he sought to provide a glossary of outrage and aestheticism. George Melly, in his introduction, noted that Core's commentary on the "queens of the gay ghettos may well turn out to be an elegy".

Latterly Core found a niche writing obituaries for the *Independent*, notably of those who had died from Aids, an affliction to which he himself succumbed.

Philip MacCammon Core was born at Dallas, Texas, on June 7 1951, and spent his early years in New Orleans and India. He was educated at the New Orleans Military Academy, the Middlesex School in New England, and then at Harvard, where he wrote about French Symbolism and painted.

As an undergraduate he spent a year in Paris, where he became a protégé of Philippe Jullian, the French art historian and biographer, through whom he met such *monstres sacrés* as Violet Trefusis and Marie-Laure de Noailles.

After a spell at the Ruskin School of Drawing, Oxford, Core became an acclaimed figurative painter, and had one-man shows at the Francis Kyle Gallery, the Whitechapel and the Camden Arts Centre in London, and in San Francisco. Among his commissions was a large mural above the Piccadilly entrance of the Ritz Hotel in London, a nudgingly camp view of the hotel in its heyday, completed in 1984 but subsequently removed.

In 1983 Core was the subject of a BBC *Omnibus* documentary, which examined his two 120-ft long commissions for the Henley Festival, as well as a remarkable crucifix sculpture. Core subsequently contributed large decorative screens for the programme's set.

As a journalist, Core wrote knowledgeably for *Harpers & Queen* and *Vogue* magazines on subjects ranging from Degas to Egon Schiele and Carl Van Vechten – he was credited with having given the latter his first English appreciation.

His illustrations for *Vogue* were much influenced by

his favourite neo-romantic artist, Christian Bérard. Core also translated the English edition of Boris Kochno's large format biography of Bérard, which was published in 1988.

Recently Core became something of a spokesman for the "alternative arts", appearing on such programmes as Channel 4's *Club X* and BBC2's *Did You See?* to comment on avant-garde art and artists.

He was also a lively source of "copy" for journalists writing about the house sales of such aesthetes as Edward James and Stephen Tennant. Core would deliver his own judgement of their particular appeal which, while not always strictly accurate, was occasionally amusing.

November 15 1989

YANA

YANA, the voluptuous British songstress, who has died aged 57, had a powerful voice and enjoyed a meteoric success in the 1950s.

A glamorous blonde whose plunging necklines provoked complaints from agitated television viewers, Yana was a household name for several years. Besides her pert and prominent bust, she was celebrated for her pack of poodles and her "personalised" number plate "YG1" – which, she announced with pride, was appropriated by the Russian astronaut Major Yuri Gagarin during his visit to London in 1961.

She had her own television show, appeared in lavish West End pantomimes, Royal Variety performances and in films such as *Cockleshell Heroes, The Ship That Died of*

Shame, and *Zarak*. Her biggest hit was the song "Climb Up the Wall".

Once, when performing this torrid number on television, Yana picked on the unsuspecting Lord Mayor of Newcastle in the audience. She pulled him on to the dance floor where she proceeded to cuddle and kiss him during her rendition.

The Lord Mayor, and the Lady Mayoress, took it all in good part, though one local councillor was outraged, describing the incident as "an affront to civic dignity". Yana observed that the other burghers were "just jealous" and offered to kiss the whole city council to put things right.

She was born Pamela Guard on February 16 1932 at Billericay in Essex, though her publicity people liked to maintain she was "Cornish-born". She began life as a hairdresser's assistant and went on to become a fashion model.

One evening, a night-club owner heard her singing at a private party and booked her for a cabaret act. Soon she was appearing on television and touring the Moss Empire circuit.

Yana's *annus mirabilis* was 1956 when she starred in *The Yana Show* on BBC TV and went to America to appear on the Bob Hope and Ed Sullivan Shows. Asked what was the first thing she was going to do in Hollywood, she replied: "Buy myself a monkey, darling . . . I am crazy about animals."

In 1957 she starred in *The Kings of Skiffle* at the Prince of Wales Theatre, "encased", according to *The Daily Telegraph's* reviewer, "in a white gown that fitted like a bandage and clinging so closely to a hand microphone that one could be forgiven for mistaking it for a mouthspray."

In 1958 she acquitted herself well in Harold Fielding's production of *Cinderella* at the Coliseum, tackling the lead role in a cast that included Jimmy Edwards as the King, Kenneth Williams as one of the Ugly Sisters and the young pop star Tommy Steele – furthering his ambition to be an "all-round entertainer" – making his West End debut as Buttons.

The next year she was chosen to sing two numbers in *Set to Music*, one of the pioneering Eurovision programmes, and in 1960 she played Alice FitzWarren, the Alderman's daughter, in *Turn Again Whittington* at the London Palladium, opposite Norman Wisdom's Dick. At one performance a dancer failed to catch her when she leapt from a 7ft platform but, despite cutting her tongue, she pluckily carried on.

During the 1960s, which saw the emergence of quite a different breed of pop star, Yana faded gradually from view, though she continued to crop up in provincial pantomimes.

By the 1980s she was working at Boots, the chemists, in Marylebone where she was "rediscovered" to play the Good Fairy in *The Wonderful Wizard of Oz* at Crewe. In 1984 she was featured in the ITV programme *Where Are They Now?*

She last worked professionally in cabaret two years ago and had latterly been demonstrating a slimming machine in Harrods.

Yana was thrice married.

November 23 1989

BILLY WELLS

BILLY WELLS, who has died aged 80, was a stalwart pantomime dame and one of the British variety stage's best-loved *monstres sacrés*, whose characters included a haughty Queen Victoria.

A pocket-sized, roly-poly comic with a technically assured style all his own, he learned his craft in the bawdy atmosphere of the music-hall before perfecting such regularly revived roles as Mother and Widow Twankey in Aladdin. Wells's pantomime career spanned some 60 years, beginning in Cardiff with *Babes in the Wood*, and ending at Crewe in the same show. Besides playing dames he also, somewhat unusually, filled the role of principal boy in panto – a part traditionally reserved for long-legged thigh-slapping females.

Latterly Wells toured the night-club circuit as a full-bosomed Gaiety Girl or an imperious Queen Victoria, a cameo role in which he was last seen in August in the finale of a British Music Hall Society concert given to celebrate his 70 years in showbusiness.

Billy Wells was born in Eastbourne in 1909, to a doting mother who put her seven-year-old boy wonder on the stage in local concert parties. His first employer was the Cardiff-born Scots comedian Sylvester Stuart, who cast him in his *Oh Joy!* concert party tours as a light comedian when he was still in his mid-teens.

He then toured with their Cardiff-based successor *The Welsh Follies* in which he polished the "camp" convention that was to bring him acclaim as a drag *artiste*.

During the Second World War he served with the

RAF and also toured with ENSA. He appeared at home and abroad in Ralph Reader's Gang Shows, and in the *Soldiers In Skirts* and *Forces Showboat* revues.

In 1964 he launched the *Billy Wells Music Hall* at the Rainbow Room in Jersey, where it ran for nine seasons, featuring Wells himself and Mrs Shufflewick (*alias* Rex Jameson).

Shortly before his death Wells gallantly participated in a publicity stunt, swathed in a bombazine dress and red wig, at the first night party of the farcical *The Vicar And The Tart* at London's Mermaid Theatre. He remarked: "I've been a tart on stage for 50 years and I'm still getting paid for it."

He was unmarried.

December 29 1989

TERRY-THOMAS

TERRY-THOMAS, the comedian, who has died aged 78, perfected the role of the amiable cad whose winsome gap-toothed smile, over-familiar manner and rakish moustache concealed a devious nature, capable of treachery on a Machiavellian scale.

Of the legion of counter-jumpers, poodle-fakers and lounge-lizards he played so memorably on screen, perhaps the one which best epitomised the Thomas persona was the handlebar-moustached Sir Percy Ware-Armitage, Bart, in the international farce *Those Magnificent Men in Their Flying Machines* (1965) The bounderish baronet, an unmitigated cheat, was determined, as he put it, to "nobble" the competition in the London to Paris air race. Assisted by his bungling manservant Courtney, played by Eric Sykes, Sir Percy reserved his most venomous ploys for the American competitor ("If he can't land on one wheel, he shouldn't be in the race").

The double-act he fashioned with Sykes provided some of the modern cinema's most richly comic moments. As he steps on his underling's cupped hands, Sir Percy snarls: "I trust your hands are *clean*, Courtney"; and when, in between belabouring the hapless Courtney with his riding-crop, he allows him to witness the consequences of their sabotage, he says: "Don't expect treats like this all the time."

Thomas also cropped up in other less hilarious ensembles of international stereotypes such as *It's A Mad, Mad, Mad, Mad World* (1962) and *Monte Carlo or Bust* (1969). His own favourite film was another big American picture, *How to Murder Your Wife* (1965), in which he played Charles, the magnificently misogynous butler to Jack Lemmon.

But to his British admirers Thomas did his finest work in the 1950s in a string of engagingly parochial home-grown comedies, many of them made by the Boutling Brothers. The era of the minor public school chancer, ex-officer and "temporary" gentleman, clad in a fancy waist-coat and spinning his sports car into a roadhouse off the Kingston bypass, suited Thomas's style to a tee.

After establishing himself as a comedian on wireless and television, Thomas first made his mark in the cinema in *Private's Progress* (1956) as the silly ass of a CO pronouncing – in tones often imitated but never matched – that his men were "a shower! An *absolute shower!*"

The next year he contributed a scene-stealing cameo as a con-man in *Brothers-in-Law* (1957) and he went on to score a series of successes in such films as *The Naked Truth, Blue Murder at St Trinian's, Lucky Jim, Too Many Cooks* and *Carlton-Browne of the FO*.

Two of his best-loved popular British pictures were *I'm All Right Jack* (1959), the Boultings' telling trade union satire — still considered too controversial to be shown on television during the General Election campaign 20 years later — and *School for Scoundrels* (1960), the "one-upmanship" saga in which he was at his most laughably bumptious.

Thomas Terry Hoar Stevens was born at Finchley, north London, on July 14 1911 and educated at Ardingly. He began life as a clerk with Union Cold Storage Co before drifting into films as an extra and supporting himself as a professional ballroom dancer and cabaret *artiste*.

The 1930s musical, *Rhythm in the Air*, in which he played an intoxicated exhibition dancer, allowed him to draw on techniques he had learned as a paid dancer at the Cricklewood Palais.

When he adopted his first two Christian names for stage purposes he found that people thought he was related to Ellen Terry. He therefore reversed them and inserted a hyphen to secure a "trade mark"; he was always insistent that the hyphen be used to remind people of the distinctive gap between his two front teeth.

During the Second World War he served with the Royal Corps of Signals and, like many showbusiness figures, achieved his big break through Forces entertainment.

He was talent-spotted in the revue *Stars in Battledress* and by 1946 he was appearing with his mentor Sid Field in the show *Piccadilly Hayride* at the Prince of Wales as well as in the Royal Command Variety performance.

In the austere Attlee years Thomas's cheerfully fruity humour – with his drawling catchphrase, "How do you do?" – proved immensely popular on the wireless, where he had his own programmes, *To Town with Terry* and *Top of the Town*. And in the early 1950s he became British television first "star comedian" through his show *How Do You View?* which ran for two years.

After his film successes of the later 1950s and early 1960s Thomas's career gradually declined, though his was a more than welcome presence in such pictures as *You Must Be Joking, The Abominable Dr Phibes* and *The Last Remake of Beau Geste*.

In the mid-1970s he was diagnosed as suffering from Parkinson's Disease but rallied with characteristic courage and in 1977 made a moving television appeal for the Parkinson's Disease Society. In 1984 he was obliged to sell his villa in Ibiza and move to more modest premises in Majorca and by last year, when a special benefit gala was held in his honour at the Theatre Royal, Drury Lane, Terry-Thomas was in pathetically straitened circumstances.

He was much supported by his second wife, Belinda, whom he married in 1963, and his two sons.

January 9 1990

GORDON JACKSON

GORDON JACKSON, the character actor, who has died aged 66, became a national institution through his splendid portrayal of Hudson, the rigidly loyal butler, in the long-running 1970s television series of an upper-class household, *Upstairs, Downstairs*.

His soft rich Scots burr, unfailingly deferential attitude to what he steadfastly regarded as his "betters" and benevolent exercise of discipline made Hudson as memorable as – though entirely different from – such great fictional butlers as Beach of Blandings Castle and the Admirable Crichton. Jackson's scrupulous interpretation of the central figure in this nostalgic series helped to ensure that *Upstairs, Downstairs* became a television classic on both sides of the Atantic.

A craggy, reserved, supremely dignified figure, a little on the prim and prissy side though not without a certain pawky humour, Hudson exercised an unquestioned authority over the servants' hall, and was avuncular to the "*gir-r-r-ls*" under his command. By way of relaxation from his duties he would retire to peruse an improving volume in his parlour.

Beginning at the turn of the century, the series followed the Bellamys through the lavish opulence of the Edwardian era; the loss of Lady Marjorie in the *Titanic*; the Great War (for which the over-age and short-sighted Hudson gallantly attempted to volunteer); and its frenetic aftermath. The storyline, though, which latterly revolved around the increasingly hopeless figure of Captain James, had fizzled out long before the 75th and final episode.

But Jackson's performance opposite the redoubtable Mrs Bridges (played by Angela Baddeley), with whom "Angus" had a rather unlikely "understanding", always made *Upstairs, Downstairs* compulsive viewing. By general consent the apogee of the whole series was when King Edward VII came to dine at the house in Eaton Place, when Hudson ensured that the elaborate occasion went off without mishap.

It was a measure of the affection in which *Upstairs, Downstairs* was held that a pastiche by Stanley Baxter in one of his comedy spectaculars struck such a chord. One of the wickedest touches was Baxter's outraged Mrs Bridges, admonishing a maid for referring to "the old Queen", which she mistook for an allusion to Mr Hudson.

Behind the extraordinarily solid-seeming persona of Hudson was a real-life actor of considerable versatility. Having made his name as an endearingly callow Scots youth in such 1940s films as *Millions Like Us, Nine Men* and *Whisky Galore,* Jackson went on to play Ishmael in Orson Welles's celebrated stage production of *Moby Dick,* and Maggie Smith's stolid admirer in the film of *The Prime of Miss Jean Brodie.*

He showed that there was life after Hudson by winning a new television following – though the critics were unenthusiastic – in the violent and fast-moving spy series *The Professionals.* As the crusty Cowley of "CI5" he was obliged to keep a pair of hard-nosed operatives – Doyle, played by Martin Shaw and Bodie, by Lewis Collins – on an unrelentingly tight rein.

Jackson's finest moment in the cinema was his robust study of the patriotic poacher-cum-beater bagged by the caddish Edward Fox character in *The Shooting Party,* a markedly less sentimental view of the sybaritic world of the pre-1914 aristocracy. Summoning up his last reserves of energy before expiring, he croaks, not unmovingly: "God Save the King!"

A printer's son, Gordon Jackson was born in Glasgow on December 19 1923, and educated at Hillhead High School. He claimed that he had never had any training as an actor – and, indeed, he started work as a draughtsman in the drawing office of Rolls-Royce, where he was an apprentice engineer. But his acting talent had become apparent early when, as a schoolboy, he played small parts for BBC Radio in Scotland when a child's voice was required.

During the Second World War Rolls-Royce gave him time to go to London to appear in propaganda films made at Ealing studios, notably *The Foreman Went to France*, made when he was 17. His first stage appearance was as Dudley in *George and Margaret* in 1943 at the MSO Theatre, Rutherglen.

Jackson had completed nearly five years with Rolls-Royce when the firm told him that it was time to choose between engineering and acting. He took the risk of deciding to act, but had a painful, rather slow climb to success through repertory.

Among his numerous films were *Tunes of Glory, Mutiny on the Bounty, The Great Escape, The Ipcress File, Those Magnificent Men in Their Flying Machines* (in which he played a kilted airman addressed by the Terry-Thomas character as "Madam"), *Scrooge* and *Kidnapped*.

His recent television work included playing the lawyer in the Australian series *A Town Like Alice* and dogged father in Terence Rattigan's *The Winslow Boy*.

Jackon was appointed OBE in 1979 and earlier won Emmy and Royal Television Society awards for his acting as Hudson. A genial teetotaller, he enjoyed gardening and music.

He married Rona Anderson in 1951 and the couple had two sons.

*

Eric Shorter writes: Gordon Jackson was such a naturally sympathetic actor that it was wasteful of the theatre not to give him more chances. Those he got he made the most of.

He made a good start with his first West End part in *Seagulls Over Sorrento* (1951), but it was four years later in Orson Welles's *Moby Dick* at the Duke of York's that he felt the excitement only stage acting transmits; and the critics felt it too from his performance as the perplexed Young Actor (Ishmael). Jackson used to say that working on *Moby Dick* with Welles and on *Macbeth* with Bill Gaskill were the two most exciting theatrical experiences of his life. As Banquo, Jackson felt joyfully at ease in this stark production, in spite of the critical squall which nearly everyone else involved (Alec Guinness and Simone Signoret among them) ran into.

Jackson was sent for again when another *Macbeth* (Nicol Williamson) played at the Aldwych nine years later for the Royal Shakespeare Company. By then he had been Williamson's endearing Horatio both at the Round House and in New York. With such a whining, snarling Hamlet you wondered at Horatio's patience, but that was something Jackson never had any trouble conveying, any more than he did friendship.

As one of the ghostly occupants of a signalbox on a forgotten bit of British Railways in Brian Phelan's *The Signalman's Apprentice* (Oxford Playhouse, 1970) and as the Interrogator in Marguerite Duras's *The Lovers of Viorne* (Royal Court, 1971), he discovered harsher qualities than Hamlet saw in Horatio.

It is still best, however, to see an actor in his element; and as the amiable, beaming and slightly effeminate Rodney in Charles Wood's *Veterans* at the Royal Court a year later, Gordon Jackson could be his old, warm familiar self – even down to the Scots accent – as the film unit cook fussing courteously around the great actor (Gielgud), impatient to go before the camera.

He was as an actor as well liked off stage as on.

January 16 1990

BHAGWAN SHREE RAJNEESH

BHAGWAN SHREE RAJNEESH, who has died aged 58 at his ashram in Poona, India – where he had lived since being deported from America – was the notorious "guru" who drew thousands of followers from all over the world by preaching a bizarre blend of Eastern religion, pop psychology and free love.

The Bhagwan, known as Osho Rajneesh in recent years, had a dedicated following in his heyday. His enigmatic *aperçus*, encouraging the guilt-free enjoyment of wealth and sexual licence, were apparently taken as gospel by more than half-a-million "Orange people", many of them prosperous Europeans – including a not insignificant group of expensively educated Britons.

The journalist Bernard Levin went so far as to describe the Bhagwan as the "conduit along which the vital force of the universe flows". In *The Times* he described the Bhagwan's *sannyasin*, or followers, as "in general an exceptionally fine crop, bearing witness to a tree of a choice, rare nature".

Levin observed that "The first quality a visitor to

Rajneesh's ashram notices – and he never ceases to notice it – is the ease and comfort with which they wear their faith . . . The joy with which they are clearly filled is, as anyone who listens to Rajneesh must deduce it would be, directed outwards as well as in; I cannot put it better than in saying that they constantly extend, to each other and to strangers, the hands of love, though without the ego-filled demands of love as most of the world knows it. They have shed their chains, and they demonstrated their freedom easily and unobstrusively, though the results at first can be startling . . ."

Among the events organised by the Bhagwan's British followers was an "an explosion of energy and consciousness" at the Napoleon Room of the Café Royal in Regent Street. But after the Bhagwan had abruptly decamped from his original commune in Poona in mysterious circumstances in 1981 – there was talk of smuggling, drug-trafficking and prostitution, not to mention tax problems – it seemed increasingly clear that "the Bagwash" was a charlatan.

The saying was coined: "Jesus saves, Bhagwan spends". Certainly he managed to accumulate such items as a Lear jet, 35 jewel-encrusted watches and 93 Rolls-Royces.

He transplanted his operation to "Rajneeshpuram" in Oregon where, together with several thousand of his red-robed followers, he set about constructing a self-sufficient utopia. The Bhagwan would drive around the site in one of his Rolls-Royces past lines of chanting, clapping fans, but the allegedly paradisaical atmosphere was somewhat offset by his escort of helicopter and armed guards; indeed the supposedly loving community was riddled with para-noia and internecine feuds.

The advent of Aids also rather put the dampener on the free love; the Bhagwan ordered his subjects to use rubber gloves and condoms and to wash with pure alcohol before embarking on sexual activity.

The crash came in 1985 when several of the movement's leaders were jailed. The Bhagwan's principal aide, Ma Anand Sheela, left the commune with the parting shot: "To hell with Bhagwan."

The guru alleged that she had bugged his quarters, amassed millions of dollars at the commune and turned the valley into a concentration camp. Soon afterwards the Bhagwan himself was expelled from America and barred from more than 20 other countries – including Britain – as an "undesirable alien" before returning to Poona.

It was there, in 1974, that the Bhagwan Shree Rajneesh had first established his sect. It soon became controversial as a sex cult; an advertisement for the sect appeared in *Time* magazine under the headline "SEX" which urged: "Never repress it! Search all the nooks and corners of your sexuality."

In Poona followers paid to join sexual encounter lessons called "*tantras*" in which participants were encouraged to behave with the utmost licentiousness. The Bhagwan's western followers defied India's strict moral codes as they kissed and fondled each other publicly while dressed in the garb of Hindu holy men.

One Poona editor complained that their behaviour was analogous to a group of foreigners dressing up as monks and nuns and engaging in sexual activity on American streets.

The Bhagwan said celibacy was a crime against nature and that a high sex drive improved a man's creativity. "It is natural for sexual energy to need expression," he said. "You cannot find in the whole history of mankind a single impotent man becoming a great painter or musician or dancer or scientist or poet."

He said it was fortunate that man's ancestors did not listen to "the idiots who preached against sex. Had they done so, none of us would have been here."

On moving to America, the Bhagwan elected to take an oath of silence and spent much of his time watching children's programmes on television. Although by 1985 seven of the Bhagwan's followers were in jail, and 15 more were on the run, the Bhagwan pleaded divine ignorance of these matters, and was found guilty only of illegal immigration.

Under a plea agreement he received a suspended 10-year sentence, paid a 400,000-dollar fine, and agreed not to return to America for five years without the written permission of the US attorney-general.

In 1986 the Bhagwan's chief henchwoman, Ma Anand Sheela, was charged with numerous offences including poisoning 750 patrons of local restaurants; illegal wire-tapping; fire-bombing government buildings; and attempting to murder prominent members of the community, ranging from the district attorney to the Bhagwan's dentist.

Back in India, where he dropped the Hindu honorific of Bhagwan (meaning "Lord God"), Rajneesh continued to deliver religious discourses at his Poona commune and to outrage many Indians with his support for free sex.

In his most recent public statement last November, he told Indian voters that the country did not need political parties and they should refuse to vote. The Bhagwan had a love-hate relationship with India and contempt for its bureaucracy.

January 20 1990

NORMAN PARKINSON

NORMAN PARKINSON, the photographer, who has died aged 76, devoted much of his life to the study of beautiful women, whom he treated with a reverence bordering on idolatry, and was an unofficial portraitist to the ladies of the Royal Family.

A man of singular charm, "Parks" was once described as resembling "an elegant giraffe"; sporting a twirling moustache and a Kashmiri bridal cap, he liked to deck his lean 6 foot 5 inch frame in kaftans, loud beach shirts and heavy gold jewellery.

In the 1930s, when he first began "snapping", Parkinson was one of a new breed of heterosexual photographers. Rather than shoot his fashion features in studios, he pioneered a slightly surrealist method, taking his models to grimy, industrial locations. "I was one of the first to take the scent-laden atmosphere out of photographs," he explained, "and the first to get girls to run, to jump, to stretch, to let air through their knees."

In spite of his quest for the original Parkinson always insisted that photography was a craft and not an art: he liked to be seen as "the capable mechanic with clean fingernails", "a civilised chap". It was his opinion that men should be photographed only when strictly necessary, and true to this principle he concentrated upon photographing some of the most beautiful women of several generations.

"Being photographed", he claimed, "is a whole section of a woman's identity. She has to be admired." In his quest for pulchritudinous subjects Parkinson would sometimes drive round London and hand out his card to pretty girls – keeping an eye out for possessive boyfriends.

But there was no shortage of willing subjects. "Parks has got a little bit of hypnotism about him," his beautiful wife Wenda once commented. "Women will do anything for him and he loves their company, adores them." He said: "I find them the more important gender. They are more courageous, more honest, more direct."

Parkinson's popularity was no doubt aided by his consistently friendly lens. "I see no point in putting up a camera and then ... mounting your victim to do them mischief." He objected, for example, to the unflattering portraits of Duke and Duchess of Windsor by Richard Avedon, who, he said, had left "a blot on history".

If, as Parkinson claimed, "the best photographs tell the biggest lies", then his supreme fictions were reserved for royalty. Though he jokingly described photographing his royal patrons as an "awful job", he managed to invest them with a hitherto undiscovered glamour.

His 1971 portraits of Princess Anne, taken for her 21st birthday, were the first occasion on which a member of the Royal Family had been given the full treatment, with extensive professional make-up and so on – a far cry from the stiff pre-Cecil Beaton days. "Princess Anne does look quite beautiful sometimes," Parkinson observed as he set to work. "We want none of that nonsense here," growled Prince Philip.

None the less Parkinson succeeded in creating a glamorous Princess, and he continued this metamorphosis at the time of her engagement to Mark Phillips. Even he, though, could not disguise a hole in the Captain's military pullover.

He then made further explorations in the royal field,

creating some notably romantic images of Queen Elizabeth the Queen Mother, in soft focus with every jewel a-sparkle.

There were times, though, when his ingenuity gave the impression of vaudeville, as when he posed her looking through the glass window of a door; and, least successfully of all, when he posed her for an 80th birthday portrait with the Queen and Princess Margaret, each of them draped in a dark blue silk overall. The result recalled nothing so much as a publicity shot for the Supremes and was waggishly dubbed "the Windsor Sisters".

Parkinson's one regret was never to have taken a picture of the Princess of Wales – though he was once reported to have said that she had lost her youthful freshness, the "bloom the camera sees, although the eye often doesn't". He said, too, that he would have liked to portray "the loving side" of the Duchess of York, "without all the guffaws".

He liked to imbue his glamour photographs with a certain degree of titillation. He once explained, "In every photographer, there is a girlie photographer waiting to get out." His 1985 book, *Would You Let Your Daughter . . .?* was meant to teach "the delights of intelligent eroticism". It depicted a number of luscious models in pleasing states of nudity accompanied by a text in bold capitals with such memorable phrases as "MY WILL IS STRONG BUT MY WON"T IS WEAK".

"Would you let your daughter?" he asked provocatively, "play the part of Leda with the Swan? Walk through a zoo wearing diamonds? Abandon herself to sensuous fantasy?" One model was the literary biographer Rebecca Fraser; another was Wenda Parkinson, lying naked on a bed and reading a book.

A surprising contrast was provided by the "voluminous and colourful" Barbara Cartland, also described as "Rock hard, punctual and determined". She was portrayed in shocking pink, surrounded by gilded mirrors, tables, chairs and cherubs, in a bower of flowers.

In his later years, Parkinson further distinguished himself by producing the celebrated "Porkinson's Bangers", which he would occasionally bring back to England from his Tobago sausage farm, wrapped in a pair of socks. Porkinson's sausage factory was typical of his eccentric style which, he admitted, made him quite unlike the popular notion of a photographer – more like a "decaying colonel".

A barrister's son, he was born Ronald William Parkinson Smith on April 21 1913 and spent his early days in a semi-detached house in Putney. He was educated at Westminster, where he proved a popular if unacademic figure. At the bottom of one particularly dismal report his headmaster scrawled, "This is one of the worst reports I have ever seen, but I can't help liking the fellow."

Noting that photography was his son's only interest, Parkinson's father, although "a bit of a Tartar", paid for his apprenticeship to a declining firm of court photographers, Speaight and Sons of Bond Street.

At the age of 21 "Parks" set up his own studio in Dover Street with six staff and set to work photographing debutantes, which soon led to assignments for *Harper's Bazaar*, in exotic locations. Already Parkinson had developed his flamboyant style and could often be seen wearing a blood-red Harris tweed cape – though Noël Coward warned him, "People who have talent dress like stockbrokers."

During the Second World War Parkinson combined

aerial reconnaissance photography with fashion and propaganda work, while nurturing his society contacts. In 1945 he married Wenda Rogerson, a *Vogue* model discovered by Cecil Beaton.

She became one of Parkinson's favourite subjects. On one occasion he photographed her for American *Vogue* in a Mainbocher evening dress amid the rubble of the New York Ritz, which was being demolished behind her. They were both arrested by a passing policeman, but released when a crowd of admirers proved to be on their side.

The 1981 retrospective exhibition of Parkinson's work at the National Portrait Gallery displayed the vast range of his shots, from portraits of Coward, the Sitwells, and Margot Fonteyn to his fashion work for *Vogue, Queen, Town and Country* and *Life*, employing such models as Jerry Hall and Koo Stark.

In 1963 Parkinson moved from his flower-covered house in Twickenham to Tobago. He began selling postcard views of the island, mainly to American tourists; and later had the idea of setting up a sausage factory, exporting his sausages to America under the name Star-Spangled Bangers. Fearing this might offend American patriotism, he later changed the name.

On Tobago Parkinson could enjoy his hobbies, listed in *Who's Who* as "pig farming, sun worshipping, bird watching, breeding Creole racehorses" (he gave his telephone number as "none, fortunately"). This idyllic existence was marred, first by the sudden death of Wenda in 1987 and, soon afterwards, by the fire which destroyed his house, said to have been one of the most beautiful in the Caribbean.

In spite of his privileged connections, Parkinson

remained distinctly modest and once insisted, "I'm quite the most downmarket man; I'm quite unposh." He was a natural aristocrat, though, and quite grand in an insouciant way. Explaining that his remains would be interred at a private burial ground on Tobago, for example, he said, "I couldn't bear to be buried with people that I have not been introduced to."

He was appointed CBE in 1981, and is survived by a son.

February 16 1990

FREDERICK VON MIERERS

FREDERICK VON MIERERS, the leader of the New Age movement Eternal Values who has died in New York aged 42, claimed to be a visitor from the star Arcturus and made a fortune selling bogus gems to socialites.

With his bronzed face, blue eyes and pineapple-blond hair, von Mierers proved a charismatic leader. He told his disciples that he had been "sent to this planet to neutralise dark forces" and promised them a noble eternity: "Terrible storms will destroy the world, and only the elite will be saved. I am here to train the leaders of the New Age!"

Eternal Values was structured around an inner circle – "The Group" – which at its peak a few years ago numbered some 100 active members, including bankers, lawyers, television tycoons, actors and models. Von Mierers peddled a range of New Age merchandise – cassettes, videos and books, diet plans, astrological charts and psychic "life-readings". Above all, though, he was a gem salesman, unloading second-rate emeralds, sapphires and rubies at several thousand dollars apiece, assuring his clients that his baubles guaranteed survival of the coming Apocalypse.

Latterly some of the cult's members grew disenchanted with their leader's dictatorial style, and with an increasing emphasis on drug abuse and ritualistic sex.

Frederick von Mierers was born Fred Meyers in the backstreets of Brooklyn, New York, in 1947. He told friends that he was educated at the Professional Children's School, though there is no record of this. By the late 1960s he had cultivated a new name, an eclectic accent and a plutocratic background.

In his youth von Mierers enjoyed a brief success as a model; known as *le mignon*, he was much admired in fashionable homosexual circles. In the early 1970s he also made regular visits to London, where he established himself as an escort of debutantes and endeared himself to their mothers by addressing them all as "Duchess".

By 1976 von Mierers was listed in the *New York Social Register*, a copy of which he carried everywhere with him as a talisman, along with an address book full of such names as Vanderbilt and Rockefeller. Two years later, by then established as an interior decorator and astrologer, von Mierers underwent what he described as "a bewildering substitution of egos".

He experienced visions of past lives, he said, and realised that he was a native of Arcturus. He began to preach a distillation of Eastern philosophy, doomsday prophecy and New Age aphorisms; Eternal Values was founded, and soon became a success. Von Mierers "taught" at a church in Park Avenue and sold on a strictly cash basis, innumerable dubious gems.

By now the spiritual leader had a number of residences:

a Bronx loft, a pink marble palace in Asheville, North Carolina – he believed that only the Blue Ridge Mountains would survive the Millennium – a house on Nantucket and a retreat in the Berkshires.

In the early years of Eternal Values von Mierers preached sexual abstinence, but latterly he seems to have revised this doctrine. New recruits, many of them models, were obliged to undergo multiracial sex rites by way of initiation. His disciples began to rebel, and their leader grew steadily iller. He was unmarried.

Eternal Values is currently undergoing investigations for fraud, and von Mierers is suspected of having been involved in an international smuggling ring.

March 18 1990

DEXTER GORDON

DEXTER GORDON, the tenor and soprano saxophonist who has died in Philadelphia aged 67, achieved his apotheosis in the jazz film *Round Midnight* (1986) after a career blighted by heroin and alcohol addiction.

The film featured Dale Turner, a black jazz genius struggling against drink and drugs. Turner is temporarily rescued from his plight by a penniless fan obsessed with his music, and by the fan's nine-year-old daughter. But recovery only takes him back to New York and the drug-pushers; he reverts to his old ways and dies in a seedy fourth-class hotel – the classic setting for jazz tragedy.

The choice of Gordon for *Round Midnight* (produced on a "shoestring" budget of $3 million) was made only after turning aside saxophonists Archie Shepp and Sonny

Rollins, both looking too fit and exuding too much energy to be suitable.

The French director Bertrand Tavernier and Gordon established a singular *rapport*. Gordon would often change lines which, as it turned out, gave scenes greater validity.

He turned in a tremendous performance, shambling through his part with heart-rending dignity, style and pathos, whether with or without his saxophone. He was nominated for an Oscar.

But filming had its strains. "I'm doing everything I can with Bertrand to make it for real," Gordon told reporters. "It's very tiring. The concentration, uh. I get up for breakfast at 7.30, which is, uhhh, a whole different ball game."

Tavernier recalled that he had to reassure the producer that Gordon was "all there". The director found him "very articulate and intelligent. He even understood the problem of sound reproduction."

Gordon had a history that made him an enigma to medical science. During the making of the film studio doctors found that he was a diabetic, had virtually no liver and a percentage of alcohol in his blood stream that defied belief.

The average amount of alcohol content in the bloodstream is measured at 33; at over 150, a driver's licence is automatically forfeited. If it is over 250, one is considered clinically insane. Gordon's alcohol content registered at 1,200.

Yet he never had any trouble in remembering his lines. And the film featured such a wealth of music that a memorable album, *The Other Side of Round Midnight*, was produced out of those parts of the soundtrack left on the cutting-room floor.

Previously Dexter had appeared in Jack Gelber's play, *The Connection*, for which he also wrote the music. In real life he had played with such legendary figures as Lionel Hampton, Louis Armstrong and Charlie Parker.

Gordon came to jazz before "Bebop" fragmented the scene in the mid-1940s. Although he adapted to the stirring changes of the "Modern" school, his own playing retained the direct lines that owed much to Lester Young.

A doctor's son, Keith Dexter Gordon was born at Los Angeles in February 1923. His father took him to hear Duke Ellington's orchestra when he was four; he studied harmony and clarinet at the age of 13 and alto-saxophone at 15.

Young Dexter joined a local band, the Harlem Collegians, before a three-year stint with Lionel Hampton's outfit. Next he was briefly with the drummer Lee Young; then, in 1944, with Louis Armstrong's Last Big Band, followed by a year with Billy Eckstine.

Eckstine's band was a hotbed of talent, including Dizzy Gillespie and Art Blakey, and with them Gordon played his first recorded solo, "Blowing the Blues Away".

In 1945 he moved to New York where he worked with Charlie Parker, recorded with Dizzy Gillespie and with his own band, which included Leo Parker, Bud Powell and Tadd Dameron. Two years later he returned to Los Angeles to play with the drummer/singer "Cee Dee" Johnson.

At about this time Gordon began his informal partnership with the tenor saxophonist Warrell Gray – an association which was musically fruitful but ill-fated, leading as it did to Gordon being sentenced for drug offences and to Gray's death from an overdose.

But Gordon staged spectacular comebacks, those of

the early 1960s being particularly well received. In 1962 he made his first trip to Europe and subsequently settled in Copenhagen, though he was eventually encouraged by increasing acclaim at home to return to America.

In the early 1980s Gordon visited Europe again – including seasons at Ronnie Scott's Club in Soho – but was in virtual retirement until being cast in *Round Midnight*.

Latterly Gordon had a long battle with throat cancer, finally dying of kidney failure. As Sue Mingus, the widow of jazz composer and bassist Charles Mingus, said: "He actually died round midnight."

April 26 1990

MAX WALL

MAX WALL, the actor and comedian who has died aged 82, was a veteran of the variety stage, revue and panto-mime whose career enjoyed an Indian summer – both as a lugubrious stand-up comic in the music-hall tradition and as a legitimate actor in plays by John Osborne and Samuel Beckett.

Wall's divorces and his bankruptcy helped fuel his disenchanted view of show-business. "Maxie" made an almost miraculous comeback without being able to believe it; he continued to regard himself as a "has-been".

Like many of his calling, he learned to resign himself to the vagaries of the limelight. It was partly his philos-ophical reaction to his success and set-backs which deep-ened his powers as a clown towards the end of his life.

Wall won the admiration of a younger generation,

who knew nothing of the theatrical traditions by which he had earned a living between the two world wars, by simply demonstrating stand-up comedy in routines that would not have survived in other hands.

His most celebrated sketch was that of a preposterous pianist whose recital is deferred by various distractions. His solo turn at the footlights seemed to challenge the very nature of music-hall humour in its ability to button-hole an audience. He exposed for inspection an essentially frivolous art which had required in its timing and taste the gravest preparation, practice and polish.

When, in the early 1960s, he turned to "straight" acting during a spell when his fortunes as a comic were improving, he won wide critical favour – most notably as Archie Rice in Osborne's *The Entertainer* (1974). Subsequently, in the plays of Samuel Beckett, Wall's brand of wry, ruminative comedy disclosed a powerful gift for pathos.

Deprived of the rapport with his audience which a clown naturally feeds upon, Wall discovered another kind dramatic satisfaction in the spell he was casting over a silent house.

It was, however, as the solo comic remembering better days and candidly wondering how to entertain us that he won the widest affection. His style could be sentimental and self-pitiful. It sometimes verged on bitterness.

His dolorous surprise at being able to hold our attention with creaky material and techniques, and his proclaimed gratitude for being in work at all, avoided cheap pathos because his sense of irony usually prevailed, though he could never deny the flatness he felt after a performance – however successful it happened to be.

His Professor Walloffski was a turn he perfected. In a

long black wig, a tail-coat and trousers which stopped well short of his white socks, and elongated boots, he would promise us a classical interlude at the piano without progressing beyond a few chords. A casual thought would strike him, or, when he went to sit down, he would be unable to find the piano stool. This object, when retrieved, he would apostrophise with elocutionary relish.

His rolling of simple words round his tongue until they almost achieved another meaning had been part of many a stand-up comic's delight in language and its ambiguous possibilities; but Wall was among the last to work it through so wittily. Then there were his funny walks — particularly the "chicken" strut which might include the splits. His dancer's training kept him nimble.

Wall's act, even for those who had seen it often, remained a constant surprise because of his sense of timing. His way, after an anecdote, of slowly turning and leering with a ghastly grin was always unexpected.

In the middle of his solo show, *Aspects of Wall* (which enjoyed a West End run at the Garrick), he would sometimes pause so long to analyse an effect that it felt artistically suicidal. The jokes were hoary. He despised his material.

He was born Maxwell George Lorimer at Brixton on March 12 1908, to parents who were both "on the halls". Max first appeared on the stage at 14 in *Mother Goose* in Devon and Cornwall.

He went on to revues as an eccentric dancer. In 1932 he appeared with *Earl Carroll's Vanities* in New York.

Back in Britain, he became something of a celebrity and was photographed playing golf with King Edward VIII. In 1940, he played Tom Carroway in Rodgers and

Hart's *Present Arms* and the next year he led a tour of *Funny Side Up* in the Stanley Lupino role.

During the Second World War, he served in the RAF. Afterwards he led a high-spirited revue at the Duchess called *Make it a Date*, and went on to enjoy success on radio, television and the musical stage.

His first wife, Marion Pola, had been a dancer in an Arthur Askey show, *Bandwagon*. The marriage lasted 15 years and produced five children before it broke up. In 1955 he married the 24-year-old "Miss Britain".

The popular press disapproved. Wall's career crumbled. The comedian who had once owned three Rolls-Royces and a mansion in Jersey was forced to play club and cabaret circuits. Though the marriage to "Miss Britain" lasted 10 years – and there was a third, much briefer marriage after that – Wall spent his later years alone in a south London flat.

Much of his contentment arose from his return to the stage in straight roles, first as Alfred Jarry's *Ubu* at the Royal Court in 1966; then as Emmanuel in Arnold Wesker's *The Old Ones* in 1972; and, more spectacularly, as Archie Rice in 1974, before creating the one-man show which he toured widely.

He returned to Greenwich two years later in Beckett's *Krapp's Last Tape* (at the author's suggestion), stretching the long silent opening of that soliloquy beyond all daring in its banana-eating business. Then he appeared in Shakespeare's *Twelfth Night* (as Malvolio).

Wall played Vladimir in *Waiting for Godot* first at the Royal Exchange Manchester, and then at the Round House, Chalk Farm, London. When Albert Finney headed a revival of Arden's *Serjeant Musgrave's Dance* at the Old

Vic in 1984, Wall played Bludgeon; and for the Beckett celebration that year at the Edinburgh Festival he gave readings and performed a stage version of the novel *Malone Dies*.

On television he was seen in such varied fare as *Waiting for Godot, Crossroads, Emmerdale Farm, Born and Bred, An Evening with Max Wall, Jane in the Desert* and *Comic Asides*.

Channel 4 viewers were, though, denied the chance to see his portrayal of Sir Arthur Harris, the wartime leader of Bomber Command, in a controversial film, *Fireraiser*, made by a women's workshop in Brighton which even Michael Grade refused to screen.

In the cinema, Wall won more critical approval for his sinister performance as Jeremiah Flintwinch in the faithful adaptation of Dickens's *Little Dorrit* (1987) and as the father in *We Think the World of You* (1989).

Wall's summary of himself in a rare interview in 1975 was: "At heart I'm a loner. But a loner who gets on well with people. I spend much time looking out of windows, reading or wondering if I'm going to be good any more."

He said neither bricks nor bouquets could touch him any longer. "I had eight years out of favour and I just accepted them. Money means nothing to me but being accepted as a entertainer is everything."

May 23 1990

ROCKY GRAZIANO

ROCKY GRAZIANO, who has died in New York aged 71, was world middleweight boxing champion from July

1947 to June 1948 — a period when the toughest middleweights in the history of the game were in action.

Graziano had 83 professional bouts and won 67, 52 of them by knockouts. He is best remembered in boxing circles for his three bloody and bruising encounters with Tony Zale, though he gained wider fame with his best-selling autobiography *Somebody Up There Likes Me*, later made into a film with Paul Newman playing Graziano.

His first encounter with Zale, who was then the middleweight champion, was at Yankee Stadium in September 1946. A tremendous battle — described by one spectator as "a small war" — ended with a knockout win by Zale in the sixth round. The effect of the knockout punch was described later by Graziano:

"It was a big left hook, and I see it coming, but I can't stop it. It was like the ground exploded up and hit me in the stomach . . . I try to yell, but I can't make a sound. I am deaf, and I can't talk, and I can't lift my arms, and I am falling. For the first time in my life I know what it's like to be KO'd."

A return match for which the whole of New York, solidly behind the local boy, was baying, took place before a crowd of 27,000 in July of the next year. This time Graziano won the title by knocking Zale out in the sixth. But he enjoyed a reign of only a year before losing once more to Zale, this time in three rounds.

Notable practitioners in the middleweight division in those postwar years also included such formidable fighters as Jake "Raging Bull" La Motta, Marcel Cerdan and Sugar Ray Robinson — who effectively ended Graziano's career by knocking him out in a title bout in three rounds in April 1952.

Son of a boxer known as "Fighting Nick Bob",

Graziano was born Thomas Rocco Barbella in "Little Italy" on New York's Lower East Side in 1919. He grew up as a street-fighter and learned to steal before he could read.

"I quit school in the sixth grade because of pneumonia," he joked, "not because I had it but because I couldn't spell it. We stole everything that began with an 'a' – a piece of fruit, a bicycle, a watch, anything that wasn't nailed down."

At the age of 12 he was arrested for the first time when he was caught breaking into a chewing-gum machine; while on probation he stole a bicycle and was sent for the first of three trips to reform school. In 1939 a friend took him to Stillman's Gym to see if he could put his street fighting instincts to use in the ring. When a seasoned pro named Antonio Fernandez beat up the lad, Barbella swore he would never box again. Two months later, though, he was back in the ring, this time fighting under the name of his sister's boyfriend, Rocky Graziano.

He went on to win the Metropolitan AAU welterweight championship. There followed a spell in the Army, where Graziano was sentenced to a year in military prison for striking an officer. On his discharge he won the Amateur Golden Glove Championship and in 1942 turned professional.

Then the gangsters moved in, offering a $100,000 bribe and a promise not to reveal his prison record if Graziano would "take a dive" in a bout against "Bummy" Davis. He refused the bribe and knocked out Davis in the fourth round – but the New York authorities suspended his licence for not reporting the incident.

The Chicago authorities thought better of him, and though he refused to go there at first, it led him on to take the title. After his humiliation at the hands of

Robinson Graziano had just one more fight, which he lost on points to Chuck Davey, and he retired from the ring in 1952.

In retirement Graziano dabbled in painting for a time and developed an admiration for the style of Picasso. He then took up writing before embarking on a lucrative career as a television actor. He was comedienne Martha Raye's sidekick for a while, and in recent years was much in demand for commercials.

May 28 1990

FREDERICK MELLINGER

FREDERICK MELLINGER, who has died in Los Angeles aged 76, was the founder of Frederick's of Hollywood, a mail-order business and chain of shops specialising in "erotic" lingerie.

The enterprise had its genesis during the Second World War, when Mellinger was stationed in the American Midwest. Like millions of other GIs he had a pin-up picture on the wall of Betty Grable. As he gazed at her legs one day, speculating about the nature of her underwear, it occurred to him to conduct a survey among his fellow soldiers to discover what they found attractive in female attire.

The results of the survey showed that most of Mellinger's comrades liked women to wear tight clothes of singularly sparing cut, preferably made of some transparent material. Armed with this intelligence, after the war he opened a tiny office in New York, proclaiming it Frederick's of Fifth Avenue, and set about designing ladies'

135

underwear from a man's point of view – push-up brassieres, crotchless panties and the like. Then in 1947 he moved to Hollywood where in due course he branched out into sex appliances and films.

To begin with Mellinger's business was done entirely from catalogues sent under plain wrappers. But in the 1960s, by which time his mail-order business had a multimillion dollar turnover, he expanded into retail shops, eventually building up a chain of 160. He oversaw his empire from a garish purple building on Hollywood Boulevard.

Mellinger had two phrases he never tired of repeating: "I never listen to Paris designers – they don't dress women for men", and: "Sex never goes out of fashion."

Since Mellinger's retirement in 1984 the image of Frederick's of Hollywood has gradually changed. The catalogues no longer offer appliances or videos: the underwear has become less vulgar and is modelled by more wholesome looking girls; even the headquarters on Hollywood Boulevard have been painted a sober grey.

Mellinger was, *au fond*, a conservative family man. "Many people expect me to be a dirty, lecherous old guy," he once said. "I think they're kind of disappointed when I'm not."

He is survived by his wife, a son and a daughter.

June 6 1990

JOE LOSS

JOE LOSS, the bandleader who has died aged 80, was an indefatigable showman who set toes tapping for six decades on dance floors from Hammersmith Palais to Buckingham Palace.

With his huge slice-of-melon grin and the energy of a dervish, he communicated his sheer delight in rhythm with a remarkable directness, although he was habitually dismissive of his own dancing ability: "My wife says I'm the worst."

Loss's signature-tune was Glenn Miller's "In the Mood", but his repertoire stretched from the palais-glide to the finnjenka, from the rumba to jive, from foxtrots like A. P. Herbert's "A Nice Cup of Tea" to the irrepressible "Scatterbrain", and from revived waltzes like "Ramona" and "Diane", to the perennial quickstep "Jeepers Creepers", and the rejigged First World War song "Oh! Johnny, Oh!"

He had an acutely discerning ear for popular tunes and adhered to strict tempo and sharp sound rhythms. He believed in straightforward, elegant musical arrangements and did not favour over-exuberance and transient fads: he had no use for the amplifier.

Although he employed one or two jazzmen, notably the trumpeters Leslie Hutchinson and Arthur Mouncey, Loss generally eschewed improvisation and relied on straight arrangements of the melody, with heavy emphasis on such singers as the fruity tenor Monte Rey, Chick Henderson (who sang on "Begin the Beguine") and a vocal quintet called the Loss Chords.

Loss was reputed to be the Queen's favourite band-leader and often played at Buckingham Palace and Windsor Castle – at the Queen's 50th birthday celebrations, Queen Elizabeth the Queen Mother's 80th birthday, and at pre-wedding balls for Princess Margaret, Princess Alexandra and Princess Anne. He went so far as to list these "gigs" in his *Who's Who* entry – like many in the world of show business, his respect for the Royal Family was positively reverential.

Joe Loss easily outlasted his many rivals and continued a household name in the age of television, although by the late 1950s the big band business in Britain was virtually at an end, replaced by "trad" jazz bands and pop groups.

But Loss, although no longer resident in a palais, soldiered on regardless, rushing with his musicians in coaches from town to town, playing in dance-halls, in television and radio studios, at private parties, annual balls and office dances. He and his orchestra even performed in boxing-rings, an aerodrome hangar and a railway goods van.

For many years Loss wintered on the *QE2* and on one cruise in 1978, he became the first bandleader to penetrate the People's Republic of China. His zest for performance on those cruises was remarkable: even when introducing "Viva L'Espana" for the umpteenth time in a week his enthusiasm remained undiminished.

Joshua Alexander Loss was born off Bishopsgate in east London on June 22 1909, the youngest son of Israel Loss, a Russian immigrant woodworker who had been a wheelwright in the Boer War. Young Joe was educated at the Jewish Free School, Spitalfields, and learnt the violin at the Hackney Academy of Music: "My father didn't know a dance band from a symphony orchestra, but he thought it would be easier than a hammer."

At 13 he won a scholarship to Trinity College of Music, and from there he went on to the London College of Music. Proud of their son, his parents arranged for him to give a concert at Toynbee Hall, and the entire Loss family turned out to see the prodigy play Dvorak's *Humoresque*. But a practical joker had greased his bow, and all attempts to produce a sound from the strings were in vain.

Loss developed a taste for such dance bands as the Savoy Orpheans and, despite parental objections, at the age of 16 formed the Magnetic Dance Band, which played on Saturday nights at a hall in Chelsea.

In 1926 he landed his first job, helping to accompany silent films at the Coliseum, Ilford, for 30 shillings a week. Three years later he was in the dance band at the Wimbledon Palais de Danse's *thés dansants*; and at the age of 20 he founded his own seven-man orchestra at the Astoria Ballroom, Charing Cross Road.

But Joe Loss's band soon gained distinction and moved to the Kit-Cat Club, Haymarket. In 1933 it made its radio debut and a few months later topped the bill at the Holborn Empire.

Gathering widespread popularity, the orchestra made many dance records and had strings of theatre engagements. Loss had a major hit in 1936 with his recording of "Begin the Beguine", which sold a million copies, and "In The Mood" sold another million.

In 1940 he took his band to France to play for the British Expeditionary Force, and he toured extensively throughout the war. When hostilities ceased he became resident bandleader at the Hammersmith Palais.

Forging on despite changes of fashion – Loss even took the Twist in his stride – the band was voted "Britain's No 1" in 1965. Television succeeded the dying music halls – *Come Dancing, Bid for Fame* the theme tunes for *Maigret* and *Steptoe & Son* – and the band's ballroom popularity continued. In the 1970s, after making 1,000 recordings for EMI, Loss signed yet another long contract.

Many of Britain's singing stars owe some of their

success to him. Dame Vera Lynn gave her first broadcast with the Joe Loss Orchestra.

Loss declared in 1980 that dancing was best in the North of England. "People still dance for fun in the North and Scotland," he said.

In 1962 he was made a director of Mecca Dancing. He was appointed OBE in 1978 and LVO in 1984.

Although he officially retired in December 1989, when the band became known as Todd Miller and his Orchestra, Joe Loss was conducting again in London a few weeks later and up to the time of his death was planning more appearances.

He lived in a flat overlooking Regent's Park in London and amused himself by collecting watches and watching cricket: he was a life-member of MCC.

Loss married, in 1938, Mildred Rose; they had a son and a daughter.

June 7 1990

RAYMOND HUNTLEY

RAYMOND HUNTLEY, one of the best and busiest supporting actors of the century, who has died aged 86, played, with unfailing authority, a succession of imperturbable Englishmen whose pernickety and sometimes pettifogging natures enriched scores of plays, films and television dramas.

He was perhaps best known as the grumpy and pompous family solicitor, Sir Geoffrey Dillon, in the hugely popular London Weekend TV series *Upstairs, Downstairs*. When the late Russell Harty featured the cast in one of his chat-shows there was a memorable vignette of the Huntley persona. Did the actor mind, the interviewer asked, being cast as such a stuffy old git, or words to that effect. "Would you care to, ahem, *rephrase* that question, Mr ... er, Harty?" replied the unsmiling Huntley in his most tetchily magisterial tones.

Raymond Huntley made staidness funny. He himself rarely laughed. His composure was that of an orderly minded, quiet, and perhaps cold-hearted man of few words or expressions of affection whose integrity gave to all he said the stamp of truth.

The men he played lived mainly by the book, and if they seemed incapable of passion or zest, it was not so much from lack of emotion as from disdain for anything undignified or indecorous.

Huntley never vulgarised or sentimentalised these inhibitions. His portraits of officials, civil servants, doctors, diplomats and churchmen reflected his own concern for convention and good taste; if the price of that was dryness and accusations of stuff-shirtedness, so be it.

His natural economy of speech and reservation of manner added veracity to his acting – although if something sinister were called for he could supply it. Indeed he did so soon after the start of his career in the title role of Count Dracula which he played first in London and then all over America with great success.

Most of his parts, though, were somewhat anaemic, and it was his gift to make dullish, ordinary men who might otherwise be dismissed as types into arresting individuals. Huntley's stern and somewhat humourless appearance made him invaluable in comedy. Few actors could discover more dramatic mileage in a murmur or a curled lip, whether from the chairman of a interviewing board, or a clubman grunting from his armchair to his neighbour.

His stately stare or glare through his spectacles could be as cold or intimidating on the stage as off – and especially at the Garrick Club, which he haunted towards the end of his days with an undisguised contempt for the food and devotion to his role as resident grumbler.

In his mid-eighties, by chance, he was summoned to play the Judge in Jeffrey Archer's play, *Beyond Reasonable Doubt*. It was Huntley's first theatrical engagement for several years: he was – discreetly – thrilled.

After a few performances, however, he slipped and injured himself and was out of the play. During those few performances, though, he brought to the ideal Huntley role a characteristically imperious poise.

Raymond Huntley was born at Birmingham on April 23 1904 and educated at King Edward's School. He had no formal training for the stage but at 18 he joined the Birmingham Repertory Theatre for two years.

After Acis in the last part of Shaw's *Back to Methuselah*, he played the parson in *The Farmer's Wife* and then toured as Churdles Ash in it. After a spell of touring in repertory with Hamilton Deane, he scored his first resounding success in 1927 when he played Dracula in Deane's adaptation of the novel by Bram Stoker.

On his return from this international success, Huntley setted down to a steady career as a dependable supporting actor. Among the more notable plays he appeared in were *Clive of India, Cornelius, Time and the Conways, When We Are Married, Rebecca, They Came To A City, Private Lives, Black Chiffon* (in New York), *No Sign Of the Dove, Any Other Business?, An Ideal Husband* and *Getting Married*.

In 1968 he rather surprisingly cropped up as the

Paymaster-General in Rolf Hochhuth's controversial *Soldiers*.

Huntley made his cinema debut in 1934 and was subsequently seen in such films as *Rembrandt, Night Train to Munich, School for Secrets, Mr Perrin and Mr Traill*, Somerset Maugham's *Trio* and *Passport to Pimlico*, in which he played the bank manager who enthusiastically embraces the district's unilateral declaration of independence – an unusually skittish part for the actor.

His later films included *Room at the Top, Only Two Can Play, Hostile Witness* and *That's Your Funeral*.

Raymond Huntley was a shy, private man, not easy to know, but behind a mask of intolerance – his old friends maintained – was a dry sense of humour and great kindness.

June 18 1990

LYNNE CAROL

LYNNE CAROL, the actress, who has died in Blackpool aged 76, was best known for her portrayal of the waspish beldam Martha Longhurst in the early days of *Coronation Street*.

Martha Longhurst appeared in the first episode in December 1960, and with Ena Sharples and Minnie Caldwell she made up the formidable coven that held court in the snug of the Rovers Return, to the exclusion of all interlopers. All too often Ena and Martha would deliver acid tongue-lashings to the unfortunate Minnie. The verbal interplay between the three epitomised the serial's earthy Northern humanity and yielded some of

"The Street's" richest moments – perhaps never equalled since.

Martha Longhurst's renown became such that Lynne Carol's unpublicised visit, *in propria persona*, to the Ideal Home Exhibition caused a near riot: the crowds mobbed her to such an extent that the police advised her to leave for her own safety.

Aficionados of the show included Laurence Olivier and John Betjeman, who compared *Coronation Street* to Dickens's *Pickwick Papers* and declared: "At 7.30 p.m. on Mondays and Wednesdays, I am in heaven."

Alas, in 1964 after only three years in the series, Martha Longhurst fell victim to a new producer's whim – "As flies to wanton boys, are we to the gods; They kill us for their sport." Lynne Carol was deeply shocked to read in her newspaper that Martha Longhurst's days were numbered,

All through rehearsals on the date of the fateful recording Peter Adamson, who played Len Fairclough, refused to say the line "She's dead", firmly believing that some act of mercy – and wisdom – would reprieve Martha at the last moment.

But the moving finger had written. Martha "died" quietly in the backroom of the Rovers Return, to the sounds of revelry in another part of the pub. The subsequent burial took place in the Manchester General Cemetery at Harpurhey, where a special grave was dug. "Why not bulldoze Ena?" enquired the *Daily Mail*.

A descendant of six generations of actors, Lynne Carol was born in Monmouthshire in 1914 and pitchforked into the theatre at the age of three. She married Bert Palmer, a Lancashire character actor, and they made their home in Blackpool.

The house was barred to reporters on the day, May 13 1964, that Martha Longhurst's death was broadcast: Lynne Carol watched the episode alone with her husband, who made a cine-recording of the tragic events on screen. She remained bitter about Martha's demise, and believed to the end – quite rightly – that a terrible mistake had been made.

In April this year another terrible mistake was made when a hoaxer telephoned Granada Television to announce that Lynne Carol had died in a Blackpool nursing home. Miss Carol, who was then on holiday in Germany, was particularly unamused by reports that she was "aged 90".

Her husband died in 1980.

July 2 1990

PATIENCE STRONG

PATIENCE STRONG, the popular versifier, who has died aged 83, administered a rhyming counsel of strength and patience to readers of such publications as *Woman's Own* and the *Daily Mirror* for nearly four decades.

She created a unique relationship with her readers, treating every aspect of the human condition in simple, homely words that touched their hearts and encouraged them to believe that they knew the author personally. Her daily poem in the *Mirror* was read by thousands, and the verses cut out and cherished.

There were poems for all eventualities, offering help through times of hardship, sorrow and bereavement, and conveying gratitude for life's more accessible joys. Nature and Christian faith were persistent themes in her work:

Look at roses when oppressed by weariness or grief.
Look at roses and restore spent hope and lost belief –
In the meaning of this life and of a heaven above.
Look at roses if you ever doubt that God is Love.

During the Second World War Patience Strong worked tirelessly from her small study at her cottage in Kent – which virtually became an adjunct to the Post Office – writing to the Service personnel and their families who turned to her for spiritual succour. Many a British serviceman perished with a cutting of a Patience Strong poem in the pocket of his battledress.

Miss Strong admitted that there might not be a great deal of literary merit in her verses. "I just naturally think in rhymes," she said. "I do it without thinking. Now and again perhaps I do write a pot-boiler if I'm rushing to catch the 5.30 p.m. post."

The secret of her success, she believed, was sincerity. Her favourite aphorism was "Nothing's true unless you've lived it."

She was born Winifred Emma Cushing in London on June 4 1907 and started writing poetry at the age of four, when her verses, based on photographs which her uncles sent back to her from Egypt during the First World War, were invariably called "Dawn on the Desert".

It was not until she was in her mid-twenties that Miss Cushing sent some of her verses to the *Daily Mirror*. "Everybody told me that I was trying to get into the Rolls-Royce class," she recalled, "trying to follow Wilhelmina Stitch, the most famous verse writer of her time. But the *Mirror* editor said, could I do another 18 by the next day, and he'd give them a trial. They ran ever afterwards."

The editor also asked her to choose a suitable name for

herself, and that same evening a friend happened to bring her a book – a chronicle of New England life by Mrs A. D. T. Whitney. "The minute I saw the title," she said, "I knew that was it. It was called Patience Strong."

Patience Strong's poems were first published in the *Mirror* in August 1935 under the heading "The Quiet Corner", and subsequently in its sister paper, the *Sunday Pictorial* (later to become the *Sunday Mirror*). They also appeared weekly for more than 35 years in *Woman's Own*, and continue to be published in the quarterly journal *This England*.

In the course of her long career, Patience Strong published scores of books of her poems and religious thought, as well as an autobiography, *With A Poem In My Pocket*. She also made several recordings of her poems, and blossomed briefly as a lyricist. Her best-known songs included the tango "Jealousy" and "The Dream of Olwen".

In spite of the sentimental and sometimes bland content of her verses, Miss Strong was a lady of pronounced views, and occasionally asked her editors if she might extend her repertoire to write poems about her pet hates. The request was always rejected – though she was proud to have managed, in the early 1960s, to slip in "a little something about the Channel Tunnel". "I'm against that," she said: "it would fill Kent full of foreigners on motorcycles."

She was widowed twice and died childless.

August 31 1990

RICHARD MURDOCH

RICHARD MURDOCH, the actor and broadcaster who has died aged 83, is best remembered from the Golden Age of Wireless. As "Stinker" Murdoch, he played the sparring partner of "Big-Hearted" Arthur Askey in the first-ever weekly comic radio series in Britain, *Band Waggon*. A decade later he was on the air again with his acute sense of English comedy in another weekly BBC programme, *Much-Binding-In-The-Marsh*, this time with Kenneth Horne and Sam Costa.

The first show was based on the idea of a literally resident comedian at Broadcasting House, London; the second on a mythical RAF station "somewhere in England" in the Second World War.

Although Dickie Murdoch was an experienced light actor in the theatre – especially in musical comedies, concert parties, revue and pantomime – he worked in wireless when its power had in some ways as great or even a greater hold on the public imagination than television has now.

He first became a household name as the absurdly taller, better-looking and better-spoken half of a double act with the diminutive and bespectacled Askey. Though admirers of Murdoch hoped that he would somehow transfer his talent successfully to television, his heart was in the art of wireless, where the audience had to concentrate closely on what was being said.

He was paid five guineas a programme at the start of the *Band Waggon* series and 15 guineas at the end – 50 programmes later. Askey called him "Stinker" on the air because he considered him of superior formal education.

Richard Bernard Murdoch was born at Keston, Kent, on April 6 1907 and educated at Charterhouse and Pembroke College, Cambridge, where he performed with the Footlights.

He was tall, fair-haired, handsome and had a high-pitched voice which helped him to project a sense of comedy. His first appearance after the Footlights in 1926 was in a chorus line at Southsea in *The Blue Train* which transferred to the West End.

After several years in light comedies and revues for C. B. Cochran and André Charlot, he met Askey. The BBC was launching an experimental comedy series in imitation of a successful American weekly 60-minute comedy show.

Band Waggon (so spelt to distinguish it from the similarly named American production) was the BBC's first go at the form and paved the way for such other wireless shows as *ITMA, Take It From Here* and *Hancock's Half-Hour*. It was also the first comic series on the British airwaves to boast of a continuous story-line.

It caused King George VI to report his delight in it to the Cabinet and enticed Sir John Simon to assure the House of Commons just after the outbreak of the Second World War that life would be back to normal soon because *Band Waggon* starts again next Wednesday.

No one, however, had reason to believe that *Band Waggon* had a future when it was launched. The script was so bad that the producer, John Watt, cancelled the last six programmes of the planned dozen when he had seen the first three in January 1938.

Then the two comedians, Murdoch and Askey, came

up with an idea. What about the programme's "resident comedian" Askey being the resident of a flat at the top of Broadcasting House with his old pal "Stinker" Murdoch?

They used to broadcast, in fact, from St George's Hall nearby, and then, when it was destroyed, from a church hall in Bristol; but the joke about their living at the top of the BBC headquarters did the trick.

They introduced, sketchily, other characters like Mrs Bagwash and her daughter Nausea who came to clean up, as well as adopting pigeons, a goat called Lewis and (for one episode) a camel. The programme, which always went out "live", affected churchgoing as well as royal conversation and the morale of MPs.

Evensong on Wednesdays was advanced in many parishes so that worshippers could return home in time to listen in between eight and nine, and the Post Office reported a steep drop in the number of telephone calls being made at that hour.

Band Waggon came to an end not so much because of the war as because the impresario Jack Hylton had bought what proved to be the highly profitable theatrical rights which took the show round the music halls. It ended at the Palladium.

The wireless show had been immortalised. There was grief at its disappearance, but its exponents preferred to act before the new audiences every night to finding a new script every week.

Towards the end of his war service in the RAF, Murdoch, a squadron leader, met Wing Commander Kenneth Horne in the Directorate of Administrative Plans at the Air Ministry, London, and another show was born – *Much-Binding-In-The-Marsh*. With Leading Aircraftman

Sam Costa, they formed in 1947 one of the most memorable trios that have ever contributed to this kind of broadcasting. It continued until 1950.

Murdoch and Kenneth Horne wrote its signature tune and lyric in an afternoon, and broadcast it that evening. With topical variations they went on singing it for the next three years.

Although he made many appearances on television in its early days – and in one or two more recent nostalgic programmes – Murdoch preferred the wireless as an art form. He often returned to the theatre between broadcasts and rounds of golf to tour light comedies and revues, but he had never been much of a "legitimate" actor, and his performances could seem heavy and self-indulgent.

But he kept on working; some of his dames in pantomime gave particular pleasure because his delight in the work did not spoil the effect of the fun as it sometimes did in farce. Murdoch's dames had a dignity, sauciness and flourish to which his height and formal treatment of the English language gave characters like Twankey an unusual edge.

He acted William, the waiter, in Shaw's *You Never Can Tell* at Niagara on the Lake (Canada) and toured light comedy in South Africa as well as Britain. He also played in a radio series somewhat after his own heart, *The Men From The Ministry*.

He first appeared in films in 1934, and was still making "cameo" appearances in the 1980s. Murdoch made many appearances on the early television transmissions from Alexandra Palace, but afterwards returned to his first love, sound, and broadcast for 16 years in *The Men from the Ministry*.

In the early 1980s he appeared in the BBC's *Old Boy*

Network feature from the Malvern Festival Theatre, demonstrating that he was still capable of some lively tap dancing in his mid-seventies. Latterly on television Murdoch contributed a delightfully dotty study of an out of touch old barrister, Uncle Tom, in the chambers of *Rumpole of the Bailey*; and he showed that he was also capable of playing less sympathetic characters with a chilling vignette of the appeasing Lord Halifax in *The Wilderness Years*.

In 1932 he married Peggy Rawlings; they had a son and two daughters.

October 10 1990

BETTY JUMEL

BETTY JUMEL, the zestful comedienne billed as "The Bundle of Fun" who has died aged 89, was one of the last survivors of the variety halls, which she played almost continuously for more than half a century.

She was pert, petite and bouncy, and depended for much of her appeal on a fine sense of the physically absurd. With her unfailing instinct for the mildly grotesque, as she interrupted herself during a piano recital, or took a drink of water from a vase of flowers, or went down with a collapsing piano stool, Jumel perfected her simple but brilliantly timed solo or duo turns on a variety circuit which extended in her heyday into every small town in Britain.

Betty Jumel was born at Fairhaven, near Blackpool, in 1901, and made her first stage appearance aged 10 with her father Harold Jumel, who toured an act round the halls called *The Four Jumels*.

He taught her to sing and dance and throw her voice almost from infancy; and when the married foursome of two brothers and two sisters disbanded before the First World War, young Betty joined her father in a double act in which he played the piano and she sang and danced.

Very small for her age and fairly pretty, she wore a lace dress and ringlets and the act was a great success. When her father enlisted, Betty became a soubrette working in end-of-pier variety shows in the North of England.

She created her own comedy material, notably three solo turns under the heading *A Bundle of Fun*. In one of these she played a fairy in a take-off of *Swan Lake*. In another, she used her strong high voice to burlesque an opera singer; and in a third she mimicked a pompous concert pianist hitting the wrong notes.

She would sometimes make four different appearances in one evening, especially in the Manchester or London suburbs where the Empires were nearer to each other. She understood from the word go the hierarchy, discipline and rigour of a branch of the theatre which stood proudly apart from the legitimate stage.

Other performers eventually persuaded her to let them join her – and she appeared on a number of occasions with the gangling and angular Nat Jackley in a much-loved turn called *At the Ball*. Jackley's height contrasted marvellously with her small figure in an overtight ball gown, which was split up one side to reveal her funny, wafer-thin legs.

Miss Jumel spent most of her life on tour; every

Christmas she appeared in pantomime and most summers found her by the sea in concert parties.

Her first West End appearance was in a Lyceum review *Good Company* (1933) by Albert Burdon and Dan Leno Jnr; and during the Second World War she travelled with ENSA to Egypt.

In the 1940s she appeared in a number of films with Will Hay, Sandy Powell and Norman Evans which were meant to capture the style and atmosphere of the variety stage before it vanished.

At the Leeds Grand in 1945 she and Norman Evans set a record for pantomime when their production of *Humpty Dumpty* ran from Christmas Eve to Easter. Miss Jumel was impressive as a diminutive Dame Trot in *Babes in the Wood* (at Prince's, now the Shafesbury) in the 1948 pantomime season, and she appeared for the same management in *Mother Goose* at Oxford the next Christmas. At about this time she joined Norman Evans in his radio series *Good Evans*; and she was in *Humpty Dumpty* at the Palladium with Terry-Thomas in the 1960s.

Miss Jumel was married, first to Victor, one of the Arnley brothers – who performed a variety act in the 1920s. Their daughter, Georgina, broke with family tradition by becoming a legitimate actress.

Some years after the death of her first husband, she married an Italian acrobat, Bill Castagnoli, who predeceased her.

October 14 1990

CRAIG RUSSELL

CRAIG RUSSELL, the transvestite comedian who has died in Toronto aged 42, had the unique honour of being judged both Best Actor and Best Actress at the Virgin Islands Film Festival.

He won this distinction with his bravura performance in a low-budget film called *Outrageous* (1978), as a transvestite Canadian hairdresser who throws up his job to become a professional female impersonator in New York, wallowing in the borrowed glamour of Judy Garland and Bette Davis. The role bore striking similarities to Russell's own history, and he approached it with a winning insouciance and a wistful bitchiness which somehow avoided the worst excesses of camp.

"Female impersonation", he once said, "is one of the oldest traditions of theatre. I'd like to see it shake off some of the tacky associations it's picked up and recognised as an art in itself." In *Outrageous* he achieved this ambition.

An insurance salesman's son, Craig Russell was born in Toronto in 1948. At the age of 13 he fell in love with Mae West, an actress whom many would regard as the ultimate female impersonator – and who was to become the inspiration of his career.

Young Craig wrote to Miss West, claiming to have started a fan club with 25 members and enclosing the requisite number of forged signatures as evidence. Racked with adolescent guilt at this deception, he went on to found a genuine fan club which eventually rose to a membership of 2,000.

The actress and the schoolboy entered into correspondence, and then into regular telephone conversations. In due course Russell followed his father into the insurance business, but by 1967 was complaining to Miss West that the office routine was driving him mad.

She invited him to stay at her beach house, where he remained for nine months. "She taught me everything I know," he recalled. "She still had closets full of wonderful dresses, and for some reason they fitted me, so I would dress up for her, just doing routines and songs from her films. She loved it."

Refreshed by this transvestite idyll, Russell returned to Toronto where, resuming the conventional apparel of his sex, he found employment as a hairdresser. After a few years of this he found himself drunk at a Hallowe'en party dressed as Tallulah Bankhead, and was so gratified at the applause which greeted his impersonation that he resolved to turn professional.

With money borrowed from his parents he set himself up as a solo performer, beginning with a repertoire of six Hollywood *monstres sacrés*, which he gradually built up to 25.

Russell was meticulous in his preparation for each new role, and would immerse himself in old newspaper clippings to find every detail and nuance of his subject's character. "It goes deeper than just putting on a wig and a voice," he explained. "It has to come from the solar plexus if it's to be real. When I do Judy Garland I actually cry: I forget Craig and become Judy and all her problems."

His old mentor, Miss West, was greatly flattered by Russell's act but was much happier when he had worked his way up to "class joints", as she called them. "When you were working in those dives," she said, "I was afraid that people would get drunk and think it was me on the skids." Peggy Lee and Carol Channing were also among his admirers.

After his triumph in *Outrageous* Russell continued to tour with his impersonations, impressing audiences with the speed and wit of his delivery; and in 1988 he made a sequel called *Too Outrageous*. But *autres temps, autres mœurs* and in the era of Aids – to which Russell himself succumbed – it did not enjoy a comparable success.

November 11 1990

SLIM GAILLARD

SLIM GAILLARD, the Cuban-born jazz musician who has died in London aged 75, was the inventor and chief propagator of a bizarre vocalese he called *Vout*, which hit the same nerve of nonsense humour in America in the 1940s, that the Goons were to touch a decade later in Britain.

Vout (prounounced to rhyme with shout) embraced an infinite variety of meaning, as did the suffixes *o-roonie!* and *o-reenie*! The *Vout-O-Renee Dictionary*, published in the 1940s, probably shed less light on a language than any lexicon ever.

The jazz world is full of figures celebrated as much for the eccentricity of their behaviour as their musicality, but few of them had as colourful a history or as striking a persona as Slim Gaillard. His admirers included Duke Ellington and the author Jack Kerouac – who once wrote "To Slim Gaillard the whole world was just one big *o-*

157

rooni." And he worked with most of the jazz greats, including Dizzy Gillespie, Charlie Parker and Thelonius Monk.

Miles Davis, not a man to throw compliments around, said: "There are only two men that I look up to – Slim Gaillard and Dizzy Gillespie. Without them I wouldn't be playing."

The son of a German Jew and a black woman, Bubee "Slim" Gaillard, was born at Santa Clara, Cuba, on January 4 1916. His early childhood was spent cutting cane and picking bananas and occasionally going to sea with his father Theophilus who worked on the big ocean liners.

At the age of 12 Slim accompanied Theophilus on a world voyage and was accidentally left behind on the island of Crete. He never saw his father and mother again.

He remained on Crete for several months, picked up shoemaking and Greek, and then turned ship's cook and travelled the Mediterranean. After various adventures he found a home with an Armenian family at Detroit.

There, Slim worked in an abattoir, trained as a mortician and did a stint at Ford's Motor Works. For good measure, he took up boxing and became the light heavyweight champion of Michigan, sparring on one occasion with the world heavyweight champion, Joe Louis, the "Black Bomber".

He also worked at Harry the Hatter's, where he struck up an acquaintance with the Purple Gang, the equivalent of Al Capone's Chicago mob, and he soon found alternative employment with the young Jewish boys, who, he recalled, used Italians for muscle and blacks (whom they called "smoke") as drivers.

Gaillard did not forget his old friends at the mortuary

and as he drove the Purple boys in their hearse through the streets of Detroit he kept a lookout for victims of gang warfare. He would return alone in the hearse after hours to ferry the corpses to the mortuary, where "they gave me $25 a stiff, and that was good money".

He might have become more heavily involved in crime, had he not been a musician. He started to perform on street corners, where he would play the guitar, sing and tap-dance all at the same time. He also played the vibraphone, the saxophone, various brass instruments and the piano, and was a Latin-American dance champion.

In 1937 Gaillard moved to New York, where he spent most of his time on 52nd Street, the "street that never slept", and made his first recordings, on guitar, with trumpeter Frankie Newton. He then joined up with another colourful character, the string-bassist/singer Slam Stewart.

Slim and Slam made their first records in 1938, with the drummer Pompy "Guts" Dobson. The gibberish vocals – one of their titles was "Flat Foot Floogie" – were at first rejected but a month later they tried again and had a hit.

Although the lyrics of "Flat Foot Floogie" were almost completely unintelligible, the tune had a catchy rhythm and was "covered" by Benny Goodman, Fats Waller and the Mills Brothers. Craziness triumphed and Gaillard and Stewart earned a fortune in royalties.

Many of Gaillard's songs were food-related: "Avocado Seed Soup Symphony", "Matzo Balls O-roonie", "Dunkin' Bagels", Yop Hic Heresy (inspired by the table of his Armenian family in Detroit), "Groove Juice Special" and "Chicken Rhythm". Some years later, he had one of his greatest hits with "Cement Mixer Putti Putti", which was inspired by the mechanical beats of a cement mixer in a street below the recording studio one afternoon when they were short of a title.

The song was taken up by the music establishment and recorded by Tommy Dorsey's Orchestra, as well as, more surprisingly, Guy Lombardo and his sweet "society" orchestra.

In 1941 Gaillard appeared in the Hollywood film *Hellzapoppin'*. In a remarkable jazz sequence he and the other black performers, including Slam Stewart, were cast as hotel workers who suddenly create a jam session.

The next year he joined the US Army Corps Service, and when he was discovered to have an above average IQ (he spoke several languages) he was drafted into America's first black airborne–division. He and nearly 100 blacks were trained separately for three months at Shepherd Field at Texas in the teeth of ridicule from white officers.

Promoted captain, Gaillard flew B-25 and B-26 medium-range bombers over the South Pacific, hitting Japanese targets in Fiji and New Guinea. He recalled the experience with sadness: "I felt we were bombing unnecessary things. Some pilots got angry because they were forced to do it and those refusing to take a flight were locked up in the brig and reduced in rank."

He was eventually hit in the arm and leg, suffered a nervous breakdown, and was discharged. He returned at once to his musical career, playing in Billy Berg's club in Los Angeles. Dubbed "Dark Gable", he became a darling of the Hollywood set: his fans included Ronald Reagan and Marlene Dietrich.

He had first come across Reagan in the late 1930s, when the actor sought to advise the young musician on his career: "He would sit me down and tell me how to get my records in the hit-parade. He would say, 'If you do this, and that and this, you could have a number one.' I had a number one hit record already, but he kept talking so I kept listening."

Never one to conform, Gaillard was then attracted to the new bebop jazz and it was at this time that he recorded with Dizzy Gillespie and Charlie Parker on the West Coast. When he played the bebopper's anthem, "How High The Moon", Gaillard added his own inimitable touch, singing "How High The Moon, How Low You Are".

He remained busy throughout the 1950s and 1960s, working variously as Master of Ceremonies, comedian and singer. He also ran a motel at San Diego; bought an orange farm at Seattle; opened his own club, Vout City, in Los Angeles; ran a radio programme from the premises; and set up a record shop.

In the early 1970s Gaillard returned to New York, where he played regularly with Tito Puente, King of Salsa. By now his recording activities were infrequent and he went into semi-retirement on the West Coast, until in 1982 Dizzy Gillespie persuaded him to play in Europe. He eventually settled in London, where he was much taken by the rain. "As I sing in my song 'Everything's OK in the UK', over here you just have to throw anything out of the window and it grows." He made a number of television appearances in England and mingled with the jazz cognoscenti.

His striking looks (he bore an uncanny resemblance to Walt Disney's Uncle Remus), darkly resonant voice and gift for surreal comedy, ensured that he was much in demand at festivals, concerts and clubs.

Gaillard also appeared in the television series *Roots – The Next Generation*, and in 1989 was the subject of a four-part *Arena* programme, "Slim Gaillard's Civilisation", in which the BBC recreated, at great expense, episodes from his life around the world. The programme included a sequence of him at Detroit, driving a period hearse and talking to a surviving member of the Purple Gang. Charlie "Big Guns" Julian lamented the passing of the good old days when the police could be paid off, and Gaillard nodded sagely.

The series received mixed notices, *The Daily Telegraph*'s critic complaining that Slim Gaillard's thoughts on civilisation were "as momentous as those of an average saloon-bar drunk. Just about the most coherent sentiment to come from his lips was 'The world is one big *o-roonie* to me'."

Gaillard also appeared, usually as himself, in numerous films, including *Too Late Blues* (1961), directed by John Cassavetes, *Planet of The Apes* (1968), and *Absolute Beginners* (1986).

In his time Slim Gaillard dated such Hollywood starlets as Ava Gardner, Rita Hayworth and Lana Turner. He confessed to having lost count of the number of children he had fathered.

One of his daughters, Janis Hunter, was married to the singer Marvin Gaye. Gaillard used to recall an occasion when he saw Gaye's preacher father coming down the stairs in the middle of the night, "wearing a dress, with lipstick on, and carrying one of them little dogs. It was a real strange house to be in." Gaye senior later shot dead his son.

February 27 1991

SERGE GAINSBOURG

SERGE GAINSBOURG, the controversial French singer, composer and film director, who has died in Paris aged 62, was best known in Britain for his *succes de scandale*, *"Je t'aime moi non plus"*, the heavy-breathing duet recorded with his then girlfriend, the English actress Jane Birkin.

"Je t'aime" achieved huge popularity in 1969, despite – or perhaps because of – being banned by the BBC and denounced by the Vatican. Peter Cook recorded a spoof version featuring "Serge Forward and Jane Firkin".

Gainsbourg was one of the many French popular performers whose reputation as a "serious" songwriter dissolved in the Channel. In France he was celebrated for his contribution to popular *varietés*, for his film scores and for his *louche* personality

A notoriously heavy drinker, Gainsbourg maintained an awesome intake of alcohol and tobacco. After a heart attack in 1973, he continued to smoke three or four packets of *Gitanes sans filtres* a day.

Gainsbourg was fond of telling interviewers that he was in a better state than his doctors. Indeed, he outlived three of his cardiologists. According to the doctor who was treating him at the time of his heart attack, Gainsbourg stopped smoking only for three days, while he was in intensive care, "because he believed, foolishly, that his *gitane* would cause the oxygen cylinder to explode".

It was often supposed that Gainsbourg took drugs, but in truth he was naturally outrageous, and undertook most of his more contentious projects as he was approaching pensionable age. He was finally banned from live television after a series of drunken appearances on chat shows – culminating in the occasion when he made an obscene suggestion, in broken English, to the American pop singer Miss Whitney Houston.

For 10 years Gainsbourg, who had no driving licence or chauffeur, kept a 1928 Rolls-Royce which, he said, he used occasionally "as an ashtray".

Although he became best known for his collaborations with pop musicians in the 1970s, Gainsbourg acquired a considerable knowledge of the decadent movement. His house in the Rue de Verneuil, Saint Germain, was furnished in the style of the apartment of des Esseintes in Huysman's *A Rebours*, and was a shrine to decadence: next to paintings by Dali and Francis Bacon, and originals of Chopin's letters, there were pictures of Screaming Jay Hawkins and the Sex Pistols.

In his later years, Gainsbourg – in private a gentle, polite man – cultivated, with increasing success, the public image of the "dirty old man of Europe". In he 1960s – after his divorce from his Italian wife Françoise Antoinette Pancrazzi, who described him as an aesthete tormented by his own ugliness – he developed a reputation as an unlikely Don Juan. His supposed conquests included Brigitte Bardot.

Having developed, with *"Je t'aime"*, the taste for putting a nation into shock, Gainsbourg set out – with some success – to repeat the experience. In 1979 there was outrage from French traditionalists, led by *Le Figaro*, when he recruited a group of Jamaican reggae musicians and recorded a highly idiosyncratic version of *La Marseillaise*. The song was re-titled *"Aux Armes et Caetera"*, and provoked riots when concerts were disrupted by veteran paratroopers.

Six years previously there had been opposition to the release of *Rock Around the Bunker*, his collection of songs about the Third Reich. The LP included a reading of "Smoke Gets in Your Eyes", which many listeners considered to be in questionable taste.

Record buyers who were familiar with Gainsbourg's family history, however, chose to see this and other of his more controversial releases as an indication of the singer's having been born with "a skin too few". As a child, Gainsbourg, the offspring of Russian Jewish refugees, had been made to wear the yellow star, and on several occasions had narrowly escaped death.

The son of a night-club pianist, he was born Lucien Ginzburg in Paris on April 2 1928 and brought up in the Pigalle. He changed his name for one he considered to be more aristocratic while still acknowledging his Russian origins.

He trained as a painter but by the early 1950s he came under the influence of the jazz musician, Boris Vian. Gainsbourg began to work as a singer and pianist in the night-clubs of Saint Germain des Prés.

Towards the end of the decade he began a career as a film actor, playing villains in low-budget European co-productions of varying artistic merit. Gainsbourg's own performances in such pictures, typically set in ancient Rome, drew a mixed response from critics. Of one showing, when he was obliged to flee his public at a cinema in Barbes Rochechouart, he recalled that "they were shouting at the screen in Arabic: 'Die, you bastard!'"

In the 1960s Gainsbourg, whose own recordings tended towards the cynical, specialised in writing mainstream pop for such luminaries as Juliette Greco and Petula Clark. Increasingly, however, he indulged his fondness for mischief, notably in 1966 when he wrote the highly suggestive *"Les Sucettes"* ("Lollipops") for the young France Gall.

Mlle Gall, only 16, had won the Eurovision Song Contest the year before with a Gainsbourg song, and had no idea of the new song's "hidden agenda".

In the mid-1960s, Gainsbourg wrote "BB" and other "bubble-gum pop" hits for Brigitte Bardot. Then in 1968 he met the coltish Jane Birkin, who had already acquired some valuable experience of minor scandal (as a result of her nude nymphet role in Antonioni's film of *Blow Up*).

Birkin lived with Gainsbourg for more than 10 years before leaving him in the early 1980s. "We were a public couple," Gainsbourg recalled. "We went out a lot. The trouble was, I didn't always make it back . . ."

After Birkin left him, Gainsbourg lived with his "little Eurasienne" wife – Caroline von Paulus, whom he addressed as "Bambou". They had a son, Lucien, known as "Lulu". On his last album Gainsbourg prefaced a song: "When I die, at least throw a few nettles on my tomb, my little Lulu."

As his career progressed into the 1980s, Gainsbourg discovered that his capacity to outrage was increasingly hindered by public tolerance. But nevertheless he achieved his aim in 1984 with "Lemon Incest", an unusually sensual reading of Chopin's Etude No 3 in E Major, Opus 10. The video for the song showed Gainsbourg in bed with his 14-year-old daughter, Charlotte, who subsequently embarked on a successful career as a film actress.

By the time he released *You're Under Arrest*, in 1987, Gainsbourg was visibly suffering the effects of his four decades of hard living. In 1989 he was rushed to hospital for a six-hour emergency operation on his liver.

Although an enthusiastic Anglophile, Gainsbourg never made concessions to the English-speaking market. Apart from *"Je t'aime"*, none of his witty, urbane songs ever achieved significant success in Britain.

His films like *Je t'aime moi non plus* (made in 1976, starring Gerard Depardieu), or *Equateur* (1983), were mainly screened in pornographic cinemas in Britain.

Perhaps surprisingly for a man widely supposed to be on terms of only nodding acquaintance with his face flannel, Gainsbourg also directed advertisements for Lux soap and Woolite.

Though he enjoyed moments of spectacular public disgrace, Gainsbourg was also celebrated for his extravagant acts of kindness and generosity. Bardot described him as "the best and the worst. He struck me as a little Jewish Russian prince reading Andersen and Grimm, who came face to face with the tragic reality of life: a Quasimodo, touching or repugnant depending on his mood."

Gainsbourg was appointed an officer of the French Order of Arts and Letters. The Minister of Culture, Jack Lang, called him "one of the greats of French music and poetry".

March 4 1991

ARTHUR MURRAY

ARTHUR MURRAY, who has died in Honolulu aged 95, built a chain of 500 dance studios in the United States and later expanded to Britain, Germany, Austria, Mexico and Canada.

Eleanor Roosevelt reportedly learned to dance the Arthur Murray way, as did the Duke of Windsor, John D. Rockefeller Jnr and Jack Dempsey. To these and countless other pupils his organisation passed on the secrets of the tango, waltz, foxtrot and – Murray's particular favourite – the bossa nova.

His studios were not above controversy, though. In 1960 the Federal Trade Commission ordered the studios to put a stop to bogus contests and high-pressure recruiting.

Later the same year a 74-year-old widow lodged a claim in Los Angeles for £9,000, said to have been paid for 2,480 hours of dance instruction. She was promised that as a result of the lessons she would become irresistible to men, perform on television and be invited to parties in Mexico, Palm Springs and Hollywood.

There were several such unsavoury cases, but Arthur Murray always maintained that they were the result of employees taking too zealously his injunctions to flatter and reassure the students.

The son of poor Jewish immigrants from Austria, Murray was born Moses Teichman in New York on April 4 1895. He was an unattractive schoolboy, tall, gawky and extremely shy. After a young woman had told him that he danced like a truck driver, Murray determined to prove her wrong; a classmate took pity on him and offered to show him some steps.

Transformed by the self-confidence his new skill brought him, he began to sell footprint patterns by way of mail-order dance instruction.

Murray opened his first studio in 1913. In the 1920s he started to broadcast dancing lessons over the radio and advertised in magazines. By 1950 there were 400 Arthur

Murray Dance Studios, and Murray was employing television to bring in even more customers.

In 1955 the Arthur Murray School of Dancing opened in London, then reeling under the Cha-Cha-Cha craze, which had already swept New York and Paris. Although he sold most of his dance studios in 1952 for $5 million. Murray continued to manage them until 1964, when he sold his remaining interest.

His books included *How to Become a Good Dancer*, *Let's Dance* and *Arthur Murray's Dance Secrets*.

Murray married, in 1925, Kathryn Kohnfelder; they had twin daughters.

March 5 1991

WILFRID HYDE WHITE

WILFRID HYDE WHITE the actor, who has died in Los Angeles aged 87, made a point of never seeming to take his profession seriously – the important business of his life, he would assert, was racing – but he never succeeded in disguising the fact that he was one of the most accomplished light comedians of his time.

Probably he achieved widest recognition as the genial old buffer Colonel Pickering in the film of *My Fair Lady* (1964). Although this role was essentially that of foil to Professor Higgins – exclaiming "Nonsense!" and "Disgraceful!" at appropriate moments – it seemed entirely credible that Hyde White should share a house with Rex Harrison.

In "You Did It", the song they sang after the ball, Hyde White discovered the same ability as his co-star to transcend the demands of musicality. And in so far as the part afforded him any opportunities – when, for example, Pickering rang up his old chum in the Home Office – his comic timing was equal to Harrison's, with the bonus of understatement.

Between 1934 and 1983 Hyde White appeared in more than 100 other films, many of them forgettable, although there were notable exceptions. In *The Third Man* (1949) he played some sort of British Council representative in Vienna; in *Two Way Stretch* (1960), with Peter Sellers, he was a phoney vicar; in *Let's Make Love* (1960), with Marilyn Monroe, he was Frankie Vaughan's agent.

But he took scant pride in his work for either the large or the small screen, and complained that he was entirely at the mercy of directors and editors. He was a man of the stage to his fingertips, one of the last great practitioners of the drawing-room comedy epitomised by Gerald du Maurier and A. E. Matthews.

Hyde White more or less dispensed with acting, making his entries as if he had no idea what kind of play he had wandered into, but all the comic points were effortlessly taken, and when it came to scene-stealing not even a dog or a child stood a chance against him.

Sleek, natty and silver-haired, Hyde White required no more than a gleam in the eye, or a gesture with a cane, to convey the sly and sinister underside to characters of apparent probity. If he generally played lovable cads, there was a suggestion that not so lovable ones would have been well within his compass.

The indolent style he cultivated on stage bordered on narcissicism; the yawning laugh was not so far removed from a sneer; the rich, fruity voice froze out emotion in the style of an affable clubman.

Yet the charm survived because Hyde White was incapable of conducting his life to any lasting advantage. Even his choice of plays was capricious, liable to depend less on the quality of the piece than on the proximity of a racecourse or a good hotel.

He turned down the opportunity to appear in two successful plays by his friend William Douglas Home, *The Jockey Club Stakes* and *The Secretary Bird* (although he later took over from Alistair Sim in *The Jockey Club Stakes*). On the other hand he eagerly seized the opportunity in 1971 to act in James Bridie's *Meeting at Night*, which closed after six weeks, despite considerable critical approbation for Hyde White's performance.

"This famous charmer must have been the original strolling player," wrote John Barber in *The Daily Telegraph*. "His silken good manners and his whimsical low chuckle are well known – a player who could give lessons in relaxation to a sleepy cat."

The son of a canon of Gloucester Cathedral, Wilfrid Hyde White was born at Bourton-on-the-Water, Gloucestershire, on May 12 1903, and educated at Marlborough, which he detested. "We were all frightfully unattractive individuals," he recalled, "embarrassingly self-conscious, hateful products of a hateful system."

In reaction, young Wilfrid opted for the stage. Alarmed at this decision, his family packed him off to London to receive cautionary advice from an actor-uncle, one J. Fisher White. When, however, Hyde White found this worthy living, not in the company of his aunt but with a young girl who evinced a particular enthusiasm for breakfast and champagne in bed, he was confirmed in his thespian ambitions.

Hyde White proceeded to the Royal Academy of

Dramatic Art, where, he said, he learnt two things: in his first year that he had no histrionic talent whatsoever, and in his second that this did not matter a damn.

His first professional stage appearance was at Ryde on the Isle of Wight in 1922. Known in those days as "Dasher" White, he remained in the provinces until 1925 – "the year Manna won the Derby with Steve Donoghue up" – when he made his West End debut in *Beggar on Horseback*, with A. E. Matthews.

Over the next half-century he was seldom out of work. In 1936 he gave up the theatre for four years to make films, but then returned to the London stage in the revue *Rise Above It*.

Hyde White made his first New York appearance in 1947 as Sir Alec Dunne in *Under the Counter*. In the 1950s he enjoyed a string of West End successes, notably in *The Reluctante Debutante* (1955) by William Douglas Home, and *Not in the Book* (1958), which ran for 500 performances at the Criterion.

On the whole he steered clear of the classical repertoire, although he did act with the Oliviers in their 1951 season at the St James's, as Euphronius in *Antony and Cleopatra* and more appropriately, as Britannus in Shaw's *Caesar and Cleopatra*. Later he enjoyed himself as Ralph Bloomfield-Bonnington in Shaw's *The Doctor's Dilemma*, and as Lord Augustus Lorton in Wilde's *An Ideal Husband*.

Hyde White's life took another turn after 1960 when George Cukor lured him to America for *Let's Make Love*. Marilyn Monroe's displays of temperament kept him in Hollywood for eight months instead of the eight weeks that had been envisaged, and during this time American producers marked him down as the perfect celluloid Englishman.

The job offers flowed in: "I couldn't turn them down," Hyde White declared, "particularly when you consider what a lousy actor I am." A more convincing reason was that he was eternally in debt to the bookmakers.

He had also acquired an American wife, whom he had met during the Broadway run of *The Reluctant Debutante*, so it seemed natural to settle in Palm Springs. It was a decision he never ceased to lament. "If I've made one big mistake in my life," he said, "it was leaving England. Because once an Englishman leaves his home he is never quite the same."

However great his income, it never kept pace with his rate of expenditure. In 1977 the Inland Revenue started bankruptcy proceedings against him for a claim of £10,000. "Is it only £10,000?" Hyde White imperturbably enquired. "I thought it was much more." He showed some reluctance to attend the proceedings, which eventually led the Registrar to declare that he was "trifling with the court".

When he did eventually appear his dealings with the court lost nothing in the telling. Apparently the Official Receiver asked: "If you cannot tell us how you spent such a large sum in so short a time, perhaps you can tell us what will win the Gold Cup at Ascot this afternoon?"

"Of course, dear fellow," Hyde White replied, and named the winner, although he warned the Receiver to limit his investment. "We don't want to have to change places do we?"

American television helped to rescue Hyde White from financial catastrophe. He stared as Emerson Marshall in the series *The Associates* about a New York lawyer's chaotic practice, and also portrayed Dr Goodfellow in *Buck Rogers in the 25th Century*.

At the end of his life Hyde White declared that he had been too materialistic. "I've owned 12 horses, seven Rolls-Royces, and I've had mistresses in Paris, London and New York – and it never made me happy."

Wilfrid Hyde White married first, in 1927, Blanche Aitken, who died in 1960. He married secondly, in 1957, Ethel Korenman (whose stage name was Ethel Drew); they had a son and a daughter.

William Douglas Home writes: My first recollection of "Uncle Wilfrid", as I always called him, is of the first night of *The Reluctant Debutante*'s pre-London tour in Brighton. He was sitting at the breakfast table with Celia Johnson as the curtain rose, after which there was a long silence broken by Wilfrid's voice shouting to the prompter: "Come along, boy, give me the line, boy, give me the line."

From then on until the final curtain fell he did not put a foot wrong, although I learned later that as he came forward at the end of the play with Celia and Anna Massey to take a curtain call he whispered to the former: "Let's get in front of that bloody girl, she's too damned good for us."

One other memory of him is not so happy – of his performance as Claude Johnson, the middle man between Rolls and Royce in my play *Rolls Hyphen Royce*. Although I had written an introductory speech for him he decided to ignore it on the first night, preferring to come on and say: "I'm surprised to see you all here tonight with all these one-way streets around the theatre. In fact I doubt very much if you'll ever get away afterwards, so we'll look forward to seeing you again tomorrow night."

And not content with that, he went on to say: "By the way, they tell me the roof fell in on this theatre last year. Let's hope it doesn't do it again tonight." Then he reverted to the text – in my opinion far too late.

But I forgave him for it, as one always forgave Wilfrid, disarmed as one always was by his incomparable charm. Sometimes one had to bargain with him – as, for example, in *The Jockey Club Stakes*, when he came on stage one night saying "Anybody seen my hat?" knowing full well that it was on his head.

He only agreed to abandon this regrettable addition to the script after I allowed him to rename some of the fictitious horses mentioned in the play with the names of some of those he had owned himself during a lifelong flirtation with the Turf.

"Do you know when I met my first bookie, me boy?" he said to me once. "Well I'll tell you. I was playing with my bricks when I was a little boy at home in Gloucester when the front door bell rang and my father said: 'Go and tell him I'm not in, me boy.' Down I went, and there was a fellow on the doorstep in a check suit holding my father's betting account."

But my favourite tale of all concerned an occasion when he and I both lunched with Robert Morley at Buck's Club, and Wilfrid started talking very loudly during the meal, much to Robert's embarrassment. "Lower your voice, Wilfrid, for God's sake," he said. "This is a gentlemen's club."

"Is it, me boy?" said Wilfrid. "Nothing written up to say so anywhere."

From now on, alas, there will be no new stories to recount about him, although happily he left behind enough to last a lifetime. Dear old Uncle Wilfrid was full of eccentricity and charm, and could put it all across whenever he felt like it.

This was not always the case. I told him once that I thought he had underplayed the part of Colonel Pickering in *My Fair Lady*. "Well, why not?" he answered. "What's the point of trying to compete with that old bugger Rex?" Of course he managed to compete with everyone in his own inimitable way.

May 8 1991

EDWINA BOOTH

EDWINA BOOTH, the American film actress, who has died aged 86, shot to fame after starring as the "White Goddess" in the classic African adventure *Trader Horn* (1931), but never appeared before a camera again.

For the next six years Miss Booth was confined to her bed in a darkened room, plagued by a series of mysterious tropical maladies she claimed to have contracted while making the film in the African jungle; and she was dogged by rumours of her death.

A doctor's daughter, she was born Constance Booth Woodruff at Provo, Utah, on September 13 1909, and began her career as a Hollywood extra in silent movies.

In 1928 Metro-Goldwyn-Mayer embarked on a film version of *Trader Horn*, the story of a white trader overcoming tribal hostility in Africa. The director, W. S. Van Dyke, announced that he wanted "a milk-white blonde with a brunette's temper, or better yet a redhead's" to take the female lead.

After days of fruitless auditions, Van Dyke recalled that Edwina Booth had a "temper like a spanked cat". She got the job, and duly set sail with the company for Mombasa.

The trouble started at Murchison Falls, near Victoria Nyanza on the River Nile, where the first scenes were shot. Clad only in a monkey skin, she was bitten mercilessly by insects while crawling through long elephant grass. The sun scorched her body, and she was frequently laid low by sunstroke.

Miss Booth rejoiced when a cloudburst destroyed their camp but, after hippopotami trampled on the debris, Van Dyke ordered the company to remove to the Belgian Congo. There Miss Booth, still wearing garments of singularly sparing cut, was assaulted by the malignant tsetse fly; she fell ill with malaria and then with dysentery; and hardly had she recovered when she fell out of a tree and nearly fractured her skull.

To make matters worse, the picture, initially intended as a silent movie, was transformed mid-production into a "talkie", and cast and crew had to wait for many weeks in the jungle while new sound units were shipped from Hollywood.

On her return home Miss Booth suffered a nervous breakdown, and then collapsed completely. Specialists were summoned from all over America to her bedside, to no avail.

Nor was the patient's condition improved when, in 1933, she was sued by the wife of Duncan Renaldo, who had played the lead in the film. Mrs Renaldo alleged that during their protracted stay in the African jungle Miss Booth had played the role of vamp all too well and stolen her husband's heart.

The jilted wife claimed £12,000 damages, though the "White Goddess" was absolved. "I have won my case," she said afterwards. "I have even forgiven the woman who caused me such misery."

The next year Miss Booth filed a claim for more than $1 million against Metro-Goldwyn-Mayer on the grounds that her health had been ruined by the hardships she had been subjected to.

She alleged that during the 10-day voyage from Naples to Mombasa she had been ordered to sunbathe naked on the ship's deck, and that the film's company had failed to provide her with protective clothing in the jungle.

Still languishing behind closed shutters in her bedroom, Miss Booth drew up a list of 10 separate ailments caused by her ordeal: "Impairment of metabolism; depletion and partial destruction of nerve centres; sunstroke; low blood pressure; malaria; dysentery; wounds on the head and back; contusions of feet and legs; loss of vitality, vivaciousness, beauty of form and other physical attributes essential to motion picture actresses."

Miss Booth's lawyers attempted to speed up her case, explaining that their client was by now almost destitute and urgently required financial assistance. The result of the case was never disclosed; it was thought that MGM made an out-of-court settlement.

In 1935 Dr Woodruff, who had been forced to take early retirement to care for his daughter, brought her 7,000 miles on a stretcher to Britain for treatment at the London Hospital for Tropical Diseases.

Her conditon appeared to improve during the eight months she spent convalescing at a flat in Marylebone. Every day Dr Woodruff would wheel his daughter, black-veiled against the sun which had destroyed her nerve centres, to Regent's Park. "She is slowly emerging from the darkness of the tomb," a friend told *The Daily Telegraph*.

But in 1936 Miss Booth suffered a relapse, and her father was obliged to take her to Europe to consult a physician in Vienna. By 1937, seven years after her return from Africa, Miss Booth – now a brunette – could finally pronounce herself cured.

She immediately declared that she would be dedicating all her future leisure and a large proportion of her earnings to the alleviation of human suffering. "My years of illness have not been wasted," she informed the national press. "I have learned to love mankind."

Miss Booth never revived her cinematic career, although she continued to receive fan-mail right up to her death. Latterly she worked at a Mormon temple in Los Angeles.

Booth was twice married. Her first husband, Anthony Schuck, annulled their marriage soon after her return from Africa; her second husband, Reinold Fehlberg, died in 1983.

May 24 1991

CORAL BROWNE

CORAL BROWNE, the actress who has died aged 77, was one of the most elegant and sophisticated players of her time – notable almost as much for her waspish wit and sexual candour off-stage as for her allure on it.

She will be remembered especially for two films. In real life, on tour in Moscow, she had met the spy Guy

Burgess, and in Alan Bennett's brilliant treatment *An Englishman Abroad* (1983) she recreated this incident, including some of the original conversation.

Burgess, who found solace in his exile by continually playing the music of Jack Buchanan, asked Coral Browne if she had known him. "I suppose so," the actress replied, "I almost married him."

The other film, *Dreamchild* (1986), was about Lewis Carroll. In it Miss Browne gave an affecting account of the later life of Alice Liddell, who inspired *Alice in Wonderland*.

On the stage Miss Browne excelled at playing duchesses or dragons – or, above all, Edwardian women with a past. With her striking dark looks, lustrous brown eyes, blitheness of spirit and ability to remain poised in a crisis, she had tremendous stage presence, which saw her safely through anything from light comedy to Shakespearean tragedy, from farce to melodrama.

As for her off-stage persona, her irreverent witticisms, real and apocryphal, became legendary. She had a deep, throaty voice and impeccable timing. It is not difficult to imagine the effect of her whispered but reverberating aside as a giant golden phallus was unveiled at the end of Peter Brook's production of *Oedipus*: "Nobody *we* know, darling."

No less memorable was her description of her affair with Cecil Beaton during the Second World War. When doubters queried the photographer's romance with Greta Garbo, Coral Browne would indignantly defend his masculinity, recalling that "Cecil was very passionate, and I should know. I've been under the bridges in my time. He asked me to lunch and then to dinner. But I really was extremely surprised when the great leap took place. I didn't even have time to say, 'Gosh!'"

Another story has her casting a lubricious eye over a

young actor, only to be assured by a friend, David Dodimead, that the cause was hopeless. Undaunted, Coral Browne bet Dodimead £1 that she could gain her end that very night. Her friends waited anxiously for the outcome. "Dodders," the actress drawled when she saw him across a crowded room the next morning, "I owe you twelve and sixpence."

The only daughter of a restaurateur (who spelt his surname without an "e"), Coral Edith Browne was born in Melbourne, Australia, on July 23, 1913 and educated at Claremont Ladies' College. Her theatrical career began by chance. Studying at art school, she was suddenly seconded to the Melbourne repertory theatre when the stage designer died.

Shortly afterwards the actress playing a woman "living in sin" in Galsworthy's *Loyalties* succumbed to sickness, and Miss Browne, still only 16, replaced her. At 18 she played Hedda Gabler, and by the time she was 21 she had appeared in a number of productions, including *Dear Brutus*, *The Quaker Girl*, *Hay Fever* and *The Apple Cart*.

As a 21st birthday present her father gave her £50 to visit London, on condition that she returned home as soon as it was spent. For a time it looked as though this promise might be kept.

With her theatrical experience, energy, looks – and an introduction to Marie Tempest – Coral Browne must have been disappointed to land nothing better than understudy to Nora Swinburne in a play called *Lover's Leap*.

It was seven years before she made a real mark. Good parts in two successful American comedies, *The Man Who Came to Dinner* (1941) and *My Sister Eileen* (1943), resulted in leading roles in such celebrated revivals as *The Last of Mrs Cheyney* (1944) and *Lady Frederick* (1946).

The period after the war, though, proved to have little to offer an actress whose trademark was elegance. For a time no new dramatists appeared, and when they did they showed scant interest in drawing rooms. The far-sighted Browne must have noticed the red light looming, for in 1951 she made her first appearance in Shakespeare, joining the Old Vic Company to play Emilia in *Othello* and Regan in *King Lear*, parts in which her fine voice and flamboyant manner won acclaim.

This venture into the classics was interrupted when she landed a part in *Affairs of State* (1952), adapted from the French, which ran for 18 months. There followed a spell in New York, where she played Zabina in *Tamburlaine the Great*. Back with the Old Vic Company in 1956 she appeared as Lady Macbeth – she also toured America in that part – and as Helen in *Troilus and Cressida*.

In the 1957–58 season she played Gertrude in *Hamlet*, Helena in *A Midsummer Night's Dream* and Goneril in *King Lear*; and joined the Stratford-upon-Avon company for another season as Gertrude. It was in that role that she undertook the fateful trip to Moscow, where she met Burgess.

Back in London she appeared to great effect in *The Pleasure of His Company* (1959), making an unforgettable entrance in some superb creation by Molyneux ("I've just put on a rag"). Another American play, *Toys In The Attic* (1960), followed, and the next year she played in a French import, *Bonne Soupe*.

By now she was equally in demand on Broadway, and when *The Right Honourable Gentleman* (1964), in which she played Mrs Rossiter, ended its run at Her Majesty's she took the part over to New York. Coral Browne's performance as Mrs Erlynne in *Lady Windermere's Fan* (1966) suggested that she would have made an admirable Lady Bracknell, but the nearest she ever came to such a role was in Edward Bond's *The Sea* at the Royal Court in 1973.

In 1969 she appeared as the nymphomaniac wife, acting mainly in her underwear, in Joe Orton's *What The Butler Saw* (1969), brilliantly balancing anxiety and poise. Her performance was rendered all the more effective by ribald interruptions from the gallery. Unable to retaliate, she took comfort in the elegant underwear which the management had allowed her to buy in Paris for the production. "Going on stage in nothing but your undies on at my time of life you've got to be wearing something pretty and delicate, otherwise you'd look like old Frilly Lizzie or a can-can girl."

What promised to be a more likely role, that of the Countess of Warwick who threatened to publish love letters from Edward VII in *My Darling Daisy* (1970), proved in fact disappointing, but in Shaw's *Mrs Warren's Profession* (1970), and in two plays by Anouilh – *The Waltz of the Toreadors* (1974) and *Ardele* (1975) – she found parts well worth the acting.

Among her better known films were *The Ruling Class* (1972) and *The Killing Of Sister George* (1968) in which she played, to the great amusement of her friends, a lesbian. One observer noted that she twiddled with Susannah York's nipple as if trying to find Radio Three.

Browne was a Catholic convert. She was once standing on the steps of Brompton Oratory after mass when a theatrical queen bustled up with the latest gossip. She stopped him with: "I don't want to hear such filth, not with me standing here in a state of fucking grace."

Coral Browne was married twice. Her first husband

was Philip Pearman, whom she married in 1950 and who died in 1964. At his funeral, she looked into his grave and is reported to have said, "See you later," before departing to a waiting car.

She met her second husband, the film actor and art historian Vincent Price, whom she married in 1974, in a studio cemetery on the set of a horror film comedy called *Theatre of Blood*. They lived in Los Angeles. There were no children from either marriage. "I've never seen myself as an old gran," she once said.

May 31 1991

BERTICE READING

BERTICE READING, the irrepressible singer, actress and revue *artiste*, who has died aged 58, was one of the last of the "Red Hot Mommas".

Bertice Reading was born – in a lavatory, by her own account – at Chester, Pennsylvania, in 1933. She started attending the *barre* at the age of three, and was talent-spotted by Bill "Bojangles" Robinson, the tap-dancer whose other *protégées* included Shirley Temple.

Reading was in the second year of pre-medical studies when her mother's illness and a consequent crisis in the family finances propelled her to enter a talent contest. Her subsequent victory earned her her first break, a place in the orchestral ensemble of the exuberant vibraphonist Lionel Hampton.

Her engagement with Hampton's Orchestra was extended after she had made a particular impact when performing at the inauguration of President Eisenhower.

While appearing in Paris she was offered a part in the all-black revue *The Jazz Train*, opening in London in spring 1955.

In the show, which took the form of an imaginary tour through black musical history around the world, Reading had a notable success playing the great blues singer Bessie Smith. *Jazz Journal* singled out her "extraordiary version of 'Frankie and Johnny', which may bring a blush to innocent cheeks, but proved a show-stopper on the opening night".

This combination of raising blushes and stopping shows was to feature largely in Reading's subsequent career. She was adept at a whole range of musical styles, from gospel to blues to musical comedy, and she added to her formidable vocal talent and striking appearance an unfeignable appetite for performance and a first-rate wit.

On her arrival in London, Reading was eager to try her hand as a straight actress – "If you can make people understand the point of a song in less than three minutes, it's not so hard to make them understand the point of a script in more than two hours" – so 1957 saw her appear in two serious plays at the Royal Court, Carson McCullers's *The Member of the Wedding*, and William Faulkner's *Requiem for a Nun*. Her performance as the nurse in Faulkner's play earned her a nomination for a Tony Award when it transferred to Broadway two years later.

The next years saw Reading spending the bulk of her time abroad, working as a cabaret *artiste*, and undergoing marriages to a Swiss impresario and a Dutch businessman.

Reading's next extended engagement in London was the Jerry Leiber and Mike Stoller show *Only in America* at the Roundhouse in 1980; she also put on *Pack Up All*

Your Cares and Woes, which was to be the first of four sets of one-woman shows at the King's Head in Islington.

Changing into a series of startling costumes in a little box onstage, Reading gave her public the benefit of her views on a range of subjects. "If you've liked it, tell your friends," she instructed the audience at the close of the show, "if you haven't, keep your big mouths shut."

"Although I talk about sex all the time on stage," Reading said in an interview given at the time, "I very rarely do it. I'm probably more pure than anybody you can imagine." She went on to appeal to "any nice bachelors who would like to have a good evening out" to get in touch.

Eighteen months later, in 1982, Sandy Wilson's inspired musical version of Ronald Firbank's novel of *Valmouth* was revived for the Chichester Festival. In the play a young black girl falls in love with a British aristocrat; in real life, Reading married Sir Richard Blake, 17th Bt.

At the uncontested divorce hearing in 1984, Sir Richard said that Reading had left him on the wedding night and not been in touch since. "I could write a book about the British aristocracy," said the *quondam* Lady Blake. "A short one. About three pages long."

The next year she put on another of her solo shows, *Every Inch A Lady*, during which she donned a pink satin tutu, danced to a version of "The Sugar-Plum Fairy" choreographed by Mr Wayne Sleep, and exited on the line: "Nobody loves a fairy when she's 40."

Cabaret remained the mainstay of Reading's work through the 1980s, an appearance in Jean-Luc Beniex's film *The Moon in the Gutter* notwithstanding. In 1987 she appeared at the Folies Bergère. Although Reading herself had reservations about the show — "I never did look especially good in plumes" — there was no denying the impact of her initial entrance, which was made by parachute.

The same year saw Reading back in London to play Bloody Mary in *South Pacific*. By now a rather matronly figure at 5 feet tall and 18 stone, Reading was a trenchant opponent of dieting and health-faddism. "What's the point in suffering so you can look like a pencil?" she asked.

Another favourite topic was the tyranny of the fashion industry. "As for those models," she would say, "those models all look to me like they've got TB."

By 1989 Reading was claiming that she had for the last 10 years given up sex in favour of champagne and cigarettes, and was all the happier for it. "I'm 56 years old," she said, "and if I never saw another man again, I wouldn't mind."

But last year she married fourthly the psychotherapist and astrologer Philip George-Tutton, 30 years her junior. "I didn't want to give up the title of Lady Blake that I had suffered so much to get," Reading admitted.

Her in-laws were initially perplexed. "You must not feel you have lost a son," she told them. "You must feel that you have gained a mother."

The newly-weds moved to a house in Dulwich called "Here Be Dragons".

Latterly she had been taking part in rehearsals for *Notre Dame* — a musical version of *The Hunchback of Notre Dame*.

Sandy Wilson writes: My first vision of Bertice Reading was as a rotund figure in a white shimmy dress and a blonde crew cut, stealing an American revue, *The Jazz Train*, at the Piccadilly Theatre.

A year or so later, George Devine and Tony Richardson, of the English Stage Company, asked me to devise a show for her at the Royal Court – perhaps a revue or a pantomime. But a friend of mine said: "Why not *Valmouth*? Bertice *is* Mrs Yajnavalkya" – and *Valmouth* it was, though not at the Court.

We opened to mixed reviews but enthusiastic audiences at the Lyric, Hammersmith, but when we transferred to the West End, Bertice had disappeared to Broadway where she won a Tony nomination in *Requiem For A Nun*.

She reappeared in my life in 1960, when *Valmouth* was produced off-Broadway and gave an even better performance of Mrs Yaj; but we closed after a week and Bertice vanished again.

She surfaced in London in 1972 and involved me in an abortive attempt to revive *Valmouth* with, of all people, Danny La Rue in Fenella Fielding's role of Lady Parbula de Panzoust.

A decade later *Valmouth* was finally revived at Chichester and Bertice triumphed again – and made the definitive recording of the show. She also acquired a new husband, an Irish baronet, and I gave her away – something, I told her, which I had been wanting to do for the last 25 years. But I failed, because the marriage was over even before the wedding night.

Our next meeting was in Plymouth where she was rampaging round the stage of the Theatre Royal in the other role she was born to play, Bloody Mary in *South Pacific*. It was during the tour that she married her last husband Philip, and we were all summoned to meet him at a party to celebrate their first anniversary.

Only the other day she rang me out of the blue, wanting me to see her new home in Dulwich, and the bedroom which Philip had painted scarlet. That was the last time I heard that wicked but girlish giggle. So all I can say now is: "I will miss you, Mrs Yaj."

June 10 1991

RONALD ALLEN

RONALD ALLEN, the actor who has died aged 56, spent 16 years in the role of David Hunter, the debonair motel manager in the legendary television soap opera *Crossroads*.

Before it folded in 1988 – after disastrous attempts to rejuvenate both its script and cast – the twice-weekly series, which recounted the ups and downs of life in a motel somewhere outside Birmingham, enjoyed a faithful following of about 26 million viewers. Even in its heyday, though, *Crossroads* was not distinguished by polished performance – for years it was made on such a punitively low budget that it was shot virtually "live", and ham acting was par for the course.

Characters supposed to be away on business would reappear inexplicably in crowd scenes; and almost invariably the person on the other end of Meg Richardson's telephone could quite clearly be heard talking from the other side of a thin partition wall. But "Ronnie" Allen, with his male model good looks, his transatlantic smile, his wide Seventies suits and his perfectly coiffed hair – just a hint of grey at the temples – was in his element amid all the bland roadside sophistication.

He first joined the motel staff in 1969, and was

promoted manager in 1981, when Noele Gordon's part – as the tight-lipped manageress Meg Richardson – was written out. From then, until Hunter was himself written out in 1985, Allen glided gracefully through a welter of farcical tragedies – fires, blackmailings, murders, kidnaps, armed robberies, frauds, threats and inter-staff tiffs – without having so much as to straighten his tie.

The crises were sometimes extreme – as, for instance, when his son Chris plotted the successful kidnapping of Hugh Mortimer, the millionaire husband of the proprietor of the motel, Meg (by now Mrs Mortimer). But even at the height of the tension Allen – whose acting technique was characterised by frequent pauses between phrases, often supplemented by sighs – contrived to seem blissfully unaware.

As Hilary Kingsley put it, in her seminal study *Soap Box*: "David was the most famously dull character in the history of soap operas . . . with the charisma of an ashtray and all the life of Sooty without Matthew Corbett's hand . . . To describe him as wooden would bring a libel suit from the Forestry Commission." But if Allen had doubts, he was careful never to show them. Far from lamenting lost opportunities, he always maintained that he preferred television serials to stage plays: "You get a real sense of involvement with the audience."

Certainly, Allen received letters daily from viewers seeking a job at the Crossroads Motel, and enclosing details of their work experience. Most of his correspondence, though, was from fans asking, "How much is David Hunter Ronald Allen?"

To this he would reply: "How do you divide personality from appearance? I look the same way and I talk more or less the same way. Those things are an important part of what personality is like, but the character qualities are very, very different indeed."

His protests seemed less convincing, though, when Allen proposed marriage to his screen wife, Barbara, played by Sue Lloyd (of *The Bitch* and *The Stud* fame). Six months later the wedding was called off, though the couple finally married earlier this year.

When the Hunters were dropped from *Crossroads*, Allen did not conceal his bitterness. But he could console himself with having had his role immortalised in Noele Gordon's *Crossroads Cookbook*. Introducing "Beef Chasseur", she pointed out that the French word: "*Chasseur*" translated into English as "Hunter" – adding, "but I don't mean *you*, David!!"

Ronald Allen was born at Reading, Berkshire, in 1934, and trained at the Royal Academy of Dramatic Art, where he won the John Gielgud Scholarship.

He worked in repertory before joining the Old Vic company, where he played Benvolio in *Romeo and Juliet*, Mountjoy in *Henry VI* and Paris in *Troilus and Cressida*, which went to Broadway. Back home, Allen appeared in a number of television plays and made a notable impression as the honeymooning husband in *A Night to Remember*, a poignant film about the *Titanic*.

Allen's first big television break came in the late 1960s in *Compact*, the twice-weekly soap opera in which, for more than three years, he played the editor of a women's magazine. He then spent seven months in the rather less probable role of the manager of a football club in the serial *United!*

After leaving *Crossroads*, Allen's matinée-idol demeanour endeared him to a new wave of comedians, and he made frequent guest appearances in the Comic Strip television films, notably as the lubricious Uncle Quentin in *Five Go Mad in Dorset*; as the Dracula-crazed policeman in *Supergrass*; and, more recently, as the denim-clad English don in *Oxford*. That he performed these roles with such relish said much for his sense of humour and gallant self-parody.

In recent years Allen also went to Hollywood, where he gained a part in the serial *Generations*, as an English tycoon who spent his time clinching impossible business deals. But the period was not a happy one; unable to obtain a work permit, he had to return home.

Allen was highly regarded by his fellow actors, who thought it a pity that for much of his career he never quite fulfilled the promise of his early classical roles. Only last year he returned to the London stage and showed theatre-goers what a fine and under-rated player he was, with a bravura performance as the leading man in Tom Stoppard's sunny play, *Rough Crossing*.

Allen's hobbies included gardening and collecting antiques. He is survived by his wife.

June 20 1991

MICHAEL LANDON

MICHAEL LANDON, the Hollywood actor, producer and director, who has died aged 54, made his reputation as cute "Little Joe" Cartwright, the youngest son of the Ponderosa Ranch in the popular Western series *Bonanza*.

After 14 years of this he went on to play "Pa", the wholesome patriarch of the Ingalls clan in the saccharine series *Little House on the Prairie*, and then ascended to virtue on an angelic scale in *Highway to Heaven*,

In that series, which he wrote, directed and produced, Landon played an angel despatched to earth to give chosen people a second chance to redeem their lives. Unusually for one of the heavenly host, his character was notable not for his halo and robes but for his bouffant hair-do and denim jacket.

Despite repeated claims that his programmes would "make the world a better place", Landon was often criticised by his colleagues for his relentless interference in all aspects of production. Landon did not deny accusations that he was bad-tempered and dictatorial, and evidently found it difficult to replicate the exacting moral standards set by his characters.

Twice divorced and father of nine children, he was publicly harangued by his second wife Lynn Noe for ending their 18-year marriage to marry a make-up artist 30 years his junior. "I am a driven man," he once remarked, "because ever since I was a kid I wanted to show myself and others that I was somebody."

He was born Eugene Maurice Orowitz on Long Island, New York on October 31 1936. His father was a theatre agent and his mother a Broadway actress. "My father was a Jew who didn't care for Catholics," he recalled, "and my mother was a Catholic who was anti-Semitic." He described his childhood as "wretched".

He was a scrawny, reserved boy, but through determination and practice began to shine on the games field: he eventually set the American high-school record for the longest javelin throw. In spite of graduating from high school 300th in a class of 301, he was offered a number of offers of athletic scholarships. He chose to go to the University of Southern California, which was obliged to pay another student $10 to take his entrance examination for him.

Over the years Landon had come to believe that, like Samson, his strength was somehow connected with his luscious curly hair. Not long after his arrival on campus, a group of jealous jocks cornered him and subjected him to a crew cut. This did indeed affect Landon's track prowess, and he lost 50 feet off his average javelin throw.

He dropped out after his freshman year, and worked as a blanket salesman, a canner at a soup factory and a car-wash attendant. In 1952 he began taking drama classes at the Warner Brothers acting school, and chose his stage name from the Los Angeles telephone directory.

The class was closed down four months later, but Landon gained a role in the television production, *Telephone Time*. With his hirsute good looks restored, he was soon in demand for cowboy roles in such television Westerns as *Tales of Wells Fargo*, *Wanted Dead or Alive* and *Cheyenne*.

He made his film debut in *I Was A Teenage Werewolf* (1957), a risible horror movie. The next year he appeared as the albino, Dave Dawson, in *God's Little Acre*, and then as a gallant soldier in *The Legend of Tom Dooley* (1959). Then he was offered the role of Little Joe in *Bonanza* which became the most popular programme on NBC.

In the early 1960s Landon had begun to take an interest in the production of the show. He began to write scripts and went on to direct more than 30 episodes. After *Bonanza* expired in 1972, he was avalanched with offers of work, but turned them all down to concentrate on a script he had written which dealt with bed-wetting (a problem he had suffered from as a child).

Unable to find a buyer for the script, he continued writing and directing, before landing the lead role in *The Little House on the Prairie*, a story of 19th-century Minnesota life, which ran for the next nine years. "The ingredients on our show," Landon once remarked, in an attempt to explain its success, "are the little things nobody seems to care about any more, the simple needs of people."

Landon became increasingly obsessed with authenticity, and the film crew complained of his insistence on using his own story lines. He had an unusual way, too, with awkward actresses, for whom he would keep a live tarantula under his hat – at opportune moments he tipped the brim to let the hairy creature walk over his face.

By the mid-1980s he was spending most of his time with his new family. He admitted that during that decade he had "put on too much weight and stopped working out". He began dieting and exercising, dyed his grey-streaked hair brown, and was due to start work on a new television series *US*, when he was diagnosed with cancer in April.

"I want my agent to know", he joked, "that this sure shoots to hell any chance of doing a health food commercial."

Landon married first, in 1956, Dodie Levy; secondly, in 1962, Lynn Noe; and thirdly, in 1983, Cindy Clerico. He had nine children.

July 3 1991

ARTHUR PENTELOW

ARTHUR PENTELOW, the actor, who has died aged 67, was one of the longest-serving members of the cast of Yorkshire Television's soap opera *Emmerdale Farm*, in which he played – or rather masterfully underplayed – the gruff, pipe-smoking landlord of the Woolpack pub.

Pentelow's appearance as Wilks dated back to *Emmerdale*'s creation in 1972, when it was proudly presented as a series about rural family life, free of what the scriptwriter Kevin Laffan condemned as the "sex, sin and sensationalism" of its counterparts. With time *Emmerdale*'s original "ordinary, non-hysterical" storylines – which roved between such conservation issues as the ignominy of battery farming, and such human questions as the virtues of warming the pot before "brewing t' tea" – were inevitably replaced by a grittier script.

But in the role of the blunt, kindly Henry Wilks, Pentelow remained a stalwart representative of the Woolpack's old guard, dispensing wisdom with solemn, interposing puffs on his pipe. A retired Bradford wool merchant who settled in the village after his wife died, Wilks provided the voice of reason – the counterpoint both to the burly, irascibly sideburned figure of Amos, his landlord partner at the Woolpack, and to the sheep-shearing Beckindale folk, invariably inquiring if there was "'owt oop?", on the other side of the bar.

Wilks was the character employed to cause Amos's copious mutton chops to inflate with rage by putting a damper on his grandiose schemes, and to expose the landlord's meanness – he was forever wincing under the lash of Amos's tongue for giving away free pints of bitter beer. Indeed Wilks's curious love-hate relationship with Amos came to fascinate the programme's 12 million viewers. Amos's insistence on addressing his partner as "Mr Wilks" instead of "Henry" was one of numerous *Emmerdale* enigmas left frustratingly unexplained.

Wilks also played an important conciliatory role outside the pub. He stood by his friend Annie Sugden through thick and thin. And when a family row broke out at Emmerdale and Jack threatened to leave, it was Wilks who secured the future of the farm: he bought the freehold and organised the family into a limited company.

Wilks featured prominently in recent episodes, when, after Amos left the programme, he moved out of the Woolpack to make way for the new landlord, Alan Turner, and went to live at the Sugden farmhouse.

Arthur Pentelow was born at Rochdale, Lancs, on February 14 1924. He originally planned to become a policeman and joined the force as a cadet clerk, but the Second World War intervened, and he found himself in the Royal Navy instead.

Afterwards he returned to Rochdale and for a while worked as a schoolteacher. He had dabbled with amateur dramatics before the war, and before long decided to become an actor.

He trained at the Bradford Civic Theatre School, before going into rep at the Bristol Old Vic, Nottingham and Birmingham. He was also in Orson Welles's production of *Othello* in the West End.

Besides *Emmerdale Farm*, Pentelow's television credits included *Z Cars*, *Armchair Theatre*, *The Troubleshooters*, *United!* and *Coronation Street*. He appeared in such films as

Privilege, with Paul Jones and Jean Shrimpton, and Albert Finney's *Charlie Bubbles*.

Pentelow lived mainly in Birmingham, but had a weekday cottage in a Leeds suburb, where he stayed during filming. He enjoyed gardening and playing tennis, and once remarked that, in spite of his years behind the Woolpack bar, he was not a pub person at all.

Of the many times he was set upon by fans, he cherished one occasion on which an old man tugged his sleeve in a Leeds shopping mall and said: "I'd like thee to know, tha's given me an hour or two of *real* pleasure."

Pentelow is survived by his wife, Jacqueline, and two sons.

August 7 1991

Victoria Sanger Freeman

VICTORIA SANGER FREEMAN, who has died aged 96, was a legendary figure in the circus world where she was known as "the Queen of the Elephants".

Young "Vicky" established her reputation before the First World War as a bareback rider and went on to work with a big elephant act comprising several magnificent pachyderms known as Annie, Betty, Tiny and Jinny.

"Vicky" Sanger Freeman was the last of the great Sanger circus dynasty which proudly bore the title "The Greatest Name in Circus" – a billing never repeated since she and her brother, George Sanger, toured the last Lord George Sanger's Circus in the early 1960s.

The show finally expired in 1962, at a court hearing, when her brother was petitioner for the compulsory winding-up. Thus came to an end the Sanger circuses which had spanned 117 years.

Victoria was a Sanger on both sides of her family – her father having married a cousin. On her mother's side, she was a great-granddaughter of the original "Lord" George Sanger – who had bestowed upon himself this courtesy title out of pique when faced with a court battle with "the Honourable" Bill Cody, alias "Buffalo Bill".

Indeed, Mrs Sanger Freeman was the last person who could claim to have known the great Lord George, upon whose knee she had sat as a child at his home in East Finchley. Lord George was eventually to meet a brutal death in 1911 at the hands of one of his own servants.

On her father's side, Victoria was a great-granddaughter of Lord George's brother, John. For many years she travelled with the Lord John Sanger Circus (formed by her uncle John) until this ceased to operate before the Second World War.

Mrs Sanger Freeman appeared in other circuses as well as Sanger's. For the first two or three years of the Bertram Mills Circus at Olympia, west London, which started up in 1920, the Sanger family provided the nucleus of the performance – she was the last surviving performer from the very first Mills show.

After working for Mills, the Sangers went on to provide the backbone of the annual Christmas Circus at the Crystal Palace in south London.

Victoria Florence Sanger was born on September 28

1895 into a family which was commanded to appear at Windsor Castle by Queen Victoria, and which took its show under the Big Top to every part of the British Isles and beyond.

In 1917 she married James Freeman, who worked for Sanger as a rider, highwire walker, trapeze *artiste* and clown. Freeman was considered the most versatile of all British circus performers in his heyday and as a clown under the name of "Pimpo" was one of Britain's most popular jesters.

But George Sanger had taken exception to Pimpo's courtship of his daughter and the couple had to meet clandestinely. On one occasion the hapless clown had to creep away under the seats in a cinema when they suddenly realised her father was sitting in the row immediately in front.

The wedding was secret, and they rode to Burstow Church on bicycles. But after the service they bumped into Mr and Mrs George Sanger and while accompanying them back to the circus winter quarters, broke the news to them.

They were forgiven, and Pimpo continued to be Sanger's greatest all-round performer.

The Freemans had a son, Pat, who followed in the family's footsteps as a clown, rider and animal trainer. His comedy dog act as "Old Regnas" (an anagram of Sanger) was to gain fame in the leading continental circuses but he died at an early age while performing with Circus Knie in Switzerland.

Mrs Sanger Freeman's gandsons, however, both continue the tradition – Mike Sanger is currently at Conny-Land in Switzerland and Peter Sanger ("Old Regnas") is with Circus Barum in Germany.

Mrs Sanger Freeman's husband died in 1961 and she

spent her last years quietly in Brixton. Her ashes are to be placed in the family plot at Margate where Sanger's "Hall by the Sea" was at one time one of the seaside town's delights.

August 21 1991

VINCE TAYLOR

VINCE TAYLOR, the British-born rock musician, who has died in Lausanne aged 52, was known as "*Le Diable Noir*" on account of his all-black leather wardrobe and was once cited by David Bowie as the inspiration for Ziggy Stardust, Bowie's celebrated alter-ego.

Taylor and Stardust did not actually share any physical characteristics apart from their mutual fondness for heavy eyeliner – Ziggy Stardust was a space-age "Pierrot", while Taylor proved the archetypal black leather-clad, chain-wielding rocker of the Gene Vincent variety. But there is every reason to believe that the legend of Ziggy's rise and fall was based on the period in Taylor's life when his career suddenly nose-dived, and he shed his Gene Vincent persona to adopt that of Jesus Christ – he took to dressing up in white\ robes and walking up to people on the Left Bank to bless them.

Although even by rock 'n' roll's standards Taylor's voice often lacked range and control, such was the sheer magnitude of his presence and his matinée idol good looks that, had his luck held, he would arguably have become one of the world's great rock stars.

He was born Maurice Brian Holden at Hounslow, west London, on July 14 1939. His family moved to

California when he was a boy, and did not return to Britain until 1958.

By this time Vince Taylor (as he now called himself) was already an accomplished musician, and he soon assembled his first backing group, the Playboys. It included the guitarist, Tony Sheridan (soon to team up with the Beatles) and Brian "Licorice" Locking and Brian Bennett (future members of the Shadows).

Although he performed on Jack Good's "Oh! Boy" and cut a handful of singles, including "Watcha gonna do", "Jet Black Machine" and the now classic "Brand New Cadillac", Taylor did not benefit from the kind of pro-motional muscle that boosted such contemporaries as Cliff Richard. Moreover, there was an undercurrent of violence in his stance which prevented him from effectively crossing over into mainstream pop.

Taylor's break came when he filled in for an ailing Gene Vincent during the latter's French tour in 1961. When Parisian fans smashed up the Palais des Sports after his show, Taylor's future seemed assured.

The Anglo-American rocker was immediately signed up by a local impresario, and was hailed as the one person capable of dethroning France's "King of Rock 'n' Roll", Johnny Halliday. For a short while, Taylor fulfilled the critics' promise: as his records – on the Memphis label – hit the charts, his exploits hit the headlines all over the Continent.

But just as rapidly as he established himself, his career began to self-destruct, leading to sojourns in psychiatric clinics and jail. Vince Taylor was last heard of working in a Swiss factory.

September 2 1991

JEAN ROOK

JEAN ROOK, the journalist, who has died aged 59, revelled in describing how she had "clawed and scrambled" her way to become "the First Lady of Fleet Street ... Britain's bitchiest, best known, loved and loathed woman journalist".

Rook also owned up to having been the original model for *Private Eye*'s female columnist, Glenda Slag. "I never minded the *Eye*'s caricature of me as the scurrilous hackette Glenda Slag," she wrote, "mainly because I didn't regularly read it. I daren't. It was too near the mark. If any more of wittily written Glenda had rubbed off on me, I'd have ended up as the carbon copy, instead of the other way round."

And in truth Rook never did allow the parody to outstrip her original self. She loved the privileged position of a newspaper columnist, and if she dressed in extravagantly brassy style – legendarily clanking with chunky accessories – she had the opinions and language to match.

In her weekly column in the *Daily Express*, crammed with superfluous punctuation and an excruciatingly alliterative mixture of mangled metaphors, she wrote exactly what she thought of those in public life. Lefties and feminists – indeed any manifestation of post-Sixties Britain – aroused particular scorn: "Those women who go boobing and bouncing around with hairy legs make me feel *yuk*!"

The fact that Rook's own success in a male-dominated world could be seen as a feminist victory – where hairy legs failed, furs and fragrance were sure to succeed – was neither here nor there. But then Rook was nothing if not inconsistent. Her never less than outrageous column became the vehicle for wild swings of opinion – a vacillation she considered necessary to reflect the public mood.

Thus, one week Rook would hold Prince Philip in favour; the next she would think nothing of describing him as "a snappish OAP, with a temper like an arthritic corgi". The Duchess of York was treated with similar schizophrenic hyperbole. "Sarah Ferguson looks like an unbrushed red setter struggling to get out of a hand-knitted potato sack," wrote the rancorous Rook – only to temper her description with the revelation that she was also "great fun, powerfully sexy, tremendously boisterous and thrilling to men"; as for the Duke of York, his taste, "let's face it, is about as subtle as a sat-on whoopee cushion".

Even Rook's adoring readers sometimes professed to find her unashamed vulgarity too much to bear. She received her heaviest mail-bag after referring to Mary Whitehouse as "a whited sepulchre who hands out black marks to programmes she doesn't watch through her half-closed fingers". Of 1,000 letters, six expressed agreement with this view, but 994 wanted Rook sacked. Of course this only added to her provocative reputation.

During nearly 20 years on the *Daily Express*, Rook remained a much-vaunted institution. Besides producing her column, she interviewed scores of public figures – ranging from Margaret Thatcher and Indira Gandhi to Elizabeth Taylor and Barry Humphries – and adopted what she referred to as "the same down-to-earth approach" with them all. "You know why I'm popular with the readers?" she once said. "Because I'm as ordinary as they are. They like me because I have the same reactions, the same simple view of the world. I ask the same questions. If they were interviewing Elizabeth Taylor, they would look at her hands to see if she was wearing the Krupp diamond."

Sometimes, though, for all the stylistic infelicities, traces of Rook's degree in English literature could be descried. On one occasion she launched into a discussion about W. H. Auden and Sir John Betjeman, which resulted in another sackful of abusive letters, notably from a reader who derided the article as "Literary Criticism for imbecile housewives in the same gushing but ill-natured style."

But Rook was happy to admit she had no great novel to write. She simply believed that if people chose to preach to the public, then they must expect counter-attack. She could certainly take it herself.

For all her faults and vanities, Jean Rook was an indispensably conscientious member of every team on which she worked – someone who gave as good as she got, with true Yorkshire grit. She missed her deadline for her *Express* column only twice in two decades – once, when her son was born, and the second time, when she was diagnosed as suffering from cancer.

In typically candid and courageous style, she went on to announce her illness to her readers in her next piece. She wrote her last column only two weeks ago.

The daughter of an engineer and an usherette, Jean Rook was born in Hull on November 13 1931. She enjoyed a carefree childhood in the East Riding, and later in life would sometimes dream about giving up Fleet Street to return to a more peaceful existence in the North.

She was educated at Malet Lambert Grammar School

and Bedford College, London, where she became the first woman to edit the student newspaper, *Sennet*. She began her career on the *Sheffield Telegraph*, where she met her future husband, Geoffrey Nash.

Rook moved on to the *Yorkshire Post* and then to *Flair*, a fashion magazine, and in 1964 launched herself on Fleet Street as fashion editor on the new *Sun*. She recalled that when the woman's editor told her to check out a photograph of a skinny teenager called Lesley Hornby, she did not bother. Next week the *Daily Express* had renamed the unknown girl from Neasden, "Twiggy".

Already, though, Rook's "killer style" was in evidence. In 1965, when it was still customary to describe royalty with glowing respect, her remark about Princess Margaret's "fuddy-duddy feet" caused a sensation.

Next she moved, as woman's editor, to the old *Daily Sketch*, where she distinguished herself by her "Save our Mini-skirt!" campaign. When the *Sketch* was subsumed in the *Daily Mail*, Rook became woman's editor of the new tabloid. But after 18 months on what she described as the "morose *Mail*", she crossed the Street, amid recriminatory heat, to become woman's editor of the *Daily Express*.

Over the next 19 years, she survived eight editors; she was also the first journalist to enter the same cage as a pair of man-eating Bengal tigers. With uncharacteristic modesty she denied having actually "discovered" Mrs Thatcher, but she did not forswear to note that back in 1974 she had predicted her potential as "Britain's first woman Prime Minister".

She also described her as "the English rose who, in her dew-drenched days, looked like a long-stemmed thornless pink bud, still in its Cellophane wrapper". Denis Thatcher was apostrophised as "a balding golf-ball".

Some felt that Rook met her match in Larry Lamb, who took over the *Express* editorship in 1983. Relations were fraught from the start. As she put in her lively memoirs, *The Cowardly Lioness*: "I bear three scars – my Caesarian, my lumpectomy and Larry Lamb."

In that book Rook also showed a touchingly vulnerable streak. She led two lives: one as Jean Rook, the abrasive columnist, the other as an understanding wife, mother, daughter and friend. She could play "Fleet Street's First Bitch" because it was a professional act, and she often said she would have preferred to have been an actress. She would dress up for the role every day, play it way over the top, then go home to a blameless family life.

But last month, talking to Anthony Clare on BBC Radio Four's *In the Psychiatrist's Chair*, she also confessed to being addicted to work. If she had the choice between time with her husband (who died in 1988) or an assignment, the assignment always won.

After discovering that she had cancer Rook made a resolution to lead "a good and pure life", but this was not her style: "You have to be superhuman to do that," she said. "Anyway it's boring."

She is survived by her son, who was educated at Eton.

Dame Barbara Cartland writes: Jean Rook was a close friend of mine for many years. I admired her courage – and she had a great many difficulties in her life.

I admired also the way she always told the truth even if it was not particularly pleasant, and, above all, the way in which she managed to give those who knew her, some of her own enjoyment and zest for life.

She will be a loss to the Press, which she raised to a

very high standard of journalism, and her friends will never forget her.

September 6 1991

MARGARET RAMSAY

MARGARET RAMSAY, the West End literary agent, who has died aged 83, was responsible for discovering much of the talent which produced the post-war revival in Britain's theatre.

For more than three decades the redoubtable "Peggy" Ramsay championed playwrights whose style might at first appear obscure, or whose message controversial. In a mutitude of cases, however, her judgement was eventually vindicated.

Among the names which were not names when she came across them were Robert Bolt, Alan Ayckbourn, John Mortimer, Peter Nichols, Christopher Hampton, Howard Brenton, David Hare, Edward Bond, David Mercer, Willy Russell, Caryl Churchill, Charles Wood and Stephen Poliakoff. She also introduced Eugene Ionesco to the English-speaking world.

Nor was she content merely to discover talent. Alan Ayckbourn was told to write more serious plays: "At the start, all he wanted to do was entertain; but I mean, you don't want to look after an author who's just an entertainer, do you, dear?"

Edward Bond, on the other hand, was instructed to try a lighter vein: "For God's sake, stop taking yourself so seriously. Get yourself a little red sports car and drive up and down the King's Road with a blonde."

The most notorious of all her young hopefuls was Joe Orton. The sensational manner of his life and death – although Ramsay herself was never one to be shocked by sexual frankness – brought her into the public eye.

In *Prick Up Your Ears* (1987), a film based on John Lahr's biography of Orton with a script by Alan Bennett, Vanessa Redgrave played the part of the ill-fated play-wright's encouraging and concerned agent. The actress was far too tall for the role, and the impersonation hardly reflected Miss Ramsay's essentially private personality.

But the scene in which the agent opens her purse and bestows a wad of banknotes upon Orton was certainly typical. Many impoverished writers benefited from Ramsay's generosity; the rich and successful, by contrast, often failed to engage her sympathy.

She believed that talent seldom lasted more than a decade, and that after that writers tended to repeat themselves. "You can tell real talent at once," she would say. "There is an originality, a vitality. Real talent should surprise you. No, it should *alarm* you."

Inevitably, given the acuity of her taste – which was frequently years ahead of that of the theatre-going public – she was involved with several commercial failures, but such disasters never altered her opinion of a play. And although writers in her stable might never become rich, they at least gained reputation.

Oddly enough, Ramsay, herself an intensely theatrical figure with a penchant for pithy one-liners and flamboyant hats, rarely went to the theatre, unless it was to see a new client's work. Then she might travel hundreds of miles to a provinical theatre.

Her special talent was her ability to visualise in her mind how a play would work in performance. "Peggy," the critic Harold Hobson observed, "can read a play as a musician can read a score." She liked to compare her work to that of a director, but unlike many directors she was quite content that her authors should have all the glory.

Yet Miss Ramsay could also be acerbic about her protégés. "Saw *Lawrence of Arabia*," she is said to have remarked to Robert Bolt on the telephone. "Lovely camels, dear. Bye-ee."

Her legendary indiscretions could be as alarming as Sir John Gielgud's gaffes. In conversation with one of her authors, she expressed her sympathy for the matrimonial difficulties of another client – "he's got that awful so-and-so to deal with". "But she's *my* wife," her unfortunate interlocutor was obliged to interject.

Her candour, unintentional or otherwise, was inflicted on male and female alike; and some of her authors proved unable to stomach her stinging criticisms. But she did not want to be loved. Her devotion was reserved for the task of stimulating art, however many egos might be bruised in the process.

Amid the schmaltz of "showbiz", Miss Ramsay adopted rigorously unsentimental attitudes. She did not believe in cushioning either herself or her clients; writers should starve rather than accept subsidies.

The daughter of an Army doctor, Margaret Ramsay was born in Sydney, New South Wales, on May 28, 1908, and brought up in South Africa, where she indulged in ostrich-riding. She studied psychology and philosophy at Port Elizabeth University, where she married one of her professors. They moved to London, only to separate after a year.

After a spell in the Carl Rosa opera chorus – "I had a very noisy voice" – she turned to acting, earning a prediction from Noël Coward that she would soon be a star. But one day the director William Armstrong asked her to explain Kafka's *The Castle*, a task she performed so fluently that he suggested she should become an agent.

She began by reading plays for the theatrical agents Dorothy and Campbell Christie. After she had provided them with a string of West End hits they gave her £1,000 to start her own firm in Goodwin's Court, a narrow alley off St Martin's Lane in the heart of London's theatreland.

Peggy Ramsay never moved premises thereafter. The building had formerly contained a brothel – "But you never hear the sounds of slashings and whippings now," Ramsay remarked.

Her second-floor office was lined with theatrical posters, and organised to minimise any impression of business. She conducted most of her meetings from a green chaise longe: "horizontal is my favourite position," she said.

In 1990, when Peggy Ramsay was celebrated in the *Arena* television programme on BBC2, one of her authors summed up both the affection and the awe that she inspired: "She's a cross between Auntie Mame and the Red Queen."

September 7 1991

OLGA SPESSIVTSEVA

OLGA SPESSIVTSEVA, the Russian ballerina who has died aged 96, was generally reckoned the equal of the legendary Pavlova until her obsessive pursuit of artistic perfection drove her out of her mind.

In the 1920s Spessivtseva danced for Diaghilev, who said of her and Pavlova that they were "two halves of the same apple, and Spessivtseva was the half turned to the sun". She was at her best in the great classical roles, and her interpretation of *Giselle*, the village girl whose mind gives way because of her lover's duplicity, was unrivalled.

Many dancers regard the part as unbearably demanding and avoid it. Spessivtseva, though, felt a tragic affinity with *Giselle*. Before performing in the role in Leningrad in 1919, she visited an asylum several times to observe patients.

She played the part again at the Savoy Theatre in 1932, in a performance which established the Camargo Society and the beginnings of British ballet. The part of Albrecht was taken by Anton Dolin, and the cast included Ninette de Valois and Frederick Ashton.

Spessivtseva's dancing in the mad scene was especially – and ominously – haunting. When Margot Fonteyn tackled the role for the first time with the Vic-Wells ballet five years later she adopted the Russian's halting faltering style for that scene – although in general the two dancers bore little resemblance to one another.

Spessivtseva had been suffering from nervous strain for some years when, one night in the Roosevelt Hotel in New York in 1942, she completely broke down. Her rich "protector" arranged for her to enter a private sanatorium, where she could make a slow but comfortable recovery.

But such was not to be: her protector died, and his executors cruelly disclaimed responsibility for the beautiful, brilliant but temporarily broken dancer. Spessivtseva, whose English was poor, was transferred to a state hospital for the insane. The staff there knew nothing of the new inmate's history and took her references to *Giselle* as *folie de grandeur*. When she berated them for their ignorance she was strapped to her bed and given electric shocks through her skull.

This treatment did not help and she languished in the asylum for more than 20 years before a new drug and the intervention of her old friend Anton Dolin secured her release in 1963.

Olga Alexandrovna Spessivtseva was born on July 18 1895, the daughter of an opera singer. After her father's death she was sent to an orphanage in St Petersburg with theatrical connections.

She was enrolled as a member of the Russian Imperial School of Ballet in 1905 and graduated in 1913, when she joined the Maryinsky Theatre Company. Within three years she was established as a soloist.

In 1916 Diaghilev invited her to take Karsavina's place as Nijinsky's partner for a New York season. She returned to Russia just before the 1917 Revolution, where she was promoted ballerina.

For the next few years she enjoyed enormous success in such ballets as *Giselle*, *Esmeralda*, *La Bayadère* and *The Corsair*, establishing herself as the finest dancer in Russia.

She was still almost unknown in the West when Diaghilev brought her to London in 1921 to dance Princess Aurora in his great revival of *The Sleeping Beauty*. Anton Dolin, who as a boy of 16 danced in the ensemble, described the effect achieved by the shy ballerina when she reported for practice at Maestro Cecchetti's academy.

"No sooner had she started her exercises at the *barre* than they all realised they were in the presence of genius. When they were called up in groups of four to do the *adagio* exercises, the three others in line with Spessivtseva fell back one by one and left her dancing alone."

Ballet lovers remember the production as the most perfect ever staged, but it was financially ruinous. Spessivtseva was not seen again in London until 1929 when she danced Act II of *Swan Lake*.

In 1924 she left Russia for the Paris Opera, which revived *Giselle* especially for her. One colleague from that time recalled that when she practised the mad scene, "the rehearsal room seemed more like a church in its solemn and holy atmosphere of religion".

A number of roles were created for her, among them parts in *Soir de Fête* and *Les Rencontres* at the Paris Opera and the title role in Balanchine's *La Chatte* for the Diaghilev company. She left the Paris Opera in 1932.

During a tour of Australia in 1934 the first signs of mental instability appeared. Spessivtseva announced her retirement on her return to Paris in 1935, although she danced in Buenos Aires in 1937. She moved to New York, with her elderly cosmopolitan protector, at the beginning of the Second World War.

After her return to the world in 1963 Spessivtseva went to live at the Tolstoy foundation farm in Rockland County, New York State, which had been founded by Countess Alexandra Tolstoy, daughter of the novelist, as a rest home for Russians. There she was occasionally visited by old friends from the world of ballet.

In 1964 the BBC put out a short programme about her life, and two years later Anton Dolin wrote a book about her. The title of both was *The Sleeping Ballerina*.

September 20 1991

CAROL WHITE

CAROL WHITE, the actress who has died in Florida aged 49, was celebrated for her powerful performance in the title role of *Cathy Come Home*, Jeremy Sandford's coruscating account of homelessness on BBC Television, which caused a national sensation in the 1960s.

Cathy Come Home was not so much a television play as fierce propaganda. Sandford traced the painful downhill journey of a young couple who began their married life full of hope and gaiety and ended it, separated from their children, as casualties of the Welfare State.

After an accident cut the husband's earnings, the couple lived with unfriendly relations, were evicted from squalid tenements, were driven out of a caravan site and found refuge in a rat-ridden hostel. For all its over-emphasis, the production showed with compassion the raw degradation of hostel life. In a *tour-de-force* of naturalistic acting the highly photogenic Carol White succeeded in making Cathy likeable and eventually extremely moving as the courage and optimism in her wasted away.

The diminutive Miss White, a London scrap merchant's daughter who had already made her mark in the television version of Nell Dunn's *Up the Juction* (1965), consequently became something of a Sixties icon. She went on to bring warmth and a plausible innocence to the film *Poor Cow*, a raw and realistic picture of South London life which opened with a graphic scene of Miss White giving birth while reflecting on the shortcomings of her absent husband ("He's a right bastard").

Subsequently Miss White was rather miscast as a jolly

virginal girl in Michael Winner's all too forgettable *I'll Never Forget What's 'Is Name*. However, she made a good impression – when she remembered to substitute a Gloucestershire accent for her native Cockney – as a comely country lass in *Dulcima* (1971) adapted from a story by H. E. Bates.

Miss White showed promise of better things as an actress opposite Alan Bates, Dirk Bogarde and Ian Holm in the film of Bernard Malamud's *The Fixer*. Her performance as Raisl Bok won her a Hollywood contract in 1968 to make *Daddy's Gone-A-Hunting*.

But from then on nothing seemed to go right, and the rest of her career was distinctly chequered. Miss White's attempts to establish herself in America were dogged by ill fortune. Her name – forever bracketed with her role of *Cathy* – became more familiar in the press in connection with her *amours*, divorces, court appearances, drink and drugs than with her acting.

"I came to America thinking I was at the very top," she recalled shortly before her death from liver failure, "and that no one could touch me. But pimps, pushers, liars and ex-husbands brought me crashing down."

In 1982 she returned to London to take over the role of Josie from Georgina Hale, in Nell Dunn's play *Steaming*, but her comeback ended unhappily when her contract was terminated following several missed performances.

Carol White was born in Hammersmith, London, on April 1 1942. She described her father as "a scrap-metal merchant and a spieler in a fairground and a door-to-door salesman of the elixir of life". At the age of 11 Carol heard about theatre schools from a hairdresser and thereafter attended the Corona.

Miss White made her film debut three years later in

Circus Friends and went on to appear in *Carry On Teacher*, *Beat Girl* and *Never Let Go*, in which she played Peter Sellers's girlfriend. "In those days in British films," she recalled, "brunettes were ladies and blondes were bits. I wore my hair white and painted my lips red and my eyes dark."

She then married Michael King of the King Brothers singing act and gave up acting for a few years. She returned, this time on the smaller screen in *Emergency – Ward 10* and, more notably, as a bright Battersea girl in Nell Dunn's exhilarating sketch of South London life, *Up the Junction*.

Miss White's later films for the cinema – not a distinguished collection – included *The Man Who Had Power Over Women*, *Something Big*, *Made*, *Some Call It Loving*, *The Squeeze*, *The Spaceman and King Arthur* and *Nutcracker*.

She wrote a racy volume of memoirs, *Carol Comes Home* (1982), in which the Swinging Sixties of purple hearts and Courrèges boots gave way to the excesses of Hollywood ("the assault course of a hundred different bedrooms . . . with broken hearts and broken promises left at every corner"), as well as a beauty book, *Forever Young*.

After her divorce from King she married Dr Stuart Lerner, a psychiatrist, and then Michael Arnold, a musician. She had two sons from her first marriage.

Jeremy Sandford writes: In her early films Carol captured powerfully the quality of the urban girl-next-door from the less prosperous areas. And in *Cathy Come Home* she seemed the archetypal young mother, every mother who has ever struggled not to be separated from her children.

I last saw her some 10 years ago when she had come

over to London and asked me to help her write her autobiography. She had devastating tales to tell about double-dealing Hollywood psychiatrists. Unknown to her, she told me, hers had been paid double her fee by an ex-boyfriend, to "muck her up". She told me she had come home for good to live the simple life back in Hammersmith, and I never dreamed she would go back to America.

She later wrote the book with help from another writer and I have regretted since that it wasn't me. It seems the classic tale of the pretty but unsophisticated girl who goes to Hollywood. There is no simple moral, though, because Carol, besides being pure and straight, was always reckless, always something of a life-gambler.

September 20 1991

MILES DAVIS

MILES DAVIS, the American trumpeter, bandleader and composer who has died at Santa Monica, California, aged 65, was probably the most influential and financially successful of all jazz musicians — as well as the most controversial.

Davis was the innovator of more distinct styles than any other jazz musician: he pioneered "cool jazz", hard bop, modal playing, free-form explorations and the use of electronics. "To be and stay a great musician," he wrote in his autobiography, *Miles* (1989), "you've got to always be open to what's new, what's happening at the moment. You have to be able to absorb it if you're going to continue to grow and communicate your music."

Davis enjoyed the respect and admiration of musicians

but every time he changed direction his audience divided between loyal and disenchanted listeners. He ignored them.

He was by no means universally admired. The poet Philip Larkin, for example, loathed his work, and described his trumpet style as "corpse-walking" and a "passionless creep".

Admittedly Davis's music never suffered from an over-abundance of warmth. But his terse, introspective playing possessed an undeniable emotional authority, and he had a remarkable knack of putting himself in the perfect setting.

He was constantly reinventing himself, and the number of incarnations of Miles Davis are legion. He began as a shy 19-year-old youth with a faltering trumpet technique but an extraordinary tone who was talent-spotted by Charlie Parker.

Then, in the mid-1950s, he emerged in sharp Italian suits and driving a white Ferrari. Mesmerically poised and elegant, he led one of the most stylishly original jazz groups ever assembled.

His brilliant quintet and sextet contained such musicians as John Coltrane and the incomparably crisp drummer, Philly Joe Jones. Davis also starred in large misty ensembles organised by the arranger Gil Evans, making such classic records as *Kind of Blue* and *Miles Ahead*.

The 1960s proved a thin time for jazz in general and Miles Davis in particular: record sales fell and audiences dwindled. But by the early 1970s Davis had taken on board the funk-rock of James Brown, Sly Stone and Jimi Hendrix, under whose influence he created the prototype jazz-fusion albums *In a Silent Way* and *Bitches Brew*.

These albums introduced a new generation to jazz and

spawned an entire movement, spearheaded by such Davis *alumni* as pianists Herbie Hancock, Chick Corea and Joseph Zawinul, and the guitarist John McLaughlin. Davis's counter-attack into jazz rock was accompanied by a radically new wardrobe. The Italian suits were replaced by skin-tight trousers and the brightest of pied-piper gear.

The crackle and the needle-point precision of the 1950s were gone as Davis continued to appeal to the youth market throughout the 1980s, although he always retained the melancholy, sultry essence of his musical personality.

Determined that jazz should not lose contact with the mainstream of black popular music, he used synthesizer music extensively on such late-1980s albums as *Tu Tu* and *Amandla*, restlessly shifting his context but never abandoning his piercing muted sound.

He explored disco rhythms, which he played against backings concocted on a synthesizer, and recorded with the pop group Scritti Politti. His success was phenomenal, and by the time he published his autobiography Davis could boast that he had more fans than at any previous point in his career.

Davis's tape-recorded confessions, however, did not make edifying listening. They told of drug-addiction and wife-beating. "That was the first time I hit her – though it wouldn't be the last," he said of one wife.

And he revelled in having played the pimp in order to feed his drug habit, claiming that he "had a whole stable of bitches out on the street for me" and he justified every action with reference to the "racist, white motherfucker" – an omnipresent ogre. Not for nothing was Davis dubbed the "Prince of Darkness".

The son of a prosperous dentist, Miles Dewey III

Davis, was born at Alton, Illinois, on May 25 1926. A year later his family moved to East St Louis, a small town on the Mississippi River.

Young Miles's mother was deeply conscious of her family's middle-class status and cherished hopes of her boy becoming a violinist. Davis later refused to attend her funeral. His father was made of somewhat sterner stuff, and gave him a trumpet on his 13th birthday.

In 1944 he left St Louis for New York after a visit to his hometown by Charlie Parker and Dizzy Gillespie, two of the first and foremost exponents of the new bebop jazz. They were both in a band led by the singer/trumpeter Billy Eckstine and Davis replaced an ailing trumpeter and sat alongside his idols.

Jazz music was now in the melting pot, New York the crucible, and Davis eagerly wanted to be involved. But although he was married with a child at the age of 16, he was still under parental control himself, and was prevailed upon to continue his formal music studies in New York. Davis duly enrolled at the Juilliard School of Music, and lived off an allowance given him by his father. In this respect, he was a privileged youth among his "scuffling" contemporaries.

But although he put in a certain number of hours at school Davis was more often to be found in one of a string of seedy clubs on 52nd Street – "The Street That Never Slept" – listening and playing rather than learning harmony and composition at the Juilliard.

He played and recorded with Charlie Parker, and by the late 1940s he had eschewed the brassy stridencies of bop trumpet, electing for a "cool" approach and keeping within the soft middle range of his instrument.

It was an association with a white, one-time dance

band pianist, Gil Evans, that led to Davis making records with an unorthodox instrumentation that included the French horn and tuba. These Nonet recordings, later issued on an LP under the title of *Birth Of The Cool*, inspired a host of imitators, principally on the West Coast.

Heroin addiction was common among the beboppers; they believed it helped them to negotiate the complex chord sequences played at breakneck speed often in breathtaking unison. In 1949 Davis, the non-smoker and non-drinker from the black middle-class, became hooked and for the next four years he worked only occasionally.

Then he cured himself: "I spent 12 days looking at the ceiling. I threw up everything I ate. My pores opened. I smelt like chicken soup. Then it was over."

Davis emerged triumphant from this period of self-destruction to make a series of outstanding albums in the company of young turks hell-bent on changing the sound of jazz. They included the tenor saxophonists John Coltrane and George Coleman, and drummers such as Art Blakey, Philly Joe Jones and Max Roach (who said of Davis that he "seemed to be able to turn anything into something good").

In 1955 he made a memorable appearance at the Newport Jazz Festival. His sensational improvisations, which were lyrical and tonally pure, created excitement without screaming and made him the hit of the show.

A further association with Gil Evans produced three classic albums – *Miles Ahead* (1957) *Porgy and Bess* (1958) and *Sketches of Spain* (1959). Using an orchestra of more than 30 pieces, the albums produced an unambiguously new sound and sold in their thousands.

Some critics carped. John S. Wilson of the *New York Times* wrote: "Evans has created a rich, exotic, hanging sound through which emerges the languid pained sound that Davis squeezes from his trumpet . . . for the listener in search of jazz there is mighty little of that commodity." Most people, however, accept that Davis made an enormous contribution to jazz, although his later departures did alienate many of his followers.

He was totally uncompromising, refusing to bend to public opinion; throughout his career Davis was insistent that he be accepted solely on the intrinsic value of his music.

He delighted in the luxuries of the materialistic white society he so roundly condemned. Davis owned a lavish house on West 77th Street in Manhattan, a house in Hollywood and a vast wardrobe of flamboyant clothes and accessories that included diamond-studded wristbands and numerous pairs of high-heeled shoes. He was constantly demanding advances from his record company, Columbia.

Despite his famous hatred of whites – he used to make such absurd statements as "Jazz is a white man's word" and "The blues is a white man's invention" – Davis was frequently seen in the company of Caucasian girls and often used white musicians, incurring the wrath of black players.

When he engaged the white guitarist John McLaughlin he rounded on his critics: "If you can show me a nigger who can play better I'll hire him." At the same time he teased the pianist Bill Evans (whose playing he much admired) with comments like: "Man, we don't want to hear no white opinions."

On one occasion Davis was involved in a violent fracas with a policeman outside the Birdland Club on Broadway, when his head was split open. He was eventually exonerated and considered suing the New York State.

Davis renounced showbiz conventions on the stage; he never smiled; turned his back on audiences; left the stage without acknowledging applause; and he frequently played for only a few minutes before leaving the stage.

"People come to see me because they've heard I'm so bad," he used to say. "Ain't that a bitch?" But Davis revelled in his notoriety and one of the reasons for his ungracious behaviour was that his audiences were white.

Davis's whispery, raspy voice was caused by his yelling at somebody in 1956 after surgery to remove polyps on his vocal cords. He was plagued by illness much of his life, at various times battling with diabetes, pneumonia, a stroke, and hip joint problems caused by sickle cell anaemia. He broke both legs in a motor-car accident in 1972. Although he overcame heroin addiction in the early 1950s, he continued to use cocaine until 1981.

Davis was married and divorced three times: to dancer Frances Taylor, singer Betty Mabry and actress Cicely Tyson.

The Prince of Darkness was a highly talented, somewhat bizarre figure. He was perhaps best summed up by the critic Leonard Feather, who wrote: "Miles Davis – black, volatile, rebellious and resilient as jazz itself".

"My thing," Davis was fond of saying "is *time*." He was alluding both to his conviction that correct tempo is fundamental to any piece of music as well as to his own spectacular creative longevity.

September 30 1991

JACK TREVOR STORY

JACK TREVOR STORY, the writer who has died aged 74, was the author of 400 short stories and 40 novels, among them *Live Now, Pay Later* and *The Trouble With Harry*.

In the 1940s Story was working on the assembly line at Marconi in Cambridge when his writing ability was recognised and he was promoted to the public relations office; he did not stay long. He began to write stories of cowboys and Indians and then went "up market" to write Sexton Blake thrillers, of which he wrote 20.

In 1949 he thought his fortune was made when his comic novel, *The Trouble with Harry*, was bought by Alfred Hitchcock, who paid him $500 (then £120). Story thought there would be further payments, but there were not.

Annoyed, Story telephoned Hitchcock at Claridges and explained that he had the bailiffs in the house and was desperate. Hitchcock replied he would buy the next novel unread, and Story said he had one. The bailiffs gave him a ride to Claridges, but Hitchcock had left the hotel for the boat train at Victoria Station.

The bailiffs drove Story to Victoria, where he boarded the train; but Hitchcock handed the typescript back to him and said he would have none of it.

Story had better luck with *Live Now, Pay Later*, which sold well and was much appreciated as a satire on Britain's hire-purchase society; he sold the film rights for £12,000 in 1962. But money flowed through his hands. He did not drink excessively or gamble but he loved women. He was surely one of the oldest, ugliest and most penurious lovers of young and beautiful women.

He went on to write a string of comic novels: *Something for Nothing*, a sequel to *Live Now, Pay Later*; *Hitler Needs You*, a tale of pre-war Cambridge life; and *I Sit in Hanger Lane*, featuring Horace Spurgeon Fenton.

In the sequel, *One Last Embrace*, Horace became a novelist. *Dishonourable Member* was an unsuccessful attempt at political satire. And in 1979, in the middle of bankruptcy proceedings, Story published *Up River*, a novel about going bankrupt.

His novels were called satires by his publishers but they lacked a cutting edge, as he could not bring himself to hate any of his characters. They are full of good things, though – introducing a policewoman, for example, he describes her as "fair, bit pretty, but plump and sexy, good at neck-locks".

Story was much admired by reviewers, who liked reading his novels because they were so enjoyable – but they failed to give him full literary marks. His favourite review called one of his books "devoid of bullshit"; he had that pinned on his wall.

Jack Trevor Story was born at Hertford in 1917, the son of a baker's roundsman and a domestic servant. His father was killed in the First World War, and his mother moved to Cambridge, where she worked as a college bedder. Story spoke with a Cambridge accent and had a townie's prejudice against the University.

As a lad he worked as a butcher's boy making deliveries to the colleges. Years later, invited to speak at the Cambridge Union, he startled his audience by saying: "I propose that this house is full of shit".

His early education, he used to say, was derived from *The Modern Boy*, *Melody Maker* and *Action*, the journal of the British Union of Fascists, which he read to annoy his Communist friends. He later became a ferocious autodidact.

Story regularly produced 4,000 words a day, and took only two or three weeks to finish a novel – he wrote one in 10 days. His output was accordingly uneven, but from time to time he made a great deal of money, although neither he nor the Inland Revenue knew exactly how much. He went bankrupt twice.

He spent his money on big motor cars, which displeased the tax examiners and bank managers. He said he liked "Detroit road boats" because there was plenty of room in them, and he kept a table in the back to write on when the mood took him.

Often he was supported by girlfriends, to the amazement of his men friends, for he had teeth, someone said, like Stonehenge. Story made something of a celebrity of one of his mistresses – Maggie, a Scottish girl 30 years his junior. At the time he was writing a weekly column in the *Guardian* about his life with her, and the newspaper's circulation rose when she left him, as the readers wondered if Maggie would come back.

He said his readers could see what she looked like if they bought a copy of a certain "girlie" magazine. She went to Brussels to work for the Common Market and never returned.

Story found another girl, Elaine, whom he married and educated well enough to send her to Oxford, from where she did not return. He wrote a book about Maggie, *Letters to an Intimate Stranger*; and another about Elaine, *Dwarf Goes to Oxford*.

When he was penniless in the 1970s he was made writer-in-residence at the new town of Milton Keynes, where he was given a flat above the Museum of Rural Life.

He was to stay one year, but remained for the rest of his life.

Story could play the guitar and sing, and in the early 1970s he was given his own series, *Jack on the Box*, on ITV, consisting of his personal views and interviews with eccentric or colourful characters. He acquired an Equity card, played Galileo in a television advertisement and was taken on the books of a model agency called Ugly.

Story married three times, was divorced once and had no more than eight children. Two of his wives predeceased him, and he wrote the dates of their deaths on the wall of the room he worked in, which he said was a better reminder than a tombstone.

December 9 1991

WALTER HUDSON

WALTER HUDSON, who has died at Hempstead, New York, aged 46, was once listed in *The Guinness Book of World Records* as the heaviest man on earth.

About 6 feet tall and 9 feet around, with cherubic features set off by pigtails braided in the Cherokee style, he long devoted himself to the pleasures of the table. Four years ago Hudson – then tipping the industrial scales at his top weight of 85 stones – gained worldwide notoriety (as "Whopping Walter") when he became stuck in his bedroom door. He was wedged there for some four hours; it took eight firemen to free him.

Walter Hudson was born at Brooklyn in 1945 and, as he recalled, "began gorging at the age of six". At 15 he was so obese his legs collapsed underneath him and he was confined to bed.

Indeed, except for the time when his family moved to Hempstead in 1970 and he was transported by motor car (his then 42 stones broke the seat), he remained inside. "I'm just a foodaholic," he once confessed. "I have no excuse."

Hudson's eating habits were fuelled by food brought in by members of his family. He would generally start his day with a breakfast of two pounds of bacon, 32 sausages, a dozen eggs, a loaf of bread, jam and coffee.

For luncheon Hudson favoured four Big Macs, four double-cheeseburgers, eight boxes of fried potatoes, six pies and six quarts of Coca-Cola. He would dine off six corns on the cob, three ham steaks, half a dozen yams and another six or seven baked potatoes, ending with a whole apple pie.

Between these principal repasts he would despatch a fowl or two, chased by macaroni, string beans, six large bottles of soda, not to mention colossal sandwiches and copious snacks such as Ring-Dings, Yodels, Yankee Doodles, Twinkies and assorted candy. "All I cared about," he recalled, "was food, *food*, FOOD!"

When not eating and sleeping he would watch television, listen to tapes and read the Bible – he had a particular penchant for the Psalms and was apt to recite Psalm 121: "I will lift up mine eyes unto the hills . . ." Hudson, though, was advised against sitting up for longer than five minutes because of the risk of being smothered by flab. The only exercise he engaged in was when he attended to his ablutions; it took him an hour to negotiate the six yards to the bathroom from his bedroom.

Then, in 1987, he found himself wedged in the

doorway. "The day I got stuck in that door," he recalled, "that's when the Lord got me the help I needed." The help to which he referred was offered by Dick Gregory, a comedian who masterminded the Slim Safe diet scheme.

"We think what might have happened," said Gregory about his new client, "is that in 27 years of lying around he might, because of the reading of his Bible, have taken on the same characteristics as Buddhist monks – slowed down the biological processes. But we don't know."

Gregory placed Hudson on a 1,200-calorie-a-day diet of raw fruit and orange juice. For exercise he was advised to lie in bed waving his arms about like a conductor.

Hudson soon lost some four inches off his knees, and within three months had shed 28 stones. It began to look as if he might fulfil such ambitions as visiting his mother's grave, riding on the New York subway, driving into the country – and even flying to a clinic in the Bahamas, from which he envisaged emerging as a sylph of 13 stones.

But it was not to be. At the time of his death, of an apparent heart attack, Hudson reportedly weighed 80 stones. Rescue workers had to cut a large hole in the wall of his bedroom to remove the body.

He was unmarried.

December 28 1991

FREDDIE BARTHOLOMEW

FREDDIE BARTHOLOMEW, the British-born child star, who has died aged 67, melted the hearts of millions as the angelic boy in the Eton collar in the early talkies.

At the age of 10, while on holiday in New York with his aunt, he was spotted by David Selznick of MGM, who cast him in the lead role in *David Copperfield* (1934). Aunt Ciss accompanied him to Hollywood, where the boy's curly hair, dimpled cheeks and somewhat wistful expression, combined with his quavering voice and "quaint" English accent, made him one of the first millionaire child stars.

David Copperfield, in which Bartholomew held his own opposite such stars as Basil Rathbone, Edna May Oliver and W. C. Fields, was hailed as a small miracle of compression, and became a huge success at the box office. Even English audiences, more than ready to condemn the film as a Hollywood travesty, were enthralled.

Contracts, fame and fortune were heaped upon young Freddie; in the next few years he starred in a number of films, including *Anna Karenina* (1935) – as Greta Garbo's screen son – *Little Lord Fauntleroy* (1936), *Captains Courageous* (1937), *Kidnapped* (1938) and *Tom Brown's Schooldays* (1940).

The story of Little Lord Fauntleroy was eerily echoed in his own life. Throughout the 1930s his parents fought a long and bitter legal battle with his aunt over his guardianship.

Bartholomew himself was always quite clear that he wished to remain with his aunt, who had brought him up from a young age. In 1935 he made the first of many appearances in a Californian court. Dressed in a grey knickerbocker suit with woollen socks and bare knees, he was asked by the judge what he thought happened to "little boys who tell lies".

"They probably go to hell," replied the boy solemnly. A compromise was eventually reached whereby his aunt became his legal guardian but a proportion of his earnings was handed over to his parents. But most of his money (at his peak he was earning £1,000 a week) was swallowed up in lawsuits – there were 27 in all.

Unlike many child stars, young Freddie remained unspoilt, a circumstance which the novelist Anthony Powell, who met the young star when seeking a scriptwriting job in Hollywood in the late 1930s, attributed to the good influence of his formidable aunt. In his memoirs, *To Keep the Ball Rolling*, Powell described Aunt Ciss as "a splendidly sensible and unassuming English woman," who, in the midst of all the legal wrangles, "remained quiet, firm, unfussed, entirely dedicated to what she looked on as best – not solely with an eye to professional advancement – for her nephew, a lady of whose bearing in the circumstances any country might be proud."

Powell was charmed by the boy, who insisted on showing him "the complex cat's cradle of delicate wires and filaments installed in the furthermost caverns of his jaw, purposed to remodel the back teeth in whatever form was regarded as most appropriate for a child-star of his eminence".

But, like most boys, Freddie grew into a gangly adolescent with a squeakily breaking voice. His film career declined from the beginning of the 1940s and by the end of the Second World War he had ceased to act altogether.

He was not, however, unduly cast down by this change of fortune, and went on to enjoy some success as a television chat show host and director in the 1950s before becoming a dapper executive in Benton & Bowles, a leading New York advertising agency.

Frederick Bartholomew was born in Dublin in 1924. He spent his early years with his grandparents and aunt in

Warminster, Wiltshire, where he appeared in church theatricals and a couple of films being made locally, *Fascination* (1930) and *Lily Christine* (1932).

He left for America two years later and never again lived in England. After the success of *David Copperfield* he received a seven-year contract from MGM at £250 a week.

After appearing successfully in *Professional Soldier* and the first part of *Lloyd's of London*, both in 1936, he showed that he was master of more than just the pious platitude when he played the spoiled brat in an adaptation of Kipling's *Captains Courageous* (1937) – opposite Spencer Tracy's moving performance as the simple-hearted Portuguese fisherman.

In 1938, aged 14, Bartholomew took the lead in *Kidnapped* and starred with 16-year-old Judy Garland in *Listen Darling*. The same year saw the release of *Lord Jeff*, about a schoolboy jewel thief, and then in 1939 he appeared with the American child star Mickey Rooney in *The Spirit of Culver*.

Bartholomew's star began to wane shortly after the release of *Tom Brown's Schooldays* and *The Swiss Family Robinson* in 1940. He was given progressively smaller parts in less good films, such as *Junior Army* (1943) and *The Town Went Wild* (1944)

In 1943 he joined the American Air Force and adopted American citizenship. But his career as a serviceman was short-lived; he was discharged on medical grounds after a year.

In 1946 he left the aunt who had devoted her life to him to marry his press agent, Maely Danielle. The marriage was dissolved some years later.

After the war he toured the United States in vaudeville, spent some time in Australia, working in a Sydney night club, and appeared in the films *Sepia Cinderella* (1947) and *St Benny the Dip* (1951).

But by then he had become attached to the rising new medium of television. He began by introducing commercials, but was soon attracted to the technical aspects of the work, and became a director.

Although he always said he enjoyed his Hollywood childhood – "All kids love dressing up, don't they?" – Bartholomew never allowed his early fame to cloud his later career. He always expressed astonishment when film buffs sought him out.

After the dissolution of his first marriage Bartholomew married, secondly, Mrs Aileen Paul, a television announcer. They had a daughter.

January 25 1992

FRANKIE HOWERD

FRANKIE HOWERD, the comedian who has died aged 70, was a master of the lubricious leer and the outraged double-take, and over the decades perfected a classic music-hall persona – genteel, portly and camp.

He sustained this character on the air, in pantomime and revue, as well as in *Carry On* films but he was perhaps best known as Pseudolus, the ingratiating and salacious slave in the long-running musical *A Funny Thing Happened on the Way to the Forum*. Howerd later played much the same character as Lurcio, in his television series *Up Pompeii!*, which was one of the most successful comedy shows of the 1970s.

With his Humpty-Dumpty appearance – shiny-apple

face, wig perched like a squashed dead stoat on top –
Howerd belonged body and soul to the variety stage. He
thrived on stream-of-consciousness patter; and his savour-
ing of the quirks and quiddities of language stemmed
from a conventional music hall concern for the intricacies
of speech.

With his gift for innuendo and suggestive bluster, he
contrived to raise the status of low comedy. He gave his
whole expressive personality over to the defence of propri-
ety, turning into something like an exasperated camel, the
mouth pouting and bursting with lugubrious disgust at
mankind's dirty-mindedness.

Like Max Miller, he seemed to disdain ribald humour
but could direct his audiences in such a way as to be able
later to reprove them for it. Congratulating himself that
they had got quite the wrong end of the stick, Howerd
would try to put them right with a growing sense of alarm
and panic. As the gales of laughter blew about him, he
would interrupt himself with desperate denials: "No,
missus, oooh, aahhh, I mean, the very idea. *No!*"

When Howerd was on a run, it seemed that nothing
could touch him. But, like all stock acts, his brand of
provocative indignation went in and out of fashion; and
beneath the bombastic exterior, he remained profoundly
susceptible to critical slights. Cripplingly nervous in his
youth, he later became prone to bouts of devilish
depression and never learned to weather the swing between
acclaim and rejection.

Such sensitivity could make for moments of poignantly
comic self-mockery. In 1990, when Howerd enjoyed one
of his many revivals, he embarked on an 18-month tour of
his show, *Frankie Howerd at his Tittermost*.

He told the audience that there would not be many

laughs, and regretfully explained his material was "the same old tired stuff".

"Imagine you're all on a coach outing," he advised. "It's the only way you'll find the evening bearable."

Francis Alix Howard (he later adopted the spelling Howerd) was born at York on March 6 1922, the son of a Royal Artillery sergeant and a Scottish mother. He lived at Eltham, south-east London, from the age of two, and won a scholarship to Shooters Hill Grammar School, Woolwich.

Young Francis's early ambition was to be a saint. He became interested in acting in his early teens as a result of an attempt to cure a stammer.

His Sunday school teacher offered him a part in the nativity play and he doggedly stuttered through his few lines. He was a surprise success. "The churchwarden said I should take up acting," Howerd remembered. "It was an electrifying moment for me. My fate was sealed."

Howerd said that from that moment he had a "sense of destiny, almost manic in its obsessive intensity". He joined every drama group he could and spent all his free time acting and putting on concert parties for charities.

As an adolescent his incorrigible stammering led him, in reaction to embarrassment, to say "the first thing, anything", that came into his head. He later maintained that his act developed as a means of coping with his painful shyness.

At 17, Howerd auditioned at RADA. In the audition room, clutching a packed lunch, he was told to read the soliloquy from *Hamlet*.

He was so scared his left leg started to tremble uncontrollably and continued to twitch throughout his speech. ("To be, or um, not to be, that's the, well that's the question isn't it?") Desperate to stop his leg "oscillating", Howerd hit his knee. He was still holding the packet of sandwiches.

"I was mortifed," he said. "The bag split and showered everyone with bread and cheese." Howerd was not accepted and was so depressed by his failure that he spent hours "sobbing in a field". He took the disaster as a sign from God that he was meant to be a comic.

Howerd started to work as a clerk, which he hated, and spent his days learning comedy scripts he had hidden in office files. In desperation he had changed his name to Ronnie Ordex and did a "turn" at Lewisham Hippodrome as a stand-up comic.

He recalled being in such an advanced state of nerves that when the spotlight hit him he was illuminated, "gaping and shaking and squinting", and retreated tearfully from the stage without saying a word.

The comedian repeatedly tried to join ENSA but to no avail. Instead he enlisted in the Army and became a sergeant in the Royal Artillery. Howerd recalled that he often went AWOL with a couple of friends so that they could perform concert party "turns" dressed as three ATS girls.

Their main problem was that they had no ATS uniforms. "We'd roam the streets looking for victimesses who'd fall for a sleazy line," Howerd remembered. "Then we'd charm the clothes off them and do the show while they stood shivering in toilets."

Despite Howerd's reputation as a *risqué* comedian, he did not smoke or drink and said that in his middle 20s he was still ignorant of "the facts of life".

After the war, Howerd was talent-spotted while giving a free show at the Stage Door Canteen in Piccadilly. He auditioned for Frank Bernard, but his pianist was taken ill and did not arrive. As a result Bernard kept him waiting for five hours.

Howered was, by this time, "hopeless and vengeful". He said his act was an "explosion of concentrated vituperation against Frank Bernard. I was venting years of disappointment, and there was Frank telling me I'd given a hoot of comic performance."

Howerd made his professional debut in *Just For The Fun Of It* at the Sheffiled Empire in 1946. He was billed as "Frankie Howerd The Borderline Case", at the bottom of the bill. From there, he went on to appear on the wireless programme *Variety Bandbox* doing a patter act with his "deaf" pianist, Mme Blanchie Moore.

In 1948 Howerd was top of the bill at the Palladium and earning £85 a week. He had employed Eric Sykes as a scriptwriter the previous year and maintained that his success had been due to Sykes's "surrealistic and superbly written" material.

During the 1950s, Howerd was a huge success: he continued to star on *Variety Bandbox* on the wireless and to appear in pantomime, usually as Simple Simon. In 1951, he co-starred with Eric Sykes and Hattie Jacques in *Fine Goings On* for the BBC.

After going to Korea to entertain the troops, he starred in his own television show, written by Sykes, Galton and Simpson. The comedian made his film debut as a courier in *The Runaway Bus* (1953), opposite Petula Clark and Margaret Rutherford. He went on to star in Bernard Delfont's topless revue *Pardon My French*, with Winifred Atwell, a contortionist, and the Four Congaroos ("an alarmingly energetic black dance group").

In 1957 he suffered a breakdown. In an ill-fated bid

to extend his range as a serious actor, Howerd next took up an opportunity to appear as Bottom in *A Midsummer Night's Dream*. Neither the critics nor the public could accept him in his new role.

In the hope of restoring his flagging popularity he returned to his old terrain, in *More Goings On*, alongside the successful Sykes/Jacques team. But this time the show flopped badly; as did *Further Up the Creek* in 1958.

Howerd then tried his hand at television, appearing in Molière's *School for Wives* for the BBC. The show was a disaster and, as Howerd recalled, "the sound of switched-off sets was like a thunderclap across the land".

He went on to suffer one of his most spectacular failures ever, in *Mr Venus* (1958), a surreal work about a visitor from another world, in which he played opposite Anton Diffring – dressed in "sequinned jock strap and a pair of wings".

By the time the show reached the Prince of Wales Theatre in London – it had opened at the Manchester Opera House – Howerd claimed he was "ready for the padded cell".

Howerd then tried once more, unsuccessfully, to salvage his reputation with a patter act at the Palladium, but described this act as "just plain lousy".

Between 1959 and 1963 he was again prone to depressions. At one stage he planned to give up show business and open a pub. It was a wretched time.

Then, in 1963, Howerd scored a sensational hit with a beautifully underplayed send-up of the "satire boom" as a surprise guest on Ned Sherrin's cult television revue *That Was The Week That Was*. Suddenly he was everybody's favourite comic again.

Morale almost entirely restored, Howerd took on a

part in the British version of the Sondheim musical *A Funny Thing Happened On The Way To The Forum*. It enjoyed great acclaim and Howerd found himself top of the bill for two years, until 1965.

Before taking the lead in *The Great St Trinian's Train Robbery* in that year, he appeared in *The Cool Mikado* (1960), which he described as "one of the worst films I have ever seen". At the beginning of the 1970s, Howerd appeared for the second time in a toga, on this occasion playing Lurcio in the BBC's *Up Pompeii!* (1971).

It was vintage Howerd: his asides, loaded with innuendo, were followed by howls of disgust that his "innocent remarks" should have been misinterpreted. The film version of *Up Pompeii!* was followed by *Up the Chastity Belt* and *Up the Front* (1972).

Throughout the 1970s Howerd appeared regularly on television, in shows such as *Howerd's History of England*, *Up the Convicts* (made for Australian TV) and *Frankie Howerd's Tittertime*.

But, towards the end of the decade, and despite having been voted TV Personality of the Year, as well as appointed OBE, Howerd's popularity began to wane once again.

The audience reaction to *A Touch of the Casanovas* (1976) was mixed, and he barely received any attention for his tiny part in *Sergeant Pepper's Lonely Hearts Club Band* (1976). His television show *Howerd Reveals All* (1981) was a flop.

Howerd spent five years suffering from lack of confidence, before, in 1985, his fortunes began to rise again. He took the part of Frosch, the drunken jailer, in *Die Fledermaus*.

He returned to the West End in a revival of *A Funny*

Thing Happened (1987). The second run was as successful as the first, and was well-timed, coming as it did after a re-screening of *Up Pompeii!* the previous year.

His career latterly expanded to include "singing seriously in operas" in 1988, when he appeared as Sir Joseph Porter in *HMS Pinafore*, and as the amorous Judge in *Trial by Jury*.

Howerd never married, but he once revealed that he had had an affair with Joan Greenwood and had been in love with her all his life. "I had planned to ask her to marry me," Howerd remembered, "but she met somebody else." After her marriage to the actor André Morell, Howerd never saw her but said he was "devastated" by her death in 1987.

April 20 1992

BENNY HILL

BENNY HILL, who has died aged 67, was not merely Britain's, but the world's most popular comedian – the star of television shows which were screened in more than 100 countries and achieved audiences that even Charlie Chaplin never matched.

In America, where Tony Hancock and Morecambe and Wise made little impression, Benny Hill was a success from the moment in 1976 when Thames Television put out his programmes in New York. The secret of his appeal across the Atlantic, he reckoned, was that he made no special effort to appeal to Americans.

By 1985 not a single day would pass without *The Benny Hill Show* being screened somewhere in America, and many stations would broadcast the programme twice a night. At San José penitentiary the prisoners threatened mayhem unless they were allowed to watch him.

Hill's American earnings in the mid-1980s amounted to $5 million a year, and he was just as popular in Europe, especially in France and Italy. Indeed, his fans multiplied in countries as disparate as Cuba, Israel, China and Japan. The Russians pointed their television aerials towards Finland to pick up his show – until, under the dispensations of *glasnost*, they were allowed to receive the programme on their own network.

This worldwide response might suggest that Benny Hill's humour was essentially visual. And it was true, as he himself observed, that "I can get my face slapped in six different languages".

Yet his stock-in-trade was the lubricious *double entendre*, and his mind was concentrated upon the essentially British obsession with knickers, bosoms and bottoms, and with the faithless wives and feeble husbands to whom these impedimenta belonged. It was the world that Donald McGill had created in his seaside postcards.

Inevitably the formula aroused the hostility of the sexually correct. But the whole point about Benny Hill was that, even as he was chased all over the set by erotically dressed and nubile girls – "Hills Angels" as they were known – he contrived by his very ridiculousness to strip lust of its fury and menace.

"King Leer", accoutred in his baggy football shorts, was more of a soiled cherub than a sexual demon, a promoter of pranks rather than a purveyor of evil. The impression was reinforced by the round schoolboy's face, by the good-humoured twinkle in the eye, by the sly and collusive smirk, and by a voice which combined outrageous innuendo with yokel idiocy.

Hill would point out, a trifle disingenuously perhaps, that it was the men who came off worst in his sketches, as in real life. They appeared as complete idiots. By comparison, the girls retained their dignity.

Nevertheless, in 1986 Ben Elton took the trouble to inform the world that he could see nothing funny in a little old man running after girls. Hill, who always insisted that he was *chased* (if not chaste), ignored this offering.

The truth was that his undeniable predilection for smut obscured his considerable comic range. Only when Hal Roach – a former producer of Laurel and Hardy, who had described Hill as the only modern comedian to rival the greats of the past – expressed concern about his salaciousness did Hill make some attempt to clean up his act – cutting down both the number of dancing girls and the depth of their cleavage.

All to no avail. In 1988 the Broadcasting Standards Council denounced the shows as "increasingly offensive", and the next year the head of light entertainment at Thames Television cancelled Hill's conract.

But Hill did not mean to give up his show after a mere 34 years. Describing the decision as a blessing in disguise – "one gets complacent" – he negotiated a lucrative contract to make a new series in New York.

And by December 1991, when he was the subject of an *Omnibus* programme, English television producers were again eager to lure him back. Thames Television, meanwhile, had lost its franchise.

Benny Hill was born Alfred Hawthorn Hill at Shirley,

a suburb of Southampton, on January 21 1925. His grandfather had been with Bertram Mills Circus and his father had shown similar inclinations before abandoning the Big Top to become a surgical appliance outfitter. Alas, to young Alfred's schoolfellows it was only too evident that "Hillie's Dad sells Frenchies".

The boy was educated at Taunton Grammar School in Southampton, where his academic career was undistinguished – although the English master, Horace King, later Speaker of the House of Commons, apparently recognised his comic potential.

At any rate, while still at school young Hill joined Bobbie's Concert Party, a semi-professional group which put on lunchtime shows. After leaving school at 15, he took a number of casual jobs, including that of milkman.

He would drive his horse and cart round Southampton indulging the fantasy that it was Dodge City. This experience would bear fruit many years later, in 1971, with the No 1 hit record *Ernie* – "the fastest milkman in the West".

From the age of 13 Hill had been working in pubs during the evenings, telling jokes after the style of his hero Max Miller. At 17 he left Southampton for London, where he worked backstage on various revues and slept rough on Streatham Common, before the military police claimed him for the Army.

Hill began his military career as a driver mechanic, but was soon transferred to Combined Services Entertainment. To begin with he called himself Alf Hill, but "that sounded too much like a Cockney turn. So I changed it to Leslie Hill, only that seemed more like a cocktail pianist. Eventually, being an admirer of Jack Benny, I took his name."

After demobilisation Benny Hill played in working men's clubs, and teamed up with Alfred Marks for *Starlight Hour* on the BBC Light programme. But times were hard. In 1951 he could only find work as second comic and "feed" to Reg Varney, a role for which he competed with Peter Sellers. Varney insisted that Hill should stick to being a straight man or leave – so the job only lasted seven weeks.

Unemployed, Hill began writing comedy sketches for television. By 1954 he was enjoying considerable success as the compere of *Showcase*, a programme designed to give opportunities to new talent; and Ronnie Waldman, head of Light Entertainment at the BBC, gave him his chance in his own television show.

Benny Hill was the first great comic star to be made by television – previously comedians had transferred to the medium after success on the boards or the wireless. But the format which he created for his programmes owed something to his early ambition to be the principal comic in a touring revue – the kind of outfit which boasted its complement of girls, a juggler perhaps, and a straight man who doubled as the baritone.

And Hill's stage apprenticeship was reflected in his concern for every detail of his television shows, for which he wrote both the text and the music. For years his principal helpmeets were Henry McGee, a conventional straight "feed", the beaming, balding, gurgling comic actor Bob Todd and the irrepressible Patricia Hayes.

Hill himself built up a stock of characters. His favourite was Mervyn Twit, as camp as his creator. The best known was the bespectacled and blinking Fred Scuttle, a poor fool dressed in various shreds of authority.

Before the 1970s *The Benny Hill Show*'s popularity was

mainly confined to Britain. By the end of the 1950s Hill was a star turn at the Royal Variety Show, and in 1966 the Variety Club of Great Britain named him as the top television personality.

The year before there had been a hint of things to come when the show made a hit at the Montreux Festival – though without carrying off any of the prizes.

In the first flush of his success Hill showed no inclination to abandon the theatre. In 1955 he appeared with devastating effect in the revue *Paris by Night*; next year he took over the lead in *The Dave King Show*; and in 1959 he brought the house down in the musical romp *Fine Fettle* at the Palace Theatre.

He even, like Frankie Howerd, tackled Shakespeare, offering a well-rounded Bottom in a BBC television production of *A Midsummer Night's Dream* (1964).

Benny Hill also gave some notable performances in films, playing an officious fireman in *Those Magnificent Men in Their Flying Machines* (1965) and Prof Simon Peach, a computer expert with a weakness for amply upholstered women of a certain age in *The Italian Job* (1969). His other credits included *Chitty Chitty Bang Bang* (1968) and *The Best of Benny Hill* (1974).

Most of Hill's early television work was done for the BBC, with occasional excursions to Associated Television. In 1969 he signed a contract with Thames Television which set him on course for worldwide fame.

But his huge earnings never changed his way of life. "I don't covet images or belongings", he explained. "My television set and video are rented, my paintings aren't worth a fortune and money is of little interest."

Indeed, Hill could have earned far more than he did. He only worked for pleasure or to avoid loneliness, and turned down millions of dollars to do live shows at Las Vegas. He did the odd commercial, though, especially if it involved going abroad.

Travel, indeed, was Hill's only lasting passion, and with his fluent French and competent Spanish and German he was well equipped. He was particularly fond of Marseilles, where he would stay at the Hotel Splendide and sally forth on 20-mile walks, returning with ideas for future shows jotted down on the back of an envelope.

Oherwise Hill remained frugal to the point of eccentricity. He kept his parents' semi-detached house in Southampton, and employed buckets to catch the drops from the leaking roof when he spent Christmas there.

In London he lived in flats where chaos reigned and visitors were not encouraged. A flat in Teddington was acquired for its proximity to the Thames studios.

Hill's other recreations were watching television, listening to the wireless, and writing. He was also a keen boxing fan. Occasionally he would go shopping, carrying plastic bags stuffed with notes – although all he really wanted, he claimed, was "a roof, three meals a day, a passport, an aircraft ticket and a spare shirt".

He manifested a penchant for young working-class girls – "I get a kick out of taking them to places they would not normally visit", he explained. Educated and intellectual women he avoided like the plague, and matrimony made no appeal.

He had proposed once, he said, at the age of 23, but had been turned down. "Secretly I was relieved", he recorded. "It was like watching your mother-in-law driving your new car over the cliff edge. You have mixed feelings about it."

This disposition never changed. "I have a mental age

of about 17", he remarked in 1990. "Far too young for marriage."

April 22 1992

'AUNT JENNIE' WILSON

"AUNT JENNIE" WILSON, the banjo player and story-teller who has died at Logan, West Virginia, aged 92, played a major part in the preservation of the Appalachian folk tradition at a time when its survival seemed threatened by the twin challenges of popular entertainment and emigration.

The South Appalachian region, which covers 10,000 square miles, was largely settled by English and Scots-Irish immigrants. The inhabitants, cut off for many generations from the major east-coast centres and from waves of new ethnic arrivals, were able to preserve in almost pristine form the ballads of 17th, 18th and 19th century England, long after they had gone out of fashion in the mother country.

These include such tunes as "Barbara Allen", which Samuel Pepys records being sung by a Mrs Kipps in 1666 and which was subsequently printed in *Ramsay's Teatable Miscellany* (1724); "Sir Hugh", in which an innocent gentle boy is lured to his death by a Jew's daughter – altered to "The Duke's Daughter" in an early example of American political correctness; and "Cripple Creek", with the refrain "Somerset girls, don't you want to go to town?"

The Appalachian tradition also embraced home-grown songs, renowned for their fatalism and focus upon themes murderous. Notable among these is "John Henry" – the tale of a black superman who kills himself in his victorious quest to prove the superiority of man over machine. The "Dingy Town of Logan on the Banks of the Guyan", written by one of Aunt Jennie's numerous cousins, became one of America's minor treasures of the "jailhouse lament" tradition.

These tunes were among the few diversions on offer to the poor rural community of Logan County, into which Virginia Myrtle Wilson was born on February 9 1900.

The youngest of 11 children of Huey "Dock" Ellis and his wife, Cinderella, she rapidly lived up to the local claim that "there never was an Ellis that couldn't play a fiddle".

It was a time, she recalled, when "only loose women played music"; her brothers taught her how to play the banjo all the same.

By the time she left Henlawson Public School, at the age of 14, Jennie and her siblings were in great demand as a performing troupe. They played at weddings and at square dances.

These were often dramatic occasions, reflecting the lurid subject matter of her songs. During one event Aunt Jennie, reproved by a woman for dancing with her boyfriend, responded by lopping off a portion of her rival's bosom.

Following her marriage to J. D. Wilson, a miner, in 1918, Aunt Jennie became absorbed with the task of bringing up a family in the midst of West Virginia's brutal mining wars between the companies and the unions. In the pre-union days, miners earned a mere five cents per ton. "Nobody had hobbies back then," she recalled. "They just worked so hard they didn't feel like it."

Following the death of her husband in a mining accident in 1939, Aunt Jennie worked as a washerwoman.

Unable to afford a banjo, she was obliged to abandon her music.

It was only in 1955 – when, quite by chance, she came to the attention of a professor of Appalachian culture at West Virginia University – that Aunt Jennie resumed playing. At first she doubted whether she could even remember how to tune a "banjer"; eventually she was to recall more than 300 folk tunes of her childhood.

This was of particular importance because the advent of radio and television had popularised the "hillbilly style" – the forerunner of modern country and western – thereby almost erasing the purer Appalachian tradition. Aunt Jennie soon became a firm favourite at the West Virginia State Folk Festival and at the Arts and Crafts Fair at the Cedar Lakes, where she would play alongside the then majority leader of the US Senate, Robert Byrd – himself a champion fiddler.

But Aunt Jennie's knowledge did not always match her reverence for Appalachian tradition. One of her songs concerned Northumberland and when asked where that was, she replied: "I don't know. It may be down in [neighbouring] Mingo County."

Such was her authenticity, though, that Billy Edd Wheeler, one of the foremost songwriters of modern country and western music, requested that she record her songs, lest they be lost to posterity. An album, *A Portrait of Aunt Jennie Wilson*, was produced in 1965.

But she had no desire for stardom. When Dolly Parton expressed an interest in making Aunt Jennie's acquaintance, she found no response. Another of Aunt Jennie's numerous cousins wryly commented: "I figure all she [Parton] wanted to do was to steal one of Jennie's songs."

Nor did Aunt Jennie have a much higher opinion of

contemporary fashion. She branded the Beatles as "mop-heads" and berated them for having brought drugs, men's earrings and mini-skirts into America. She also took a dim view of women's liberation and used to recall that as a girl she always carried a gun and "took care of myself real good".

In 1986, Aunt Jennie was given the Vandalia Award, West Virginia's highest honour for contributions to Appalachian culture. This included not just music, but also patchwork quilts and storytelling – she had the details of every local murder of the past 100 years at her fingertips.

Garrison Keillor has described the folk revival as consisting of musicians who play "to flaming self-conscious radicals with poofy hair and tie-dyed bib overalls in some wealthy radical's back yard to raise money for hearing-impaired Lutheran lesbian farmers united against war and racism". Nothing could have been less true of Aunt Jennie, who embodied the folk character and was a genuine link to Britain's – as well as America's – past.

May 2 1992

JOAN SANDERSON

JOAN SANDERSON, who has died aged 79, was a redoubtable character actress with an unrivalled line in dragonish dowagers, stuck-up spinsters and suburban matrons.

She was best known on television for her performance in the long-running comedy series *Please, Sir!* as the sharp-tongued Doris Ewell, assistant head-teacher at the unruly Fenn Street Secondary School. Underneath her alarming spectacles, however, the domineering Miss Ewell nursed an unrequited passion for the dithering head, who seemed to prefer watering his plants.

Latterly she was seen in a more sympathetic, if not so funny, role as the no-nonsense live-in grandmother in the series *After Henry* with Prunella Scales.

Joan Sanderson's formidable presence on screen and stage ensured that the maximum benefit would be derived from every line (she had teaching diplomas in elocution) and gesture. As the Dean's wife in *All Gas and Gaiters*, Miss Sanderson suggested by the merest wrinkle of a nostril a tradition of Anglican disapproval.

Several television classics were enriched by her cameos, which included the virago in *Upstairs, Downstairs* who tempts the wretched kitchen-maid Ruby away from the ample bosom of Mrs Bridges in Eaton Place to the suburbs, where she exploits her mercilessly; and the bossy seaside landlady in Michael Palin's *East of Ipswich*.

She was unforgettable as the cantankerous gorgon Mrs Richards in *Fawlty Towers*, who enrages the proprietor by refusing to turn on her hearing aid – "It wears out the batteries."

In the theatre Miss Sanderson achieved her apotheosis as Delia, Lady Rumpers, in Alan Bennett's sparkling farce *Habeas Corpus* (Lyric 1973). From the moment she made her entrance – sweeping Patricia Hayes's charlady imperiously aside with the command "Out of my way, you pert slut" – Miss Sanderson dominated the stage.

Seldom can lines have been delivered with such relish, whether Lady Rumpers was recalling how her husband had gone into the Army only "to put his moustache to good purpose", or a wartime lover glimpsed by "the fitful light of a post-coital Craven A".

Joan Sanderson was born at Bristol on November 24

1912 and educated at Northumberland House and RADA. She made her professional debut at Stratford in 1939.

During the Second World War she gained experience in repertory and toured North Africa and Italy entertaining the troops. Afterwards she made her first West End appearance in the clerical farce *See How They Run*.

In 1948 she showed her versatility by playing both an Ugly Sister in *Cinderella* and Martha in Goethe's *Faust*.

Ten years later she appeared in *Simple Spymen* with Brian Rix at the Whitehall, where she was later to score another hit in John Wells's *Anyone for Denis?* as the custodian of Chequers, attired in admiral's uniform and given to announcing: "It was never like this in Audrey Callaghan's time."

Although Miss Sanderson was a superlative *farceur* – playing her haughtiness absolutely straight – discerning theatregoers regretted that she was not given more opportunities to tackle meatier roles. Her Goneril to Michael Redgrave's Lear at Stratford in 1953 was hailed by W. A. Darlington of *The Daily Telegraph* as "implacable, detestable".

In 1976 she managed to stand her ground opposite Robert Morley in the revival of Ben Travers's *Banana Ridge* at the Savoy; earlier in the 1970s she appeared in *Popkiss*, a musical version of Travers's *Rookery Nook*.

Her cinema credits included *Prick Up Your Ears* and a reprise of Miss Ewell in the film version of *Please, Sir!* "She is fair-minded and has a sense of humour," she loyally said of her best-known character, "despite being a so-and-so."

She married, in 1948, Gregory Moseley, a fellow actor.

May 27 1992

SUN BEAR

SUN BEAR, the founder and spiritual leader of the Bear Tribe, who has died at Spokane, Washington, aged 62, was one of America's first "New Age" Indian chieftains.

To his admirers, Sun Bear was a visionary who managed to achieve a synthesis between New Age and native American traditions. From his 100-acre estate by Vision Mountain in Washington State, Sun Bear dispensed a rich *bouillabaisse* of Hopi religious rites, "pop" ecology and Aquarian balm. The core of his philosophy was to teach others to "walk in balance with the Earth Mother". But Indian traditionalists suggested that the only balances that really concerned him were to be found in a string of bank accounts across America.

Yet Sun Bear – who in his younger days achieved notoriety as a gambler at Reno, Nevada – was unruffled by such accusations. Describing money as "green energy", he declared: "If the Great Spirit wants me to win at craps or keno, I figure who am I to turn down the opportunity?"

He was born Vince Laduke at the White Earth Indian Reservation in Minnesota in 1929. The name of "Sun Bear" was derived from a childhood vision of a large black bear sheathed in a vivid array of rainbow colours. The bear looked steadfastly at young Vince, stood on his hind legs and gently touched him on his head.

He learned native medicine ways from his Chippewa relations, but left the reservation aged 15 and did not practise the Medicine Path for another decade. Instead, Sun Bear – who spent much of the 1950s dodging the FBI after refusing to serve in the US Army in Korea – drifted across the country in search of employment. He landscaped cemeteries, taught journalism and sold real estate.

Sun Bear then spent 10 years in Hollywood, where, blessed with a "noble savage" look, he landed bit parts in such television shows as *Bonanza* and *Brave Eagle*. Subsequently, he worked for the Inter-Tribal Council of Nevada as an economic development specialist.

He ascribed his successes at the roulette table to the Great Spirit, who imparted his or her theories of gaming probability through a series of psychic dreams.

Later, Sun Bear assisted a Native Studies programme at the University of California at Davis, where he began to develop his powers of hypnotic charm. Combining this new-found skill with his handsome winnings, he left in 1970 to found the Bear Tribe.

This was initially based at Placerville, California, but soon moved to Spokane – where, amid the luxuriant evergreens, Sun Bear continued to develop his blend of spirituality. According to Sun Bear, only those who lived in holistic harmony with nature were destined to survive the coming "Cleansing" and he created a self-sufficient community with its own crops and livestock.

Sun Bear laboured in relative obscurity until Marlise James, a graduate of Columbia University's School of Journalism, joined the tribe in 1974. She changed her name to Wabun Wind, and set about transforming Sun Bear into a guru of the white counter-culture.

Sun Bear's books became bestsellers: *The Medicine Wheel* (dedicated, *inter alios*, to Thunderbird Woman, and completed with generous assistance from Adolf Hungry Wolf), was an astrological guide that sold more than half a million copies. Other commercial successes included the tribe's ceremonial pipes, which fetched anything up to

$150, and the quarterly Medicine Wheel gatherings, attended each year by 10,000 paying guests.

Sun Bear himself claimed only to draw a $50 monthly allowance, but he could none the less be found travelling for 40 weeks of the year. Many women joined the Bear Tribe to be his "special lady", only to find themselves part of a harem. Sun Bear could be found wandering around at night with a flashlight, visiting selected tents. "I've shared my energy," he said, "with a lot of women."

Mainstream Indian organisations, such as the Traditional Circle of Elders, took a dim view of Sun Bear's relentless proselytising among Caucasians, and were especially critical of his sale of religious artefacts – and of his habit of delaying sacred pipe ceremonies until the arrival of television crews.

Despite the substantial volume of published material, much of Sun Bear's philosophy remained vague – though he could be a fount of practical advice. For example, he rebuked an Indian friend for blaming a flat tyre on "bad medicine": "No, it's not bad medicine, brother. Look at the tyre – it's worn out because you were too stupid to change it."

In Sun Bear's last book, *Black Dawn, Bright Day*, he returned to the survivalist theme of his earlier work. He prepared a check-list for healing the earth, which included such vows as "I will stop flushing my toilet by so much each day".

He foresaw that plagues and floods would afflict much of the world, and offered pithy counsel on where, and where not, to go when the Cleansing came. "North Idaho is a good area," he said.

Sun Bear was not optimistic about the British Isles: he anticipated political unrest in the wake of tidal waves, although "sections of Scotland, Ireland and Wales, where people remember how to work the land, will fare better than other parts of this area".

September 1 1992

DENHOLM ELLIOTT

DENHOLM ELLIOTT, the actor, who has died aged 70, was one of the postwar cinema's most subtle exponents of inner turmoil, clenched anguish and well-bred rascality.

With his singularly well-mapped face – twitchy, cratered, ringed, robustly veined – he specialised in ageing rakes, sexual eccentrics, self-effacing neurotics, cowardly warriors, wine snobs, seducers, cads and con-men.

Elliott had begun his acting career by promising great things on the stage. Indeed he was once named as being among the most likely young men to inherit the mantles of Olivier or Gielgud in the classical theatre. Yet for some reason he never became a major star.

Initially he tended to be cast as a decent young chap, but there was more to him than showed on the surface. Off stage he could be distant, morose, retiring, moody – a complex character with a history of neuroses.

Eventually he settled for secondary roles in films on the grounds that they offered more regular and more varied work. Whether his talent would have risen, if called upon, to the great dramatic heights – and it did so once when he played Strindberg's *The Father* at the Open Space in 1979 – it is certain that the kind of taut quietness, wry insight and polished comedy he gave to his collection of grimacing losers and layabouts showed uncommon insight.

If he was a better actor than his "character" casting in films allowed, Elliott brought to every role, big or small, an acute sensitivity, precision of observation and ironical edge. He contrived to make each portrait touching as well as compelling, even when it verged on caricature.

"I'd rather stay in the second line," he once said. "As a character actor you get interesting parts and can be in a good position to steal the film." Certainly his cameos, however brief, would sometimes stick in the memory long after the stars had been forgotten.

Denholm Mitchell Elliott was born in London on May 31 1922 into a legal dynasty. He was educated at Malvern, which he loathed. "I used to nick things," he recalled.

One of what was to become a series of psychoanalysts suggested that young Denholm should try for the Royal Academy of Dramatic Art, in the cause of self-expression. Although at the time he enjoyed it little more than Malvern, Elliott later recalled that he never considered any career other than acting. It was, he said, like dressing up for Mummy and Daddy.

During the Second World War, Elliott served with the RAF as a radio operator and gunner with Bomber Command. He was shot down over Denmark in 1942. For the next three years, as a prisoner of war in Silesia, he developed his passion for acting, forming a drama group called the No Name Players.

Back home Elliott went straight into repertory. The next year he made his mark in the West End in *The Guinea Pig*, a play about the difficulties of a state scholar at a public school.

Soon Elliott came to the attention of Laurence Olivier, who cast him as his son in Christopher Fry's *Venus Observed* at the old St James's Theatre. Elliott learned a trick or two from the great actor and won the Clarence Derwent Award for best supporting performance of the year. Elliott went on to enjoy success in New York in Jean Anouilh's *Ring Round the Moon*.

Meanwhile, Elliott was forging a career in the cinema. He had made his debut in *Dear Mr Prohack* (1949) and earned favourable notices for his performances as the nervous young flyer in *The Sound Barrier* and as a naval officer in the popular film of Nicholas Monsarrat's novel *The Cruel Sea*.

But, apart from a notable stage appearance in T. S. Eliot's *The Confidential Clerk* at the Lyric, the second half of the 1950s proved to be rather a lean period for Elliott. His clean-cut, upper middle-class persona did not chime in with the era of the "kitchen sink".

In 1960 a season at Stratford-upon-Avon gave Elliott neither pleasure nor satisfaction, though he subsequently enjoyed playing in Arthur Miller's *The Crucible* in New York. By 1964 his career was distinctly in the doldrums.

But that year he scored an unexpected hit in the film *Nothing But the Best*, with a witty script by Frederic Raphael.

Elliott played, with endearing elan, a world-weary man-about-town advising Alan Bates on how to bluff his way in society. At a stroke, Elliott's image as a matinée idol *manqué* was banished for ever. From then on he was in constant demand for meaty character roles.

He played a seedy abortionist in *Alfie*, a corrupt PoW in *King Rat*, a Swinging Sixties Dad in *Here We Go Round the Mulberry Bush*, a moral zealot who closes the burlesque joint down in *The Night They Raided Minskys*, a platoon leader in *Too Late The Hero*; and a drunken director reduced to filming bar mitzvahs in *The Apprenticeship of Duddy Kravitz*.

By the 1980s, firmly established as a supremely dependable character actor, he found himself more than ever in demand. As he himself put it, the heavy lines now marking his face enabled him to switch from saving many a mediocre film to playing challenging roles in films of real quality.

In Alan Bennett's *A Private Function* he was a devious Northern burgher bent on guzzling unrationed pork; in *Defence of the Realm* he gave a haunting study of a drunk and suicidally disillusioned investigative journalist; and his zesty portrayal of the cheerily upstart Mr Emerson was one of the best things in the much-praised Merchant–Ivory film of *A Room With A View*. He cropped up again in the same team's film of another E. M. Forster novel, *Maurice*.

Among his outstanding later roles were an appalling, if oddly engaging, drunk in *Chilling Dad*, leching after the young Anna Chancellor; a doctor who rescues Jews from the Nazis in *Hanna's War*; and yet more winning cameos in Woody Allen's *September*, the box-office smash hit *Indiana Jones and the Last Crusade* and *Noises Off*.

Television afforded another ideal medium for Elliott's restrained style of acting. He was a memorably stylish, if flawed, "blood" in Frederic Raphael's ingenious *School Play*, in which adults played public schoolboys.

In an adaptation of Anita Brookner's *Hotel du Lac* Elliott played to perfection a sleazy, hollow character – a type he himself maintained would set casting directors to think, "That's Denholm".

In 1981 he won an award for his performance in *Blade on the Feather* by Dennis Potter, who once likened the actor to someone presiding over his own court martial — both judge and accused. Elliott also played the guilt-ridden father in the film of Potter's *Brimstone And Treacle* (1982).

And last year he gave a subtly mousey interpretation of George Smiley in John le Carré's *A Murder of Quality* opposite Glenda Jackson, for Thames Television.

Despite his busy career on the big and small screens, Elliott never abandoned the theatre. In 1970 he scored a hit in John Mortimer's study of sexual quirks in *Come As You Are* (Albery and Strand). His silken, satanic Judge Brack to Jill Bennett's *Hedda Gabler* (Royal Court, 1972) in John Osborne's version of Ibsen's play also won high praise.

Other stage roles in the 1970s included Dick, the paediatrician, in Peter Nichols's comedy about English exiles in the Dordogne, *Chez Nous* (Globe, 1974); the title role in Graham Greene's *The Return of A. J. Raffles* (with the Royal Shakespeare Company at the Aldwych, 1975); and the veteran actor in David Mamet's well-observed two-hander *A Life In The Theatre*, with Samuel West (Haymarket, 1989).

In his private life, which was far from straightforward, Denholm Elliott had many friends outside his own profession. He liked to travel, observing others and guessing at their lives.

Elliott never took his career as seriously, perhaps, as his admirers might have wished. But he admitted to taking a serious interest in neurotics. The cause of his death was reported to be Aids-related tuberculosis.

Elliott was appointed CBE in 1988. He married first,

in 1954 (dissolved 1957), Virginia McKenna, the actress. He married secondly, in 1962, Susan Robinson, an American actress; they had a son and a daughter.

October 7 1992

JOE MITCHENSON

JOE MITCHENSON, the theatre historian, who has died aged 81, assembled with his partner, the late Raymond Mander, probably the most comprehensive collection of material relating to the theatre ever known in Britain.

The Mander and Mitchenson Collection has endowed theatre practitioners, writers, journalists, publishers and film and television companies for more than half a century. The collection was enormously enhanced by the knowledge and dedication of its only begetters – two former actors universally known as "the Boys" – whose personalities and approaches were highly complementary.

Joe Mitchenson – a tall, kindly man with the slightly abstracted air of a Victorian poet – was, above all, the intermediary in their campaign, offsetting the thrusting character of his ally Raymond Mander (who died in 1983) by his own diplomatic and endearing nature.

Francis Joseph Blackett Mitchenson was born on October 4 1911, and educated privately. As a boy he built tiny model theatres from cardboard and glue, and lovingly catalogued a series of theatrical postcards his mother had collected in her youth.

Young Joe trained for the stage at the Fay Compton Studio of Dramatic Art. He made his first professional appearance in 1934 at the Playhouse, London, in a play called *Libel*.

He acted in repertory and on tour, and in 1939 met Mander while they were appearing together in *The Merry Wives of Windsor*. That same year they founded their Theatre Collection.

During the Second World War Mitchenson served in the Royal Horse Artillery until being invalided out in 1943. He then resumed his acting career, at the same time collaborating with Mander on many wireless programmes about the theatre.

After the war the two concentrated on their collection, which was housed in Mitchenson's terraced house in Venner Road, Sydenham. Here the Victorian theatre, which both particularly relished, was omnipresent, and even the smallest room bore a brass plate, proclaiming "Miss Tempest", and acquired from that *grande dame*'s dressing-room.

Tea was taken standing up, and visitors found themselves dazzled by the theatrical treasure-trove – if decidedly stiff behind the knees. The collection grew to embrace folios, play-bills, prompt-books, periodicals, gramophone records, photographs, theatrical china (including a Bloor Derby Garrick), paintings, drawings and designs, and costumes of genuine historical interest, including Irving's Wolsey robes.

"The Boys" were always on their guard against dubious relics. "We had an enquiry from an American," recalled Mitchenson, "who said somebody had sold him one of Edmund Kean's fly-buttons, and did we think it was genuine?"

The collection was augmented by gifts from the private collections of many leading figures in the theatre, such as the Terrys, Dames Edith Evans and Sybil Thorndike (who observed that "the *Boys* are our passport to posterity") and Sir John Gielgud.

In 1977, after the overflowing house in Sydenham had survived a threat of demolition by the local authority, the collection was established as a trust, with a governing body of distinguished theatrical devotees, and bequeathed to the nation. Seven years later Lewisham Council gave it a home in Beckenham Place Park.

Besides assisting many writers on theatrical subjects, the two discerning magpies were responsible for numerous books, several of them in collaboration with the late J. C. Trewin. Among the most widely read were *The Theatres of London* (1961), which found considerable popularity in paperback; *The Lost Theatres of London* (1968), an impressive excavation of vanished playhouses from the Victorian age; *A Pictorial History of Gilbert and Sullivan* (1962); and *British Music Hall: A Story in Pictures* (1965).

The most comprehensive of their compilations were three *Theatrical Companions* to the work of leading British playwrights of the early 20th century: Shaw (1954); Maugham (1955); and Coward (1957). Somerset Maugham encouraged them to undertake an account of his collection of theatrical pictures (bequeathed to the National Theatre), and Sir Terence Rattigan wrote an appreciation of Coward for them.

Sir Noël Coward himself (who dubbed them "Gog and Magog") described their work as "accomplished with consummate skill and accuracy. Whatever information or illustrations are required, from Mrs Bracegirdle and earlier, to Tuesday Weld and later, they will produce in a trice. The best compliment I can pay them is that we all turn to them and their famous collection when in trouble. And they never fail us."

Mander and Mitchenson were dedicated "first-nighters", and with their distinctive costuming could be described as much a part of the traditional first night as the Galleryites and the free programmes. They were also devotees of the Players Theatre, underneath the arches of Charing Cross, and added greatly by their idiosyncratic style to the essentially Victorian atmosphere – artificial but never affected – of that high-spirited audience.

As the star-studded gathering at the Players Theatre on his 80th birthday proclaimed, Joe Mitchenson was every theatre-lover's friend.

October 8 1992

HAL ROACH

HAL ROACH, who has died in Los Angeles aged 100, was the last surviving giant of the silent film industry, responsible for the discovery of such legendary figures in screen buffoonery as Harold Lloyd and Laurel and Hardy.

Rotund and dapper, until the end of his long life Roach retained the appearance of a Hollywood mogul of the old school. He made more than 1,000 comic "shorts", most of them two-reelers, including a number of early "talkies". In the mid-1930s he gradually shifted to feature production and went on to make such films as *Of Mice and Men* (1939) and the *Topper* series.

Hal Roach was born at Elmira, New York, on January 14 1892. His career began in picaresque style when he ran away from home at the age of 17. He walked and hitch-hiked to Seattle, where he was taken in by a kindly aunt and found a job selling ice-cream.

His ambitions were modest enough: "I thought I'd stay out West for a year, hitch-hike back to Elmira, become an engineer, marry a local girl, and live there for the rest of my life."

Before the year was out, however, he had made his way to Alaska, where he spent several months running mule trains and prospecting – unsuccessfully – for gold. He then moved on to California, where he worked first as a truck driver in Los Angeles and then on a construction site in the Mojave Desert before stumbling into the film business.

Roach appeared as a cowboy extra for Bison Films for a dollar a day, and spent the next two years as a bit player in countless one-reelers. In 1914, while working as a stunt man and odd-jobber at Universal Studios, he met Harold Lloyd, another struggling nobody.

Roach decided that he could make Lloyd a great comedian and in 1915, after inheriting $3,000, he formed his own company and hired his friend to play a character called Willie Work in a series of comedy shorts.

But Roach failed to sell his films, and when his money ran out he went to work for Essanay as a director, while Lloyd tried his luck at Mack Sennett's Keystone. Roach soon found a sponsor and distributor in Pathé, however, and formed the Rolin Film Company.

Lloyd was re-hired and given the new screen character of "Lonesome Luke" – together with a pair of round, glassless spectacles. The ensuing *Phun-Philms* series was a great success and turned Lloyd from a Chaplin imitator into a comedy star in his own right.

Roach and Lloyd enjoyed a remarkably happy partnership, and stumbled on their best ideas accidentally. The classic *Safety Last* (1923), for instance, in which Lloyd performed a number of extraordinary stunts, was conceived by Roach after a film was wrongly developed so that Lloyd appeared to be dangling from a building in Los Angeles.

Generally, however, the Roach comedy formula emphasised story and structure over visual gags. The result was that Roach prospered as cinema audiences grew more sophisticated in the 1920s and 1930s, while his rival, Sennett, declined.

In 1921 Roach initiated the *Our Gang* comedy series, inspired by the sight from his studio window of a group of quarrelling schoolchildren. Using young players such as Mickey Rooney, Mickey Daniels and Jackie Cooper, the series was a runaway success and lasted until 1939.

By the mid-1920s Roach was devoting less of his time to directing and more to the administration of his growing company – although he continued to contribute to the scripts of many of his films. His stable of talent rapidly expanded to include such comedy stars as Harry "Snub" Pollard, Will Rogers, Charlie Chase and Max Davidson.

His most inspired move was to bring together an English comedian named Stanley Jefferson (who changed his name to Laurel) with a "good ole boy" from Georgia named Oliver Hardy. Roach had first come across Jefferson playing the vaudeville circuit in downtown Los Angeles, and immediately signed him up.

But after discovering that "his eyes didn't photograph good" Roach made "Stan" a writer and forgot about him. When some superior film stock came in the Englishman was photographed again – "And his eyes looked all right. So we tried him."

He already had Hardy on contract. "When we saw the two of them working together – a little Englishman and a real fat Southern heavy – we decided that they just might make a team. It was another one of those lucky hunches that made me a lot of money."

Putting Pants on Philip (1927) was the first successful Laurel and Hardy film, followed by about one a month for the next three years. Notable among these were *The Battle of the Century* (1927), *Liberty* (1929) and *The Laurel-Hardy Murder Case* (1930). The partnership continued until the late 1930s, with Roach directing such classics as *Fra Diavolo* (1933) and *Way Out West* (1937).

Roach had switched to the talkies at the beginning of the 1930s, and the addition of dialogue made Laurel and Hardy even funnier. Roach won an Oscar for his Laurel and Hardy short, *The Music Box* (1932), and another for the *Our Gang* triumph *Bored of Education* (1936).

As the Depression wore on Roach realised that the two-reel comedy was dying, as hard-pressed cinemas were offering double features to encourage attendance. He moved Laurel and Hardy into features, of which more than 20 were made in all.

In 1939 Roach happened to sign a movie co-production deal with Mussolini. "For a few months," he used to recall, "I owned 50 per cent of the Italian film industry."

The same year saw the release of Roach's first venture into serious cinema with an adaptation of John Steinbeck's novel *Of Mice and Men*. The widely praised film starred Burgess Meredith as the itinerant worker, and Lon Chaney Jr as Lennie Small, the dimwitted giant who develops an innocent but fatal obsession with a young girl.

One Million BC (1940), a depiction of life among warring tribes of Stone Age cavemen, was perhaps Roach's oddest film. A veritable grunt-and-club epic, it featured some spectacularly unconvincing dinosaurs.

During the Second World War Roach worked with the American Signal Corps, and his Culver City studio produced training and propaganda films for the US Air Force. He then returned to Hollywood, where he made a brave attempt to move into the new world of television. By 1948 he had founded the Hal Roach Television Corporation and, with his son, Hal Jr, began producing situation comedies.

In 1960 Roach found he had lost his fortune because Hal Jr had made a deal with a stock manipulator whose empire had collapsed. The company folded, and in 1963 the studio was demolished to make room for an automobile showroom.

In the late 1960s Roach emerged from retirement to produce the successful compilation *The Crazy World of Laurel and Hardy*.

In 1984 he received an honorary Academy Award for his outstanding contribution to the film industry. Clutching his Oscar, Roach recalled how his film crews in the silent days lunched on sandwiches and bananas – and the property man saved the banana skins.

Towards the end of his life Roach was dogged by deafness and used to speak wistfully of a return to silent movies. But even in his 10th decade he was full of beans, and campaigned to install infra-red subtitle systems for the deaf in American cinemas.

He is survived by three daughters.

November 4 1992

DEBBIE RAYMOND

DEBBIE RAYMOND, who has died aged 36, joined the family firm, which happened to be the soft porn empire established by her father Paul Raymond.

It was not, perhaps, a calling to which she was ideally suited by temperament. She could never really see the point of sex, she would confess in some moods: it hardly seemed an interesting activity. As for posing in the nude, she would not have done it for a million pounds. Yet in spite of youthful attempts to escape her destiny, the princess of Soho was drawn irresistibly back to her domain.

Deborah Jane Raymond was born on January 28 1956 and speedily introduced to her parents' concerns: as a child of three she would be parked in the theatre while her mother choreographed the celebrations of nakedness on stage. More formal education was conducted at Wimbledon's Ursuline Convent and the Corona Stage School. Debbie did well at the convent – "It's a shame I left" – but was determined to sample life at a boarding school, from which she was expelled for "being a bad influence, smoking and drinking cider."

At that time she was a sweet, shy, slightly goofy girl who threw generous parties in her parents' Wimbledon mansion. Neither she nor her father had any thought that she would ever be attached to the Raymond empire.

Instead she crossed the Atlantic, and sought a career as a singer, making innumerable commercial jingles and becoming the lead singer in a Canadian heavy rock band.

In the early 1980s she was hired by one of her father's

editors. Paul Raymond was sceptical at first, threatening to sack her before she even joined the staff. But Debbie Raymond proved her value and eventually became editor-in-chief of a stable of magazines that included such titles as *Men Only, Men's World* and *Model Directory*.

Miss Raymond worked in a poky Soho office, but there was nothing confined about her plans for the business. She was particularly eager to develop the group's Continental penetration.

"The French are a filthy lot," she observed; and certainly her magazine *Club Pour Hommes* quickly became France's best-selling men's magazine.

Debbie Raymond professed the code of the world which she had embraced, defending prostitution and soft pornography on the grounds that their suppression would only lead to something worse. As for the feminists who held her activities in such odium, it was disgusting what some of *them* wrote.

"There's nothing harmful about soft porn," she concluded. "It's existed since the beginning of time and will continue to flourish with or without me. Anyway, I prefer the term 'erotic entertainment'."

Paul Raymond's early doubts soon turned to delight at his daughter's presence in the firm. Debbie was involved with the property side of the business as well as with the publications, and would often be seen with him at auctions. The leadership of the group (reckoned to be worth nearly £130 million in 1990) was hers to claim whenever her father retired.

She seemed well adapted to the tacky glamour of her *milieu*, a jolly, cheerful woman, happy to alternate the affairs of Soho with the occasional Caribbean holiday. Careless of respectability, she yet served on the board of her local RSPCA and raised money for charity as a member of the Pipe-Smoking Council.

Her addictive personality, however, meant that she was always vulnerable. Recently, too, she had suffered a double mastectomy (though she seemed to have recovered) and undergone a marital breakdown.

Debbie Raymond was once engaged to the Olympic swimmer David Wilkie, and had a daughter by the rock musician Duncan MacKay. She was twice married, first to Jonathan Hodge, a musician, and secondly to John James, who works in the Raymond organisation, and by whom she had another daughter earlier this year.

November 7 1992

MICHAEL ROBBINS

MICHAEL ROBBINS, the character actor, who has died aged 62, was best known for his gloriously grumpy and gravel-voiced "Arfur" in the television series *On the Buses*.

The programme, which spawned a feature film, was one of the unexpected hits of the 1970s. With a script that was little more than a life support system for old lavatorial jokes and limited action which switched mechanically from the bus station to the Butler family's living room, *On the Buses* had little appeal for the critics.

But it became the most popular comedy show of its day and has achieved cult status through repeats. Apart from rejoicing that it was uncompromisingly crude, unashamedly common, yet curiously cosy, viewers relished the earthy characterisation.

The cast included Reg Varney as the cheery, Brylcreemed bus driver; Bob Grant as the buck-toothed, wisecracking conductor; Doris Hare as the booming mum; and Stephen Lewis, who gave the twitching, persecuted inspector, "Blakey", an eerie pathos. But many *aficionados* of *On the Buses* reserved a special place in their affections for the brilliant double-act of marital disharmony between the frankly ill-favoured Olive (played by Anna Karen) and her sullen husband.

Robbins brought a resoundingly morose quality to "Arfur". He would growl withering insults at the long-suffering Olive, in her face cream and curlers, and reject her advances ("I've got an 'eadache") with a merciless cruelty that was somehow funny.

Nothing epitomised their relationship better than the scene when Arthur, on his motorbike, took a corner at such a sharp pace that the sidecar, containing the hapless Olive, was sent spinning off on its own down a sidestreet.

The role won Robbins a huge following and a nomination as Variety Club Personality of 1970, but he had a much wider range and deeper qualities as an actor than the Eeyorish "Arfur" might suggest. For nearly 40 years he was an accomplished exponent of dry light comedy and forthright farce – whether in the West End or pantomime (he was a memorable King Rat), films or classic revivals on television.

What set Robbins apart from many of his contemporaries was his willingness to play unsympathetic roles – distraught fathers, sadistic sergeants, saloon bar bullies and other unlovable but highly actable types with a sly or shady edge. "I always seem to get the slob parts," he used to say.

Michael Robbins was born at Lewisham, south London, on November 14, 1930, and began life as a bank clerk before going on the stage. He served his theatrical apprenticeship in rep for six years, first at Machester's Library Theatre and then at Barry Jackson's Birmingham Rep.

He made his television debut as the Cockney soldier in *Roll-on Bloomin' Death*. In Shaw's *Major Barbara* his salty Cockney was to the fore again as Bill Walker, the loud-mouthed ruffian who bargained for his soul against Judi Dench.

Among his numerous other television credits were *Ross* (as the flight sergeant opposite Ian McKellen), *The Hunting of Lionel Crane, Danton* and, most recently, *Adam Bede*. On the light entertainment side Robbins proved an able foil to such comedians as Tommy Cooper and Dick Emery.

In the theatre Robbins scored a particular hit as the aggressive and lecherous brother-in-law, Graham, to Tom Courtenay's inert hero in Alan Ayckbourn's *Time and Time Again* (Comedy, 1972). Robbins also played the part in the television production.

His other stage work included musicals, such as *Liza of Lambeth* and *The Ratepayers' Iolanthe*, as well as a tour in the late 1980s of Bob Larbey's comedy about the male ageing process, *A Month of Sundays*.

Robbins's film credits included *The Whisperers, The Looking Glass War, Zeppelin* and two pictures for Blake Edwards – *Victor Victoria* and *The Pink Panther Strikes Again* (in which he played a nightclub drag queen, whose songs were dubbed by Julie Andrews).

Robbins was an indefatigable worker for charity. He was active in the Grand Order of Water Rats (being elected "Rat of the Year" in 1978) and the Catholic Stage Guild; and received a Papal Award for his services in 1987.

In one of his last television appearances, in *A Little Bit of Heaven*, Michael Robbins recalled his childhood visits to Norfolk and spoke of his faith and love of the Shrine of Our Lady at Walsingham. He died of cancer.

He married Hal Dyer, an actress; they had a son and a daughter.

December 14 1992

CARDEW ROBINSON

CARDEW ROBINSON, the comedian and character actor who has died aged 75, was one of the last stage comics to make his name with a single short variety turn.

It was a monologue in which he played a gangling, overgrown schoolboy clad in short trouserings, cap and scarf while recalling his adventures as Cardew the Cad, the bad boy of St Fanny's. With his exceptional height, lean build, large eyes, long face and goofy expression, Robinson in school uniform stirred laughter almost before he began to speak of his delinquent schoolboy experiences. He delivered these with a gravity and timing which sustained the comedian's career long after the variety halls had closed.

He was born Douglas Robinson at Goodmayes, Essex, on August 14 1917, and educated at Harrow County Grammar School. He lived next to the playing fields of Harrow School and he would observe its cricket matches with a mixture of admiration and envy.

He was attracted to the stage by his school's drama department and became addicted to the novels of school life by Frank Richards (with the ample Billy Bunter lording it over Greyfriars School and a certain Ralph Reckless Cardew getting into scrapes at St Jim's). Young Robinson went straight from school on to the halls in a sketch called *The College Boys*, and later into rep.

At the outbreak of the Second World War he joined the RAF. While serving in an entertainments unit, known as Ralph Reader's Gang Show, he was asked to contribute an item, which he composed in one verse and four choruses and entitled "Cardew the Cad of the School".

After setting it to music he begged the son of the landlord of the White Hart, Newark, to lend him the long red, green and yellow scarf he had worn at Magnus Grammar School together with the cap. The following evening at Newark's Corn Exchange, the performance, starting: "You can see by my scarf, you can see by my cap, I belong to an old public school," was warmly received.

Retaining both scarf and cap, Robinson built his act entirely round the schoolboy antics at St Fanny's, a seat of learning (headmaster Dr Jankers, BA, BO, BF, FFI and Bar), which lay "in a natural basin. My room was just over the plughole."

After the war Robinson toured in the commercial production of the *Gang Show* and, as Cardew the Cad, returned to the variety halls. It led to his own BBC radio series, *Variety Fanfare*, which offered a weekly change of episode about events at the school. Cardew the Cad also became for seven years a subject in the weekly children's comic *Radio Fun*, which inspired a feature film, *Fun at St Fanny's*.

In a wireless monologue Robinson reflected on the year 1951 in which "the Cadet Corps was put under the supervision of a regular Army sergeant. So Chomondley Minor, who had no idea of cooking, was put in the kitchen. Fatty Gilbert, who can't drive, was put in charge of transport, and I was put in the Intelligence Corps. At the end of the Christmas term we had our speech day and all the parents turned up. My father didn't have far to come – he's a member of the Sixth Form."

As the variety circuit withered in the late 1950s, the Cad disappeared, except for appearances in pantomime, although Robinson continued to work for radio and television in various capacities (including quizmaster), writing material for himself and contemporaries, and in many series.

He also took small parts in feature films such as *Sink the Bismarck, Reach for the Sky, Alfie* and *Shirley Valentine*; and from time to time appeared on the legitimate and musical stage.

In Ben Jonson's city comedy, *Eastwood Ho!* (Mermaid, 1962) he romped about wide-eyed as Sir Petronel Flash. Two years later at Drury Lane he played King Pellinore in the Lerner–Loewe musical comedy *Camelot* with a relish and a string of bad jokes which reminded *The Daily Telegraph*'s Eric Shorter of "a refugee from suburban pantomime".

Robinson himself contributed a number of humorous columns and letters to the *Telegraph*. He was a popular member of charitable fundraising organisations like the Lord's Taverners and the Water Rats.

He had two daughters.

December 29 1992

DIZZY GILLESPIE

DIZZY GILLESPIE, the high priest of bebop, who has died in New Jersey aged 75, was a true innovator, responsible, with a handful of fellow spirits, for bringing a radical new dimension to jazz music.

The social and racial origins of jazz are debatable, but the harmonic, rhythmic and tonal characteristics of bebop were indisputably Gillespie's creation. By the early 1940s black musicians had become frustrated by the fact that their white colleagues earned more money than they did. Spurred by the belief that their jazz had been shamelessly exploited by "Whitey", Gillespie and his followers, notably the alto-saxophonist Charlie Parker, set out to play music so bewildering and complex that the white man would not be able to copy it.

As it happened, white musicians rose to the challenge, and, in the changing racial climate of the time, blacks and whites joined forces in clubs, on the concert platform and in the recording studio to spread what became a universal musical message.

"As this book is being written," wrote Stewart Allen in his *Stars of Swing* (1946), "a revolution is taking place in the Kingdom of Swing. It is a revolution that is gathering force to such an extent that it will soon establish a stranglehold. One by one, musicians are being won over by the new style set by a young man in New York called John Birks Gillespie."

That bebop had so immediate an effect was in some ways surprising, for it marked a violent break with the stylistic conventions of the past. Non-melodic, dissonant, often frantic, the new music was savagely attacked by the critical establishment.

In a review of a Charlie Parker record in 1946 the American magazine *Downbeat* observed: "This record is an excellent example of the other side of the Gillespie craze – the bad taste and ill-advised fanaticism . . . this is the sort of stuff that has thrown innumerable young musicians out of their stride, and harmed them irreparably."

Dizzy and his disciples did not merely have to contend with the critics. While they were pursuing their intransigently experimental course, the other end of the jazz world was experiencing a renaissance of the "old" Dixieland style.

Before long an all-out war erupted between the two sides, and in the thick of this Gillespie blew high, rapid notes in defiance of the "mouldy fyges" (as the traditionalists were called), and set the world dancing to the tune of a new musical order.

The last of nine children, John Birks Gillespie was born at Cheraw, South Carolina, on October 21 1917; his father, a bricklayer and weekend bandleader who played bass, mandolin, drums and piano, died when the boy was 10.

Two years later young Gillespie began to teach himself trumpet and trombone. He gained a place at Laurinberg University, North Carolina, an industrial school for blacks, and practised his instruments assiduously in his spare time.

Gillespie retained strong memories of racial oppression in the Deep South: "There was this fine trombonist, Bill McNeil. Had he lived and gone to New York, he would have been a big name, but the white people said he was a Peeping Tom, killed him and put his body on the railroad track."

279

Laurinberg University was about 28 miles from Cheraw, and on one occasion, while hitch-hiking home, Gillespie stopped at a grocery store to buy some bread and cheese. A throng of white youths were slouched around a stove, spitting out tobacco.

"Hey, I'm talkin' to you, nigger!" they shouted. "You know how to dance?"

"Nossir!"

"No? C'mon, all niggers know how to dance."

One of the whites then drew his pistol and shot at the dust by Gillespie's feet. "Talk about dance!" Gillespie recalled, "I buck-danced in and out of there! They were having fun, but they would kill you, too."

Gillespie was in fact an exceptional dancer. In 1937, after a spell with Frank Fairfax's band in Philadelphia, he moved to New York, where, on exhibition dance nights at the 400 Club, he gave elegant and energetic performances of the Lindy Hop with a variety of willing partners.

He was also quite capable of standing up for himself. "Gillespie did everything in unorthodox fashion," remembered Teddy Hill, whose band he joined that same year. "When we played a new arrangement he was likely as not to interject his own ideas and not follow the score. He would speak up at the wrong time, jumping about and playing an extra bar or two at the end of a number, going through miming acts during other people's solos and putting up his horn and pretending he was playing."

Indeed, Gillespie soon gained a reputation for being "a pain in the butt". During Hill's band's stint at the Apollo Theatre, New York, he was apt to put on his derby, turn his chair back to front, and perform an impromptu dance. But even Hill had to concede that he could have been worse. Despite his wild antics, Gillespie was not a drinker or a womaniser, and he was careful with his money.

Meanwhile Gillespie's technique was steadily improving. He had come to idolise Roy Eldridge, the trumpeter and an earlier member of the band. Howard Johnson, a saxophonist in the Hill Orchestra, had transcribed Eldridge's solos for Gillespie to study and memorise. Gillespie's first recording with Hill in 1937 revealed his indebtedness to "Little Jazz" Eldridge.

When a European tour was offered to Hill many of the band threatened to leave if Gillespie was booked, but Hill held out and the dissident stayed on. They played in the Cotton Club Show at the London Palladium.

That the gig took place at all was thanks to the British Musicians' Union, which had leaned heavily on the Ministry of Labour to have the embargo on American bands playing in Britain lifted. None the less Hill's band were allowed to perform only on the condition that they played a purely accompanying role and did not "move" – beyond what was strictly necessary in playing their instruments.

Gillespie then left Hill to join and annoy ("Stop playing that Chinese music!") Cab Calloway. The association was shortlived.

One night Calloway was cavorting around the stage during a gig when he was hit by a spit ball. Calloway accused Gillespie, an argument ensued, Gillespie pulled a knife, Calloway needed several stitches in his rear, and Gillespie was fired.

The "wild man" went on to play with Ella Fitzgerald's band (she had taken over the nominal leadership of Chick Webb's band after his death in 1939). From there he joined Les Hite's band, in which he quickly fell out with the drummer, Oscar Bradley. "He used to do ratamacues and paradiddles during my solos," Gillespie complained, "and I'd tell this nigger where he could put 'em. After nickin' Cab's ass I had this bad reputation and I left."

But there were advantages in having a "reputation". Gillespie reckoned it was this that saved him from the military draft in the Second World War. Like many blacks, he had no enthusiasm for "Whitey's war".

During his stint with Calloway and Les Hite (with whom he also recorded), Gillespie had been "sitting-in" with a secret society of young black musicians, keen to try out the revolutionary ideas which their bandleaders discouraged or forbade.

The sessions took place at Minton's, a dilapidated dining-room in the Hotel Cecil on West 118th Street. Other members of this cabal included Charlie Parker, the drummer Kenny Clarke, the pianist Thelonius Monk and the guitarist Charlie Christian.

It was not long before the word was out, and Gillespie gained his big break. The musical papers – and even the national press – began publishing photographs of a pouting, posturing, preening Gillespie, sporting a lavish goatee beard, and invariably garbed in beret, dark glasses and an extravagant zoot suit. He was the grimacing Grimaldi of jazz, and his exhibitionism and sartorial eccentricities earned him rancorous criticism from the "mouldy fyges". Gillespie basked in the attention. But he was quick to refute accusations that he had sold out – by producing a series of highly charged recordings, and setting up a brash, exciting big band, founded on his own idiosyncratic ideas.

"Gillespie's style reached its maturity by the mid-1940s," recalled Ian Carr, the British trumpeter and critic.

"Never before had the trumpet been played with such speed, flexibility, dynamism and drama. The whole essence of Gillespie was his cliff-hanging suspense; the phrases and angle of approach were perpetually varied, breakneck runs were followed by pauses, by huge interval leaps, by long, immensely high notes, by slurs and smears and bluesy phrases; he was always taking listeners by surprise, always shocking them with new thought."

The diehard traditionalists never came to accept this rowdy upstart, however, and the internecine jazz war raged well into the 1950s. As late as 1956, in a review of a record featuring Coleman Hawkins, Eldridge and Gillespie, the British record producer Stanley Dance wrote: "To me the lack of continuity is one important reason why Gillespie's solos are as invigorating as a pistol shot in the head. His solo opens quietly enough with an original idea, but disintegrates into incredibly vulgar triple-tonguing and hunting horn effects. We see from the publicity pictures that Dizzy now doubles in snake-charming. Knowing this, and with the above solo in mind, I long for his entry into the circus world."

It was in something like this spirit that Louis Armstrong, on the side of the old guard, produced a mocking version of the "Wiffenpoof Song", in which he sent up the boppers, and specifically mentioned Gillespie. "Up at Birdland where Dizzy dwells, with their beards and funny hats they love so well, they constitute a weird personnel . . . They are poor little cats that have lost their way . . . like little lost sheep they have gone astray . . . Lord have mercy on them . . . BYE BYE!"

But Gillespie was indomitable. In spite of challenges from younger players, he remained the king of the modern jazz trumpet, playing with a variety of bands, appearing regularly at jazz festivals around the world, and recording incessantly.

Always on the lookout for controversy, at one stage Gillespie even contemplated running for the US Presidency, on a disarmament and global government ticket. His first act, he asserted, would be to change the name of the White House to the "Blue House". He quipped that Miles Davis had offerd his services as Treasury Secretary, but added that running the CIA would probably be more in Davis's line.

That Gillespie truly believed in bridging racial and cultural barriers was manifested, in the late 1980s, in the formation of his United Nation All-Star band, which toured England and much of Europe in 1989. The band offered a heady mixture of bebop jazz and Latin American rhythms – not least because the old veteran, sparing himself, had engaged Arturo Sandoval, the dynamic Cuban trumpeter, to take the main burden of the trumpet solos.

"We're having an awful lot of fun with this band," Dizzy declared, quite explosive with excitement. "Talk about music being an international language – man, *this is it*!"

In 1979 he published an autobiography, *To Be or Not to Bop*. He is survived by his wife, Lorraine.

January 8 1993

JEAN PLAIDY

JEAN PLAIDY, *alias* Victoria Holt, Philippa Carr and 14 others, who has died while on a Mediterranean cruise at an unrevealed age (thought to be the early eighties), was a romantic and historical novelist able to console herself for critical indifference with worldwide sales reckoned at more than 75 million.

Every year Victoria Holt is near the top of the list of the authors most in demand in libraries, while Plaidy and Carr are always in the first 100. "It's the sort of stuff one reads in the school san," young *literatae* loftily declare – although the period of convalescence is often protracted.

Jean Plaidy's secret, as Antonia Byatt has observed, was that she possessed sufficient imagination to create a world for the reader, and not enough to ruin it with the complications and ambiguities with plague real life: the ideal formula for escapist reading.

Jean Plaidy, moreover, *believed* in what she wrote; there was no question of cynically writing down to her public. Although critics might sneer at her as "the Enid Blyton of historical novelists", she had Blyton's gift of making her readers turn the page.

Narrative, she held, was the secret. "It's no use trying to show how clever you are with lots of quotations and references to the classics," she observed. "You've got to get along with your story, and not hang about with it."

Her other great gift was fecundity. Altogether she wrote some 200 books. Having recognised, relatively early in her career, that she would never be noticed by critics, and having grasped also that she was building up a loyal readership through libraries, she formed her resolve. "Keep on giving them books, so they don't forget your name."

She had scant sympathy for writers who complained about the difficulty of writing: the problem, as she saw it, was that they failed to keep in trim with regular sessions at their desks.

Plaidy herself worked seven days a week, five hours a day, starting every morning at 7.30. Her average daily output was some 5,000 words, 8,000 when she was on full steam. She would have done more, save that she found the plots of her books began to encroach on each other. But restraint was a trial: "If anybody says to me, oh dear, you do look tired, it's because I haven't been at my typewriter."

Her *oeuvre* may be divided into three main categories. The 90-odd Jean Plaidy novels – with titles like *The Royal Road to Fotheringay* (1955), *The Thistle and the Rose* (1965) and *The Prince of Darkness* (1978) – were fictionalised history.

The simplicity of the narrative did not exclude emotion. "Mary was disturbed", we learn, "when Henry told her that he was going to attack the Barbary pirates."

The characters were given to expressions like "mayhap". "How feels it to be my wife?" enquired Henry V on the morrow of his marriage to his French princess. "My lord," replied Catherine, "it makes me wondrous happy." But the novels also contained philosophising of the "Who would be born royal?" variety.

Victoria Holt – a pseudonym taken from the name of the author's bank – made her debut in the 1960s, at the behest of an American agent called Patricia Myrer, who urged the commercial possibilities of the Gothic novel, "something on the *Jane Eyre* line". From the first attempt, *Mistress of Mellyn* (1961), this brand of wares proved an enormous success, especially in America. The stories might have a 19th-century background, but there was nothing staid about the fortunes of the heroines.

Consider the plight of Kate Collison in *The Demon Lover* (1982): "I, Kate Collison, had been raped by the man I most detested . . . this arrogant Baron who thought he had only to beckon to a woman to make her come running. He had followed the customs of his marauding ancestors who had lived by rape and pillage. And I . . . I had become his victim."

Alas, a few hundred pages on, Kate is all set to become the Baroness:

"He looked at me, long and steadily, and I wondered how I could ever have thought of leaving him."

Not that the author took an idealised view of men. She found them "wonderful at getting to the moon, and that sort of thing, and carrying the bags and making arrangements". But, she complained, they didn't *understand*; worse, they weren't even *interested* in people.

From 1972 Jean Plaidy's delight in history combined with Victoria Holt's melodramatic gifts under another *nom de plume*, Philippa Carr, who wrote thumping good yarns which offered plentiful opportunity for retailing colourful episodes from the past.

Annora, the heroine of *Midsummer's Eve* (1986), witnessed a witch-burning, learned about fallen Victorian women, visited Australia, observed the transportation of convicts, lost both parents, inherited a fortune, discovered she was illegitimate, lost her fortune, found she was legitimate after all, recovered her fortune, and married a tall, handsome landowner.

It was a far cry from the author's origins.

Jean Plaidy, Victoria Holt and Philippa Carr were all born Eleanor Burford *circa* 1910 – in "very humble" circumstances in Kennington, south London. Her father had no profession – "he just did jobs". However he passed on his love of reading.

Young Eleanor left school at 16 and went to work for a jeweller in Hatton Garden, where she typed, and weighed gems. In her early twenties she married a wholesale leather merchant called Hibbert. They had no children, and Mrs Hibbert made the most of her free time.

She began her writing career by turning out nine lengthy novels, in an attempt to emulate her literary heroes, Dickens, Hugo, the Brontës and Tolstoy. None of these books was published. Undeterred, Mrs Hibbert tried her hand at short stories for the *Daily Mail* and *Evening News*. It was the *Mail*'s literary editor who changed her life. "You're barking up the wrong tree," he said. "You must write something which is saleable, and the easiest way is to write a romantic novel."

Mrs Hibbert, who had not previously read a romantic novel, sat down and devoured 20 of them. She then wrote one, which was immediately accepted (and published under her maiden name) by Mills and Boon. Her subsequent efforts in this genre enjoyed a modest success. She used several *noms de plume*, Ellalice Tate and Elbur Ford among them. There was also Kathleen Kellow – "What books did she do?", she would muse in later life.

The next breakthrough came after she had written a novel about transportation to Australia. It was rejected by a number of publishers as being too long; only Robert Hale had faith, writing that "there were glittering prizes in the literary world" for anyone who could write as well as the author.

From that display of confidence his firm would draw copious rewards. The first Jean Plaidy novel was published in 1945. The author felt the need of a new name for her historical novels. She chose Plaidy because she lived near Plaidy Beach in Cornwall, Jean because it was short.

But even after Victoria Holt had added her huge royalties to Jean Plaidy's pile, Mrs Hibbert (whose husband died in the early 1970s) continued to live a simple life. Only once did she venture on a notable extravagance, when she bought King's Lodge, Sandwich. She had the house lavishly furnished in the Gothic style, complete with chests and four-poster beds, only to learn the pain of realising a fantasy. It was a "terrible mistake", she concluded.

She returned to her London flat, from which she would escape each winter on a cruise – always taking her trusty typewriter with her. Her only other indulgence was buying clothes. They had to come from the peg; she had as little time for the *grands couturiers* as for the literary critics.

January 21 1993

BILL GRUNDY

BILL GRUNDY, the broadcaster, who had died aged 69, cultivated an abrasive style that made for colourful programmes but could lead to trouble.

His most famous hour was an interview with the punk rock group the Sex Pistols in 1976. "You're more drunk than I am," he declared to the band, by way of commencing proceedings.

This, he later insisted, had been a joke. In more serious vein he invited the Sex Pistols to say something outrageous. Mr Johnny Rotten, the lead singer, duly obliged with a four-letter word.

"Keep going," Grundy urged, "come on, you've got another five seconds to say something outrageous." The youth obliged: "You dirty bastard."

"Go on," tempted Grundy.

"You dirty fucker."

"What a clever boy!" said Grundy.

"What a fucking rotter!" concluded the singer.

This exchange, which went out in the early evening on Thames Television's *Today* programme, left many viewers unamused. Though Grundy claimed to have achieved his aim of showing up the Sex Pistols as "a foul-mouthed set of yobs", Thames felt bound to suspend him for a few days.

The Sex Pistols were banned from at least seven engagements on their first nationwide tour, and EMI terminated their contract: they were well and truly launched.

The son of a factory foreman, William Grundy was born at Manchester on May 18 1923 and educated at Manchester University, where he read geology.

He began his career as a geologist, while covering football matches as a part-time journalist. When Granada Television began broadcasting in 1956 Grundy auditioned for the post of newsreader, which at first he held in tandem with his geological work.

Grundy's sporting prowess gained him a part in Granada's first play, *Shooting Star*, about a footballer. Later he graduated to such programmes as *People and Places* (for which he interviewed the Beatles on their first television appearance) and *World in Action*. He also made a number of educational programmes, notably *The Land*, for which he gave his services free.

When Granada pioneered the televising of party conferences Grundy proved a supremely able commentator, amazing colleagues with his ability to hold forth fluently for hours, even after the most convivial lunch. If he was unpredictable – he once fell asleep while reading the news – Sidney Bernstein judged him worth protecting. But Bernstein's loyalty wore thin when Grundy insulted Sir Alec Douglas-Home at a party.

At the end of 1968 Grundy loosened his links with Granada, though the company continued to pay him a handsome retainer.

He was also a sharp-witted participant in various panel games – *Not a Word, On the Line, M'Lords, Ladies and Gentlemen*. His appearances on such programmes as *What the Papers Say* or Radio 4's *News Stand* were unfailingly witty. His television career ended in the 1980s, with *Sweet and Sour* (BBC North).

Grundy also contributed to the *Spectator, Punch* and other magazines. In 1976 he published *The Press Inside Out*; his *Grundy's London* was a chatty guide, especially informative on pubs.

Bill Grundy married, in 1946, Jane ("Nicky") Nicholson; they had four sons and two daughters.

February 11 1993

JESS YATES

JESS YATES, who has died aged 74, was celebrated as the presenter of *Stars on Sunday*, a phenomenally popular religious programme on British television in the early 1970s.

Yates, a cherubic figure known as "The Bishop", would introduce the show seated at an electric organ – on which he occasionally performed in a tremulous manner – placed in front of a stained-glass window. He was prone to make such observations as "We can't see round the bend in the road, but God can."

Yates devised a restful formula of music not so much sacred as saccharine, interspersed with Bible readings by film stars and the occasional homily from a real-life bishop – whose purple cassock would clash violently with the scarlet leather armchairs. The show's *kitsch* blend of sentimentality, celebrities and cosy escapism attracted much ridicule.

Sean Day-Lewis of *The Daily Telegraph* remarked that *Stars on Sunday*, "even when seen, can scarcely be believed. Anna Neagle, regally clad, emerged confidently from an extravagant mansion and read from a colossal Bible arranged for her beside the drive; Gracie Fields seemed overawed by the same surroundings; and Harry Secombe arranged his features into a serious expression to render a hymn accompanied by 100 choirboys with candles at the ready."

Churchmen complained that the show "lacked religious content" and that Yates "painted a false picture of religion". Yates responded by claiming the programme was made "for older people who need to be comforted"; he could also cite the remarkably high ratings.

Yates – whose voice was likened by one critic to "sweet and weak tea" – cultivated a pious image for his appearances on *Stars on Sunday* and an air of sanctimony pervaded his dealings with guests. All stars were vetted for possible scandal and women were asked to appear "modestly dressed" in front of the cameras.

His own avuncular persona, however, proved unsustainable. In the summer of 1974 the *News of the World*, under the headline "THE BISHOP AND THE

ACTRESS", revealed that Yates, "a married man" (in fact, he had been separated for some years), was carrying on a relationship with Anita Kay, a showgirl 30 years his junior who had recently "starred in Paul Raymond's nude revue *Pyjama Tops*".

Amid the ensuing furore Yates had to be smuggled from Yorkshire Television's studio in Leeds in the boot of a motor car. He ceased to present *Stars on Sunday* and was subsequently replaced as executive producer of the programme.

After Yates's contract with the television company expired the next year his attempts to resuscitate his career were not helped by continuing press interest in his personal life – fanned by the celebrity of his daughter, Paula, who married Bob Geldof.

Jess Yates was born in 1918 into a showbusiness family; his mother booked stage acts. Yates joined the BBC on the production side in 1949. He was involved with such programmes as *Come Dancing, The Good Old Days* and the *Miss World* competition.

In 1958 he married Heller Toren, a former beauty queen and novelist. Their daughter, Paula, was born the next year.

Yates and his wife separated in 1965, and subsequently Mrs Yates and Paula moved to Majorca.

In 1969 Yates left the BBC and joined Yorkshire Television, where he eventually became head of children's programmes. Initially, he was asked to produce a series of six religious programmes for early evening viewing.

"I went for star names," Yates recalled, "because they would persuade people to watch." The first show had viewing figures of 600,000; at the end of the series viewing figures had risen to seven million. Yates was asked to produce a further four programmes which led to a full 12 months'-worth of *Stars on Sunday*; soon the audience was approaching 20 million.

Yates arranged for the stars to visit the Leeds studio to record their spots on videotape, then an innovation. "I'm a self-confessed despot," Yates said. *"Stars on Sunday* is the way I want it and the way I'm going to keep it."

Yates blamed his downfall on an unnamed colleague who had sneaked to the press. "Everybody knows", Yates declared, "there has been a personal vendetta on the part of a very prominent *artiste* to make sure I am removed from television for ever." .

In 1977 Yates played the organ for a gala evening at the Odeon, Leicester Square; the featured number was "Here We Are Again". During the 1980s his engagements included seasons at a Scarborough theatre playing the organ and as an entertainments officer at a beach hotel in the West Indies.

Yates, who lived in North Wales, was also in demand as an after-dinner speaker, although he said that he disliked being introduced as Paula Yates's father: "I have a great yearning not to go to my grave as 'Bob Geldof's father-in-law'."

Yates's marriage was dissolved in 1975. He continued his relationship with Miss Kay, who wrote a book entitled *All We Did Was Fall In Love* (1975). But subsequently she married a younger man and moved to Australia.

In 1976 Yates made an appearance on the panel of the television talent show *New Faces* and later that year applied, unsuccessfully, for a position as an organist at a holiday camp.

April 12 1993

LESLIE CHARTERIS

LESLIE CHARTERIS, the thriller writer, who has died aged 85, created the character of Simon Templar (The Saint) before his 21st birthday and lived on the proceeds for the rest of his life: seldom has an author been so successful in exploiting a single character.

The Saint was a modern Robin Hood, socking jaws and throwing knives with deadly effect, but never a hair out of place. He robbed only the wicked of their ill-gotten gains. Few characters in fiction can have spent more time in full evening dress or have been so punctilious in saying goodbye to lady friends, left (usually) at their bedroom doors.

Charteris himself was as much a self-constructed figure as his hero, who was essentially an idealised self-portrait. Both were healthy, tall, conventionally good-looking, sporty, champagne swigging, cigarette-holder-flourishing *bon viveurs*.

In fact, Charteris was born in Singapore on May 12 1907, as Leslie Charles Bowyer Yin, the son of a well-off Chinese doctor, who claimed descent from the Shang dynasty of the second century BC, and his English wife. The family travelled a great deal, and Charteris had been twice round the world before he was sent, aged 12, to Falconbury, an English prep school.

Young Leslie showed an early aptitude for writing, and produced his own magazine illustrated with matchstick drawings – the prototype for the vestigial figure with cigarette and halo that became the trademark for The Saint.

Although he was a successful boxer and gamesplayer, he later claimed that he had hated his school years at Rossall; nevertheless he did well enough to gain a place at King's College, Cambridge. His success in selling three stories during his first year as an undergraduate led to his abandoning university life and deciding, to his father's disgust, to earn his living by his pen. Charteris's chief model was Edgar Wallace, but his early work also owed much to Sapper's Bulldog Drummond.

The sort of money paid by magazines in the mid-1920s could not support the life Charteris aspired to, so he tried his hand at gold prospecting, pearl fishing and other romantic get-rich-quick schemes, all of which failed. He did better as a barman at English country hotels and as a professional bridge player. While touring with an English funfair he learned about knife-throwing, a speciality of Simon Templar.

His first stories had been published under the name of Leslie C. Bowyer, but he soon adopted by deed poll the name of Leslie Charteris, chosen from an enthusiasm for a certain Colonel Charteris, gambler, duellist and founder member of the Hellfire Club. And Charteris chimed well with Charles, his second name.

Charteris had created two other fictional heroes – Terry Mannering, a sort of Bulldog Drummond, and the freebooting Ramon Francisco de Castila y Esproneda Manrique (an obvious non-starter) – before he hit on Templar. The first Saint book, *Enter the Tiger* (1928), was by no means a bestseller, and it was not for a couple of years that his stories began to find popularity in a new magazine called *The Thriller*.

Enter the Saint, written in 1930, established Charteris's name, but even so the rewards were not great. *The Thriller* paid him only two guineas per thousand words. The American market seemed to offer better pickings, and in 1932 he crossed the Atlantic.

With his facility for ingenious plots and easy undemanding dialogue, Charteris was soon writing scripts in Hollywood. He graduated from producing material for the inexhaustible *Tarzan* saga to providing suitable dialogue to fill in the gaps between Deanna Durbin's songs.

All the time he was producing a steady stream of Saint books, each selling better than its predecessor. The character of Templar changed subtly as he was tailored for the American market. Soon the Saint was selling all over the world, and the money poured in.

It was inevitable that so successful a series should be bought by Hollywood. The first *Saint* film was made in 1938, with the South African Louis Hayward as the star, but it was the Russian-born George Sanders who made the part his own. His brother, Tom Conway, was later to make a series of imitation *Saint* films as The Falcon.

In the 1930s Charteris became an American citizen, and on America's entry into the Second World War, set the Saint to work alongside G-men in a new set of patriotic novels. By this time Charteris was editing his own periodical, the *Saint Magazine*, and overseeing the film, radio and comic strip versions.

By the 1950s Charteris had grown bored with the labour of writing his novels. A television series starring Roger Moore brought him £500,000 as an advance, and from then on he decided merely to supervise the writing of novels and scripts.

He made no secret of this, acknowledging the names of his ghosts and merely adding that he had "personally corrected" their work. This was a pity. None of his ghosts had the same panache, and the novels lost the tongue-in-cheek quality which Charteris had always given them.

In any case, his sales suffered from the arrival of Ian Fleming's James Bond. Charteris never approved of Fleming. He thought his bedroom scenes vulgar and his violence gratuitous. There was no torture in Charteris's novels – apart from one scene in which Templar was fed with hot curry in an attempt to make him talk.

In the long run, perhaps, Charteris came out the winner. Fleming's fame and fortune depended far more on the films made from his books than the books themselves; and the cod element in the performances of successive Bonds owes far more to Charteris than to Fleming's originals.

The fact that he wrote to a formula, and later merely operated a system of quality control, should not disguise the fact that he wrote with great gusto – and better than some of his peers.

Latterly Charteris lived in France and Britain. He could afford to indulge himself, and did so: he listed his recreations as "eating, drinking, horseracing, loafing".

He married first (dissolved 1937) Pauline Schishkin; they had a daughter. He married secondly (dissolved 1941) Barbara Meyer; thirdly (dissolved 1951) Elizabeth Bryant Borst; and fourthly Audrey Long, a former actress.

April 17 1993

LES DAWSON

LES DAWSON, who has died aged 62, exploited his corpulent figure and naturally doom-laden expression to create a television personality that was a *reductio ad absurdum* of the tradition of the "Northern comic", in the vein of Norman Evans or Robb Wilton.

Dawson's *forte* was the exaggeration of familiar music-hall jokes at the expense of the Wife: "I met her in the tunnel of love; she was digging it" and the Wife's Cooking: "I threw a bit to a bird the other day; it went into a corner and put a wing down its throat."

But it was the figure of the Mother-in-Law which – despite the wealth of existing popular satire on the subject – he made his own, building a picture of a woman of unrivalled physical repulsiveness: "I'm not saying she's ugly, but every time she puts make-up on, the lipstick backs into the tube", with aggressive tendencies: "For all that, she does possess some things that men admire; like muscles and a duelling scar."

Dawson represented himself as the preferred target for his Mother-in-Law's boundless malevolence: "As soon as I heard the knock on the door I knew it was her because the mice were flinging themselves on their traps."

He gave new life to these clichés of northern comedy with his infectious love of word-play and language in general – he published several books, including two "straight" novels – and his keen sense of the absurd; some of his reflections carried strong echoes of the more off-beat American comedians, especially Woody Allen.

His range was, however, sufficiently broad to allow him to become one of the few solo stand-up comedians to achieve consistent success on television, in shows like *Sez Les, The Dawson Watch* and *The Les Dawson Show*, not to mention *Blankety-Blank*, the dire celebrity quiz show which he sent up remorselessly in his role as compère.

His ability to pull his chin over his nose (a privilege

conferred upon him by a Mancunian youth who smashed Dawson's jaw during a fight in the early 1940s) proved irresistible to prime-time television audiences in the 1970s and 1980s.

Dawson's facility for identifying and mimicking the grotesque inspired characters like the frustrated Cosmo Smallpiece and – with the assistance of Roy Barraclough – Cissie and Ada. These matronly practitioners of "mimoing" – the Lancashire art, developed by mill-workers, of mouthing "unmentionable" vocabulary relating to reproduction or major surgery.

Dawson based the ladies on Norman Evans's "Over the Wall" sketch; he worked with Evans on the locally-networked television show *Comedy Bandbox* in 1963. One of Cissie and Ada's most memorable performances was in a television commercial for cream cakes. Asked if he would like a slice, the Dawson character simpers: "Oh, just a little, chuck"; but on seeing the breadth of the proposed cut, he grabs the knife, snarling: "Not that *ruddy little*!"

Dawson began his career as a musical turn, slipping into comedy only on a particularly grim night in Hull. Having been pilloried throughout his performance at a working men's club, he took the stage for the second show – "well in the arms of Bacchus", as he later put it. So deep was the embrace that he was unable to provide himself with his customarily execrable piano accompaniment.

Dawson first astonished then delighted the audience with his gloomy, self-deprecating patter: "I'm not saying my act is bad, but the night variety died, they held my script for questioning."

His ham-fistedness at the keyboard and calculated air of despondency proved to be, if anything, more poignant in the face of adversity. His first national success, as a comic turn on the television show *Blackpool Night Out* in 1966, came in front of a highly unwelcoming audience: the oleaginous compère Dickie Henderson had watched several acts "die" before he introduced Les Dawson.

The comedian faced his predicament head-on: "I'm about as famous as Lord Godiva . . . if you're popular in show-business they give you a dressing-room on the ground floor. To give you some idea what they think of me, my room's full of falcon droppings and the mice have blackouts."

He left the stage to an ovation. In future, however ecstatic his reception, Dawson was to adopt the demeanour of a failure facing a hostile house.

Leslie Dawson was born on February 2 1931, in a "two-up-two-down" in a Collyhurst slum. He failed the entrance exam for North Manchester High School, and, his family having moved to the Blackley area, was sent instead to Moston Lane School.

His English teacher, Bill Hetherington, encouraged him to write; consequently it was with some regret that Dawson left school at 14 for the drapery department of the Co-Operative Society. He continued to nurse literary aspirtions throughout his period of National Service in Germany in 1950: Dawson contributed stories to *The Soldier* magazine, and took a London University correspondence course in journalism.

Although he did eventually manage to gain employment on a local newspaper, he was sacked after a fortnight; Dawson's "serious" writing always had a tendency to be over-ornate. He later described how his 150-word obituary of an ex-deputy mayor was cut to read "Councillor X was buried yesterday."

Once demobbed, he travelled by train from Blackley

to Paris, where he soon decided that he had not found his niche as a pianist in a brothel near the rue de la Goutte d'Or. On his return to Manchester a year later he found a job selling insurance.

Working as a salesman for Hoover in the early 1950s, he saw a poster inviting acts to apply to join Max Wall's agency. Dawson passed the audition and moved to the capital though he maintained a traditionally northern view of London: "Poofs by the score, madmen and perverts; crooks, Lesbian wrestlers and elderly matrons brimming with lust."

He was unfortunate enough to join Wall Enterprises at one of the many crisis points of its founder's career. Before Dawson was obliged to pack his bags and return to Manchester, however, Wall did manage to send him to the singing teacher Madam Styles Allen; he shared her waiting room with Julie Andrews.

In 1956, after spectacular success on Humberside, Dawson began to build up a solid following as a comic on the Manchester club circuit and to turn his intellectual frustration to his own advantage. He would greet audiences with a cry of: "Good evening, culture hunters", before launching into self-deflating patter in an arty vein.

His daytime concerns still centred around the vacuum cleaner, though his prospects with Hoover were dealt a fatal blow when an area manager spotted him in a show called *She Stoops to Concur*.

The management considered that Dawson's contribution – a rendition of "It's Witchcraft", delivered from a melée of naked women – was incompatible with his status as a salesman of domestic appliances.

Dawson married in 1960 and, with the support and

guidance of his wife, Meg, gradually began to break into radio, in shows like *Midday Music Hall*.

An appearance on *Opportunity Knocks* in 1964 led to his triumph two years later on *Blackpool Night Out*. There followed guest appearances on shows like *The Golden Shot* and *Celebrity Squares* and then his own show.

In 1983 he launched one of his greatest successes, the Roly Polys. Dawson, with characteristic perversity, got the idea for an obese ladies' dance team while watching an emaciated *ensemble* rehearsing in Brighton. From the moment Dawson introduced them ("Let's hear it for *Les Femmes*"), Mighty Mo and her troupe were a resounding success.

His ability to overcome, even thrive on, tepid audiences and second-rate scripts made him an obvious choice to take over *Blankety-Blank*: he was host of the show from 1984 until his death.

Critical reaction to Dawson's literary *oeuvre* was more varied. *The Malady Lingers On* (1982) followed a path well trodden by Frank Muir and others with its puns on titles and proverbs; the sales were disappointing.

Hitler Was My Mother-In-Law (1982) suffered from the publisher's doomed attempt to woo the *literati* by publishing it first (against its author's wishes) under the title of *The Amy Pluckett Letters*. In a later work, a spoof detective novel, *Well Fared My Lovely*, a woman becomes convinced she is a vacuum cleaner: "She would lie for hours on the landing," Dawson wrote, "humming loudly with the cleaning hose rammed up her rectum. They took her to a mental institution where – although she still thought she was a vacuum cleaner – she started to pick up better."

Dawson got the idea for *A Time Before Genesis* while

studying Buddhism on a visit to Hong Kong in 1976. His interest in fate and eastern religions was intensified by the loss of his first wife in 1986; her death from cancer devastated him.

Although he had served a traditional apprenticeship on the Northern club circuit of the 1950s and 1960s, Dawson's humour had a degree of *largesse* not normally expected of a stand-up comic: he managed to maintain an "honest vulgarity" in an age when audiences were increasingly becoming attracted to comedians content to rely on the humour of obscenity or racial abuse.

As Arthur Marshall once said: "We could do with more like him."

Dawson is survived by his second wife, Tracy, and their infant daughter.

June 11 1993

VICTOR MADDERN

VICTOR MADDERN, the character actor who has died aged 67, had one of the most distinctive and eloquent faces in British cinema and television.

Although he was more inclined to scowl than smile, Maddern could deploy an astonishing array of expressions to characterise the heartfelt privations of the regular Cockney private soldier, the below-decks able seaman, the harassed petty crook or the average member of the British worker or – as in the case of *I'm All Right Jack* – shirker.

Heavily lined, with a prominent jaw, brooding forehead, wary eyes and ruffled hair, the Maddern visage could express yeomanlike devotion and a disciplined respect for authority (particularly if Trevor Howard's old soldier was giving the orders) yet still indicate the presence of rumbling discontent, which on occasion broke out in unequivocal insubordination.

Not that Maddern's characters always lacked official authority. Promoted sergeant major in *Cockleshell Heroes* (1955), he licked a platoon of despised conscripts into shape. But generally he was more endearing as a grumbler than as a shouter.

Inevitably Maddern was typecast. But he was able to turn each trusty or dubious minion, whether in or out of uniform, jaunty or sly, into a lively and credible persona.

Maddern knew that a skilled and reliable character actor led a busy and varied life and he rarely sought leading parts, except occasionally in the theatre. As a result he remained almost constantly in work, acting in some 200 feature films.

A short, stocky figure, he was renowned for his forthright personality. During the filming of the television series *Dixon of Dock Green*, Maddern fluffed several lines while on camera.

Given the words "It's down at Dock Green nick" he came out with: "It's down at Dick Green Dock." Trying to correct himself he then said: "It's down at Dock Green Dick."

Exasperated, Maddern eventually cried out: "Who writes these bloody scripts? Can't I just say 'down at the nick'? Fuck Dock Green!"

Born in Essex, on March 16 1926, Victor Jack Maddern joined the Merchant Navy at 15 and served in the Second World War from 1943 until medically discharged in 1946. He subsequently trained for the stage at RADA.

Maddern made his first screen appearance in *Seven Days To Noon* (1950), playing a reluctant soldier obliged to shoot a psychotic scientist. In *Time Bomb* (1952) he found himself handcuffed to a trainload of high explosive, and in *Street of Shadows* (1953) – which had distinct echoes of Graham Greene's *Brighton Rock* – he played a dithering, friendless, small-time crook, fearful both of his own gang and Scotland Yard.

Maddern also made memorable appearances in *Private's Progress* (1959) and *I'm All Right Jack* (1959), both acclaimed farces by the Boulting brothers. The latter remains a classic satire on the relationship between British industry and the trade unions.

Among his many other films were *Angels One Five, The Sea Shall Not Have Them, A Hill in Korea, Barnacle Bill* and *Carve Her Name With Pride*.

One of his earliest stage roles was Sam Weller in *The Trial of Mr Pickwick* (1952). As Helicon in Albert Camus's *Caligula* (1964) Maddern was singled out for critical praise, and in *My Darling Daisy* (1970) he brought a fine cockney bravado and arrogance to his portrait of the notorious Frank Harris. He also did two stints in *The Mousetrap*, the West End's longest-running play.

Among his television roles were Private Gross in Denis Cannan's *Captain Carvallo*; a self-deluding, habitual criminal in the *Unknown Citizen*; and old Lampwick's son-in-law in *The Dick Emery Show*.

In addition to acting, Maddern ran a printing business and in 1991 opened a public speaking school. A lifelong Conservative voter, he offered special rates to Conservative MPs and constituency workers.

After a mailshot by Conservative Central Office he

reported a flood of interest for these cut-price "Victor Maddern Scholarships". "Politicians are like actors," he noted. "They have inferiority complexes."

In recent years Maddern devoted much of his time to charitable work.

He was married, and had four daughters.

June 24 1993

PAUL CORCELLET

PAUL CORCELLET, the Paris *épicier* who has died aged 83, made a career of introducing French palates to gastronomic exotica – and even erotica – from far-flung corners of the globe.

Ahead of his time, Corcellet brought the avocado pear to Paris as early as 1934. Like Sir Walter Raleigh's potato, it remained a curiosity for years before booming into ubiquity.

In another prescient coup, Corcellet began importing the kiwi fruit to France in the early 1970s. Notwithstanding its paltry flavour, its eye-catching cross-section and pretty green colour soon made it a vital ingredient in the repertoire of the *nouvelle cuisine*.

Strange fauna were as much a feature of his culinary mission as unusual flora. Corcellet offered his sensation-seeking clientele such wonders as alligator tails, song birds in aspic and chocolate-covered termites.

One of his specialities was python. He would take delivery of whole live snakes and butcher them himself on the premises. His preferred treatment was to marinate the flesh in wine vinegar, dust it with flour, then stew it in a *sauteuse* with shallots, onions, tomatoes, white wine and a pimento or two to "bring out the flavour".

Descended from a line of French grocers, Paul Corcellet was born in 1910. Jean-Pierre Corcellet, the founder of the dynasty, had a fashionable shop in the Palais Royal where, according to legend, Josephine de Beauharnais first met Napoleon Bonaparte. Both, it was said, had gone there to buy coffee.

Corcellet liked to trace the family taste for exotica to the Siege of Paris in 1870, when famished Parisians made a virtue of necessity and explored the culinary possibilities offered by the animals in the Jardin des Plantes. Elephant trunk was served with a classic *sauce chasseur*.

After the Second World War Corcellet opened a small shop on the rue des Petits Champs, between the Palais Royal and the Opera, at a time when international air freight was expanding cultural horizons. But few can have explored the new world of culinary possibilities with more vigour or enthusiasm than Corcellet.

In the 1950s he was among the first grocers in France to experiment with frozen food. He approved of the results, and in future when a particular product was unavailable fresh he always preferred the frozen product to anything in a tin. Just before it finally closed in 1989, Corcellet's emporium was selling 42 kinds of mustard, 27 kinds of vinegar.

This was in addition to a variety of dishes to excite the animosity of conservationists, such as elephant's trunk, smoked boa constrictor, monkey in wine sauce and stewed bears' feet (which are reckoned by the Russians to have potent aphrodisiac qualities).

In 1986 the gastronomic critic, Henri Viard, published a biography: *Paul Corcellet or the Spices of Life*.

Celine, Corcellet's daughter, continues the family tradition in the south of France, selling condiments at her shop in Tamaris-sur-Mer in the Var region.

July 15 1993

ANNE CUMMING

ANNE CUMMING, who has died in London aged 75, was a sexual adventuress who wrote two erotic travelogues and in 1992 appeared topless in the *Sunday Sport* newspaper under the headline "Stunnagran!"

Cumming dressed conservatively and with style. But her conversation and behaviour were shocking. A fellow guest at a dinner party fainted when Cumming described to him in detail a sex-change operation she had attended in Casablanca.

Her candour was usually laced with wit. Asked why she had written her memoirs, she replied: "What can an old pensioner do to get by? Either take in laundry – or do your dirty washing in public."

Cumming said that she had slept with several hundred men. Her first memoir, *The Love Habit* (1977), detailed her exploits in the late 1960s and 1970s, which included a string of affairs with teenaged boys in New York. The *News of the World* bought the rights to the memoir and dubbed Cumming the "Randy Granny".

The Love Quest (1991), which chronicled Cumming's life from 1950 to 1965, was if anything more explicit.

Cumming told how she blazed a trail through Europe and North Africa, and had one sexual encounter on horseback while galloping round the Sphinx.

She spent her first night in Rabat with a professional bicyclist: "All I can remember about him," she wrote, "was his remarkable muscle tone and his beautiful strong thighs . . . I like a man from the waist down."

Feeding such an appetite was hard work. Cumming recalled a night in Paris when she stood on the street dressed only in a mink coat and fluffy slippers, baring her body to passing men. No one stopped.

A granddaughter of Grimble Groves, a Conservative MP and brewery owner, Felicity Anne Cumming was born on December 14 1917 at Walton-on-Thames, Surrey. She spent much of her childhood on a farm in South Africa, but was educated at Horsely Towers, Kent, and at finishing schools in Germany and Switzreland.

She studied drama at the Old Vic and at Dartington Hall, where she met her first husband, Henry Lyon Young. The marriage was dissolved in 1948, and the same year she married and divorced the novelist Richard Mason.

After 10 years' travel Cumming settled in Rome, where she lived for five years with the set designer Beni Montressor before deciding to devote herself to casual love affairs. She also became a respected publicist and dialogue coach in the burgeoning Italian film industry, working on films by Dino di Laurentiis and Federico Fellini, in whose *Roma* and $8\frac{1}{2}$ she also appeared.

In 1979 she moved to New York, where she taught at the Michael Chekhov drama studio.

When Cumming was diagnosed HIV positive seven years ago she stopped sleeping with men, but continued to travel. In her last two years she visited Brazil, Oman, India and Russia.

Her final public appearance, earlier this year, was on a Channel 4 nude chat show, for which she wore only a pearl necklace and drop-earrings.

September 1 1993

FRANK ZAPPA

FRANK ZAPPA, the musician who has died in Los Angeles aged 52, introduced into rock music an electronic fusion of jazz, blues and other forms, notably *avant-garde* classical, as well as elements of dadaistic political theatre.

Subversive and intellectually acute, Zappa declared that he saw "nothing reprehensible in atonal music played over a boogaloo rhythm", nor in "sonic mutilations" borrowed from modern composers. He wanted to make his audience feel that "you just have to run from the room the moment you hear us".

He led some 25 of his own rock bands, and his symphonic, chamber and ballet compositions have been performed around the world. Zappa made his name, though, as the leader of the Mothers of Invention, which existed from 1964 to 1978.

Their concerts were enlivened by such eye-catching props as a stuffed giraffe, a gallows and a box of rotting vegetables. During one show in New York, Zappa is said to have persuaded two US Marines to dismember a doll on stage, while he shouted by way of encouragement: "Pretend this is a gook baby."

But Zappa denied that he had ever eaten faeces during a concert. "I never performed this act on stage," he said. "The nearest I ever came to it anywhere was at the Holiday Inn buffet in Fayetteville, North Carolina, in 1973."

Zappa had few hits apart from "Don't Eat the Yellow Snow", the disco parody "Dancin' Fool" and the novelty number "Valley Girls" (in which he mocked the argot of the rich girls of San Fernando Valley). His lasting influence lies in such albums as *Weasels Ripped My Flesh, Chunga's Revenge* and *Hot Rats*.

Zappa's *oeuvre* did not inspire critical consensus. In 1967, when his group collaborated with 10 members of the London Philharmonic, rehearsals were interrupted when one of the string section "became nauseous and wept". But many hailed him as a genius.

Zappa's persona hardly seemed consistent with his professed abstinence from hallucinogens, but he was opposed to drug abuse, citing Flaubert's dictum: "Be regular and orderly in your life so that you may be violent and original in your work."

In the late 1980s Zappa took a strong stand against "rating", the placing of warning stickers on "offensive" pop records. The practice began after Tipper Gore, the wife of Al Gore (now the American Vice-President), bought her daughter a copy of Prince's *Purple Rain* and was horrified by the lyrics.

Zappa addressed the subject in his *Broadway the Hard Way* (1988). He also wrote a letter to Ronald Reagan: "Must all sexual practices in the United States be tested and approved by the Moral Majority? And when they test them, do we get to watch?"

As a token of his political seriousness, he set up voter registration booths in the foyers of venues on a tour of

America that year. More than 11,000 voters were signed up, while Zappa performed reggae versions of Johnny Cash's "Ring of Fire" and Ravel's "Bolero".

Zappa called himself "a devout capitalist", and his politics were fairly conservative, though he thought the essential polarity was "not a matter of conservative versus liberal" but "of fascism versus freedom". In 1990, soon after Czechoslovakia's Velvet Revolution, Zappa was welcomed to Prague by Vaclav Havel, a long-standing admirer.

The fourth child of Sicilian immigrants, Francis Vincent Zappa, Jr, was born at Baltimore, Maryland, on December 21 1940. His father was a metallurgist for the American government, so the family travelled widely around the country.

At 12 he developed a passion for the work of the composer Edgard Varèse; another formative influence was the zany bandleader Spike Jones, who specialised in comic versions of familiar songs.

In 1955 the Zappas moved to Lancaster, California, in the middle of the Mojave Desert, where young Frank attended Antelope Valley High. A classmate there was Don Van Vliet, who grew up to be Captain Beefheart.

On leaving school, Zappa moved to Hollywood, where he worked as art director for a greeting-card company and as an advertising copywriter. In the early 1960s he set up a studio in Cucamonga, California, and was arrested after making "explicit recordings". Convicted of "conspiracy to commit pornography", he spent 10 days in jail. He was also banned from consorting with unaccompanied women under 21.

Zappa moved back to Los Angeles and joined the Soul Giants; in 1964 he changed the group's name to The

Muthers. When MGM gave them a record-contract it objected to their name for its connotations of obscene abuse. "Out of necessity," Zappa said, "we became the Mothers of Invention."

In 1966 the Mothers released *Freak Out!*, a collection of songs which included "Hungry Freaks", "Daddy, Who are the Brain Police?" and "Help I'm a Rock". Their second album, *Absolutely Free* (1967), was cleverer and more complex.

David Jacobs played the group's bizarre anthem "It Can't Happen Here" on the television programme *Juke Box Jury*, where the panel voted the song a unanimous "Miss".

In the same year Zappa was photographed in drag for the *Melody Maker* and played his first concert at the Royal Albert Hall, accompanied by the Mothers of Invention and Suzy Creamcheese, who featured extensively in their lyrics.

In 1967 Zappa became an unlikely icon when he had the idea of posing naked on a lavatory. The resulting poster proved immensely popular.

We're Only In It For The Money (1968) was a satire on psychedelia; the cover was a pastiche of the Beatles' *Sergeant Pepper's Lonely Hearts Club Band*. "I will smoke an awful lot of dope," Zappa recited in a stoned drone. "I will wander around barefoot. I will have a psychedelic gleam in my eye at all times. I will love everyone. I will love the cops as they kick the shit out of me on the street."

In 1970 Zappa produced *Trout Mask Replica*, a double album by Captain Beefheart, recorded during a lull between their frequent feuds. "Zappa is an oaf," said Beefheart.

It was also an *annus mirabilis* for Zappa's own work.

The three albums he recorded that year – *Burnt Weeny Sandwich, Weasles Ripped My Flesh* and *Chunga's Revenge* – all featured a more accessible use of tonality than had been offered by the rather grim *Uncle Meat* (1969).

The next year saw the comic romp *Filmore East, June 1971*, which mixed sagas of sleazy sex over blues-derived vamps and featured the vocalists of the Turtles singing "Happy Together".

But Zappa's most successful record of the period – his personal favourite, and his most popular in Britain – was *Hot Rats*. As well as powerful and elaborate jazz, it included what is probably Zappa's best-known song, "Willy the Pimp" (sung by Beefheart).

Zappa had his ups and downs in Britain. In 1971 he was performing in London when a drunken labourer pushed him off the stage and into the pit. Zappa suffered a broken rib, shin and tibia, and a crushed larynx, which caused the pitch of his voice to drop permanently by a third. "Having a low voice is nice," Zappa said, "but I would have preferred some other way of acquiring it."

In 1975 Zappa sued the Crown in an attempt to recover expenses incurred when the Royal Albert Hall had abruptly cancelled a Mothers performance on the grounds that Zappa's lyrics were potentially obscene. Mr Justice Mocatta was required to listen to a number of Zappa's records at the Old Bailey, which he did with his head in his hands, complaining that he could not hear the lyrics.

Zappa's case rested on his claim that he could have altered the offending lines if given the chance. Accordingly, the court allowed him five minutes to make some impromptu amendments. The line: "The places that she goes/Are filled with guys from groups" was changed to "The places she goes are filled with guys from Pudsey."

"Pudsey?" enquired Alan Campbell, QC. "Pudsey? Where is Pudsey?" Mocatta (a member of MCC) interjected: "Pudsey is in Yorkshire. It is the home of many a famous cricketer."

The Daily Telegraph published an editorial about the affair, complaining of "*soi-disant* art, wholly preoccupied with the visceral, anal and genital functions. It has happened in London before, in the reign of Charles II and also in the Berlin of the Weimar Republic."

Zappa was unfazed. "I don't dislike individual Britons," he said, "but the British Isles does not feature high on the list of places where I feel comfortable or wanted."

In the 1970s Zappa tended increasingly to collaborate with classical musicians – he had earlier claimed that *Cruising with Ruben and the Jets* (1968), his pastiche of 1950s doo-wop songs, was "conceived along the same lines as the compositions in Stravinsky's neoclassical period".

The soundtrack to his film *200 Motels* (1971) was scored for "a chorus of 48, an orchestra [the LA Philharmonic], 11 dancers, four mimes and a dwarf". Tony Palmer, the film's director, said it was "a total waste of money".

After a number of successful albums, including *Overnite Sensation* (1973) and *Bongo Fury* (with Beefheart, 1975), Zappa disbanded the Mothers in 1976 and declared that future projects would be released under his name; a protracted series of legal wrangles ensued.

He eventually set up his own label, Barking Pumpkin Records, which – like his Honker Home Video concern – operated under the aegis of his parent company, Intercontinental Absurdities.

In 1983 Zappa released some recordings with the London Symphony Orchestra and was commissioned by

Pierre Boulez to write for his *Ensemble Inter-contemporain*. But Zappa was disillusioned with musicians, and came to prefer computers capable of "sampling" pre-recorded sounds.

Just before Christmas 1984, Zappa, who was a master of the electric guitar, announced that he had retired from playing the instrument in public. "Machines don't get loaded, drunk or evicted," Zappa said. "They don't need assistance moving their families around in 'emergency situations'. Digital technology is making it possible to do away with these people. I'm hoping that in the future I can just go into my studio, push a button, get it played right and not have to put up with bullshit from someone in a tuxedo."

By the end of his life Zappa was working up to 14 hours a day (or night – he became almost wholly nocturnal) in the Utility Muffin Research Kitchen, his state-of-the-art recording studio at his house in Laurel Canyon. His puppet ballets – *Sinister Footwear, Sad Jane* and *Bob in Dacron* – have been performed in San Francisco.

In 1967, having dissolved an earlier marriage to a bank clerk, Zappa married Adelaide Gail Sloatman; they had two sons and two daughters, whom they named Moon Unit, Diva, Ahmet and Dweezil.

December 7 1993

THE REVEREND NORMAN VINCENT PEALE

THE REVEREND NORMAN VINCENT PEALE, the American pastor and relentless advocate of "positive thinking", who has died at Pawling, New York State, aged 95, was spiritual adviser to President Nixon.

The plump, owlish Peale was a familiar figure at the White House during the Nixon administration, and not just to conduct religious services. In 1969 the President sent him to Vietnam as a special envoy.

Shortly before Nixon took office Peale officiated at the wedding of Julie Nixon to David Eisenhower at the Dutch Reformed Marble Collegiate Church in New York – where he had increased the congregation during his long tenure from a few hundred to more than 5,000.

Peale declined to comment on the moral implications of the Watergate scandals but defended his continued White House visits by pointing out that "Christ didn't shy away from people in trouble".

The preacher had earlier found himself in hot water over his intervention in the religious aspects of the 1960 presidential campaign when he claimed that the election of John F. Kennedy, Nixon's Roman Catholic opponent, would "place extreme pressure on the Church hierarchy".

Peale's supporters compared him to St Paul, prompting Adlai Stevenson to quip: "I find Paul appealing, but Peale appalling".

Other critics complained of Peale's gross oversimplifications and corny huckstering. His message was attacked

as moral pragmatism that watered down traditional doc-
trines of Protestantism and stresssd the materialistic
rewards of religion: "Lord, fill me with enthusiasm for my
product", he told the salesmen to pray in his film *How to
Raise Your Batting Average in Selling*.

But the minister's appeal through such organs as
Reader's Digest, regular television programmes and a steady
flow of books was enormous. The sales of his best-known
publication, *The Power of Positive Thinking* (1952), ranked
below only The Bible and Charles M. Sheldon's novel *In
His Steps* in the American list of "all-time inspirational
best-sellers". It topped the American non-fiction best-
seller charts for nearly two years, and by the time of
Peale's death had sold nearly 20 million copies in 41
languages.

Under chapter headings such as "I Don't Believe in
Defeat", "How to Get People to Like You" and "Expect
the Best and Get It", Peale presented a homely guide to
inner peace. The book is filled with "psycho-spiritual"
advice that made salvation a kind of do-it-yourself project.

Samples of Peale's practical philosophy included "Con-
ceive of yourself as a jelly-fish, getting your body into
complete looseness" and the regular ritual of saying aloud
while shaving: "I believe this is going to be wonderful
day. I believe I can successfully handle all problems . . ."

Peale expressed his formula as "prayerise, picturise,
actualise and pasteurise". He was fond of citing "before-
and-after" case histories of people who had followed such
advice with good results.

There was the despondent businessman who kept
repeating a Bible verse until he could "square his shoulders
and walk out into the night"; the high jumper who made
it after he was told "throw your heart over the bar and

your body will follow"; and the woman who could not find a husband because she was too domineering ("You have a very firm way of pressing your lips together . . .", Peale told her. "Perhaps it might help to get your hair fixed a little").

One of Peale's regular outlets was an agony column in *Look* magazine, although as far as he was concerned Freud appeared to have lived in vain. To a mother troubled because her teenage son kept pin-up girls on the wall, Peale wrote: "Ask the sports celebrities to autograph photographs for him. He will shift to manly interests and away from the so-called glamour cuties. Give him a beautiful picture of his mother for his wall."

Peale said that his own life proved true a central tenet of his teaching: "Do the best you can with what you have and you'll go far."

Norman Vincent Peale was born on May 31 1898, the son of a former physician who had become the Methodist pastor in the rural Ohio town of Bowersville.

"I thank God and my parents," Peale junior used to say, "that I was born in a beautiful little American village where love of God and country and Christian morality were practised by sturdy people who were indeed the salt of the earth."

One Christmas Eve, young Norman was stopped by a tramp, whom he shrugged aside. But his father made him go back and present the old man with a dollar together with the words: "Sir, I wish you a merry Christmas, in the name of our Blessed Saviour the Lord Jesus Christ".

"So," Peale recalled, "I ran after the man and repeated those words to him. He took off his battered hat, made a sweeping bow, and said: 'Young sir, I accept the gift of a dollar in the name of our blessed Lord Jesus Christ.'

"In the streetcar rumbling up Gilbert Avenue, I said: 'Dad, he gave me the most wonderful smile; I don't think I'll ever forget it. He is a gentleman.' Father said: 'He may be living a bum life. But he is a child of God. Never forget that.'"

Peale was educated at Bellefontaine High School, where he had "the worst inferiority complex of all". He was inspired by his fifth grade teacher George Reeves, who would write the word CAN'T on the blackboard, so that the children could chant, "Knock the T off the CAN'T".

Peale went on to study at Ohio Wesleyan University and began his career as a reporter on the *Morning Republican* and the *Detroit Journal*. While covering an apartment fire, he succeeded in persuading a scared child to move off a ledge, and an attendant policeman told Peale that he should be a preacher.

Soon afterwards Peale enrolled at Boston University's School of Theology. He was subsequently ordained into the Methodist Episcopal Church.

Through his individual style of preaching – he would begin by beaming silently in the pulpit, "just loving the audience", and then raise his voice, cut it to a whisper, laugh one moment, exude sincerity the next – Peale quickly made a name for himself during his ministries at Brooklyn and Syracuse.

Then, in 1932, he began his ministry at the Dutch Reformed Marble Collegiate Church in the heart of Manhattan. Soon people were queuing around the block to hear his Sunday sermons.

In 1938 Peale established a pioneering clinic in the crypt of the church with a resident psychiatrist. It developed into a thriving concern with more than a score of doctors and ministers.

Peale was one of America's first religious leaders to recognise the potential of the mass media; as early as the mid-1920s he had his own radio programme, *The Angelus Hour*, and by the mid-1930s he had launched his weekly multi-networked NBC show, *The Art of Living*. This was broadcast for 54 years on NBC. Copies of his sermons were mailed to 750,000 people each month.

His first book was entitled *The Art of Living* and 40-odd others followed, including *A Guide to Confident Living* (his first best-seller, in 1948); *Stay Alive All Your Life*; *Sin, Sex and Self-Control*; and *You Can If You Think You Can*.

In 1945 Peale and his wife, the former Ruth Stafford, started *Guideposts* magazine, which acquired a circulation of five million. Mrs Peale was president of the Foundation for Christian Living.

The Peales would throw grape-juice get-togethers at their farmhouse, furnished with Norwegian antiques, and holiday in Switzerland – "there's nothing so peaceful as going to sleep to the mellifluous sound of mountain cowbells," he would say.

When Peale retired from his ministry in Manhattan in 1984 President Reagan awarded him the Presidential Medal of Freedom. Peale kept busy well into his tenth decade and until a year or so ago would speak to an average of 100 business and civic groups a year.

A folksy character, Peale always found time in his hectic schedule to watch the *Roy Rogers* show on television. He had a son and two daughters.

Peale's life story was told in the Hollywood film *One Man's Way* (1963) with Don Murray taking the role of the tireless zealot.

December 27 1993

EDWARD DUKE

EDWARD DUKE, the actor who has died aged 40, made his name in the brilliant and enchanting one-man show *Jeeves Takes Charge*, for which he won the Laurence Olivier award as the most promising West End actor of 1980.

A tall, dark, slim and stately figure of considerable poise, Duke brought to his acting an assured command of pre-war manners and a subtly satirical air of self-satisfaction. This served him particularly well in the comedies of Noël Coward and in his adaptation of P. G. Wodehouse's Jeeves and Wooster stories.

Far from being simply a recitation, *Jeeves Takes Charge* was the liveliest kind of theatre. Duke affected a monocle for Wooster, a straight face for Jeeves and assorted voices for the aunts. His Gussie Fink-Nottle was wonderfully successful, and *The Daily Telegraph*'s Eric Shorter took a particular shine to the Mainwaring schoolgirl to whom Bertie unwarily gave a lift.

Duke's theatrical achievement, said Shorter, was to have organised his material "into such a nifty order that there is hardly any time for a snifter as he nips between Brinkley Court and Market Snodsbury, mainly at Aunt Dahlia's beck and call".

The show had started life as a lunchtime entertainment in a room above a pub in Putney before going to the Lyric Studio, Hammersmith, and then to the West End (Fortune and Wyndhams), where it was nominated as the best comedy performance of the year. It subsequently toured extensively, gaining a Drama Desk nomination in New York, Best Actor awards in Boston and San Francisco, a

Helen Hayes nomination in Washington and the Golden Chopsticks Award in Taiwan.

Duke also performed *Jeeves Takes Charge* privately for Queen Elizabeth the Queen Mother (a staunch Wodehouse fan) and at the 1992 Chichester Festival.

The next year he returned to Chichester in Coward's *Relative Values*, bringing characteristic comic resource, timing and authority to the seemingly unpromising role of a countess's confidant. He went on tour in the part but was too ill to join the cast in the transfer to the Savoy Theatre.

A diplomat's son, Edward Duke was born at Rudgwick, Sussex, on June 17 1953 and educated at Stonyhurst and the American High School in Tokyo, where he watched Kabuki drama from backstage. He studied drama at the Arts Educational Trust, and spent seasons in repertory at Windsor, Cheltenham and Lancaster.

Duke's first West End appearance was in the farce *Why Not Stay For Breakfast?* at the Apollo in 1973; he played a hippy living in the flat above Derek Nimmo, whom he understudied in the lead.

He was also in the Keith Waterhouse-Willis Hall adaptation of Eduardo de Filippo's *Filumena* at the National Theatre in 1977, and in the musical *Peg O' My Heart* at the Phoenix in 1984.

For much of the 1980s Duke worked in America, where he appeared in *Gilbert and Sullivan* (Kennedy Centre, Washington), as Elyot in *Private Lives* (Pacific Conservatory of the Performing Arts), as Ponce de Leon and Davy Crockett (in Shelley Duvall's Faerie Tale Theatre Series on cable television) and in *The Foreigner* (San Francisco).

On his return to England in 1990 he was in the

Aldwych revival of Coward's *Private Lives*, playing Victor opposite Joan Collins's Amanda. The production subsequently went to Broadway.

Duke was Hugh Loring in Pinero's *Preserving Mr Panmure* at the 1991 Chichester Festival and Merlin in *Chambers of Glass* at the Minerva, before returning to the West End as Ferdinand Gadd opposite Michael Hordern in Pinero's *Trelawney of the Wells* (Comedy 1992).

Duke wrote *A Marvellous Party*, a one-man show based on the life of Noël Coward. His television credits included *Sweet Wine of Youth*, *The Bretts*, the *Kenny Everett Show* and Coward's *Tonight at 8.30*.

Among the films he appeared in were *The French Lieutenant's Woman*, *Invitation to the Wedding* and *Decadence* (with Steven Berkoff and his great friend Joan Collins).

He was unmarried.

January 11 1994

DONALD SWANN

DONALD SWANN, the composer and entertainer who has died aged 70, was the musical and comedy partner of the late Michael Flanders; in their revues they epitomised English nonsense humour in the good-natured tradition of *Punch*.

Flanders's lyrics – whether about London omnibuses, gasmen or animals – were usually satirical but never bitter or heavy-handed. Swann's sprightly melodies, which he played with an admirable touch on the piano, were larded with musical jokes.

The Hippopotamus Song, with its chorus "Mud, mud,

glorious mud", was their most celebrated number and was translated into 18 languages; Swann himself sometimes sang the chorus in Russian.

Two of their revues – *At the Drop of a Hat* (from 1957) and *At the Drop of Another Hat* (from 1963) – enjoyed long runs in the West End and New York and toured around the world. Flanders' confinement to a wheelchair meant that the whole performance was delivered from a sitting position; there were no special effects, and nothing but Swann's piano and a lamp-stand for props. The entertainment rested on the songs, Flanders' monologues and the comic rapport between the pair. Swann appeared as the boyish subordinate who would listen with lively interest while his partner conversed with the audience, and then occasionally go "slightly berserk" as he tried to hog the stage with a turn at the piano.

"It is an astonishing entertainment," commented W. A. Darlington in *The Daily Telegraph*. "When the curtain rises, your natural reaction is to wonder how they will keep things going for the whole evening. But once their insidious brand of lunacy gets hold of you, you believe they might easily keep things going for a week if they wanted."

Swann was not only musically inventive and dexterous but also accomplished the rare feat of listening in an entertaining fashion. "Sometimes", Darlington noted, "he will sit quiet with quick darts of head and eyes which remind me of a big bird on a perch. Sometimes he will give a sudden plunge of restrained ecstasy as one of his partner's shafts strikes home. Sometimes he merely looks interested, but he never goes out of the picture or fails to contribute to it."

Though Swann collaborated with a number of other

artistes, the music he wrote without Flanders never enjoyed the same popular acclaim. Many of his compositions reflected both his Christian beliefs and his desire to modernise church music. These included an opera, *Perelandra* (after C. S. Lewis's allegorical story *Festival Matins*) and three books of new carols. But Swann's serious work was criticised for lacking "musical personality" and "initiative".

His sincerity was not in doubt, though. Swann was a lively participant in Church affairs, and in 1964 delivered a sermon in St Paul's Cathedral in which he claimed that satire and song could cleanse the soul from the dreariness of ordinary living. He also participated in religious programmes on radio and television. Towards the end of his life he joined the Society of Friends.

Donald Ibrahim Swann was born at Llanelli on September 30 1923. The family history was exotic. Donald's great-grandfather, Alfred Trout Swan, a draper from Lincolnshire, emigrated to Russia in 1840 and married the daughter of the horologer to the Tsars. At some point the Swans acquired a second "n" in their name.

The family, though resolutely English, was deeply involved in St Petersburg musical circles. Alfred's son became a manager in the Russo-American India Rubber company; his son, Herbert (Donald's father), was a medical student at the time of the Russian Revolution and married a Muslim nurse from Ashkahabad. Recruited into the Red Army, at the end of 1919 he escaped with his wife to Britain, where he found a job as an assistant to a doctor in Llanelli.

He then acquired a practice in the Walworth Road in London, so young Donald was raised in the Elephant and Castle. His mother died when he was 11, but he could remember her singing Russian gipsy songs and accompanying herself on the guitar, while his father played the piano. The boy learned both instruments.

He was educated at Westminster, where he met Michael Flanders and first performed in a revue with him; he also studied piano and composition as a special student at the Royal College of Music. Swann went on to read Russian and Modern Greek at Christ Church, Oxford – though his university career was interrupted by the Second World War.

In 1942 he registered as a conscientious objector and joined the Friends' Ambulance Unit. Later he transferred to the Friends' Relief Service and did three years' refugee work in Greece and the Middle East.

After the war he returned to Christ Church and took part in revues and dramatic productions. Shortly before coming down in 1948 he had a song accepted by the producer Laurier Lister. Thus encouraged, he decided to try to earn a living as a composer and accompanist.

Michael Flanders was then freelancing as a lyric writer, and together they began to contribute songs to London revues – among them *Airs on a Shoestring* (1953) and *Fresh Airs* (1956), which won an Ivor Novello award.

Swann did not work exclusively with Flanders, though. He wrote the music for the revue *Pay the Piper* (1954) and collaborated with Philip Guard for the musical play *Wild Thyme* (1955).

His first joint performance with Flanders was in a show at Whistler's Ballroom in Cheyne Walk in 1950. *At the Drop of a Hat* opened at the small New Lindsey Theatre Club in 1956, and Flanders and Swann were amazed at its success.

At first they shunned the offer of transferring to the

larger Fortune Theatre, being more concerned with their burgeoning careers in broadcasting and composing. But after "some 48 to 72 hours of no sleep" they accepted.

At the Drop of a Hat opened at the Fortune in January 1957 and ran for two years. It then transferred briefly to the Edinburgh Festival (under the title *At The Drop Of A Kilt*) before opening in October 1959 in New York, where it ran for seven months. It also toured America from 1960 to 1961, and Britain and Ireland from 1962 to 1963.

At The Drop Of Another Hat opened at the Haymarket in 1963 and later toured Australia, New Zealand and Hong Kong before returning to the Globe in 1965. After taking the show to New York from 1966 to 1967 Flanders and Swann ended their stage partnership – although they remained friends until Flanders' death in 1975.

Even during the *Hat* years Swann never excluded other ventures. In 1958 he set music to some poems by Sebastian Shaw, and performed and recorded them with Shaw in *London Sketches*. He later composed music to the poems of other writers including J. R. R. Tolkien, C. Day Lewis, and John Betjeman.

Under the pseudonym Hilda Tablet he wrote satirical music for the poet Henry Reed for BBC Radio. In addition to church music, his other work included a number of songs and operas written in collaboration with Arthur Scholey.

His concert entertainments after 1967 included *An Evening in Crete, Between The Bars, A Late Night, Swann With Topping* and *Swann Con Moto*.

Swann was a quondam president of the Fellowship Party, a pacifist political organisation, and belonged to a number of other humanitarian and pacifist societies.

He published an autobiography, *Swann's Way*, in 1991.

He married, in 1955 (dissolved 1983), Janet Oxborrow; they had two daughters.

In 1992, already ill with cancer (though the disease was still undiagnosed), he revisited Russia. Early in 1993 he went to the Greek island of Kasos. Confined in a wheelchair at the airport, he remembered his old friend Flanders.

"From this position", Swann reflected, "he wrote all the lyrics which enabled me to pay for this holiday. It heartened me", he concluded, "to think that again he had touched my life. Once more, Flanders, I tip my cap to you."

March 25 1994

KENNETH ROBINSON

KENNETH ROBINSON, who has died aged 68, was for 15 years a controversial contributor to Richard Baker's *Start the Week* programme on BBC Radio.

Robinson reduced Angela Rippon to tears by ridiculing a book she had written, argued fiercely with Esther Rantzen and provoked Pamela Stephenson into tipping a carafe of water down his neck.

In January 1984, during a discussion on a lonely heart agency for invalids, Robinson observed: "You can hear the wheelchairs banging together all night in some parts of the country." "A lot of people will be insulted by that, Kenneth," warned the programme's chairman, Jimmy Hill, "and I think quite rightly." In fact many invalids wrote in to say how much they had enjoyed the joke. Robinson, described as "unusually contrite", apologised and was temporarily suspended.

He could never bridle his savage indignation at cant and hypocrisy, and when he was finally sacked from *Start the Week* in 1986 he did not go quietly. As Richard Baker announced Robinson's impending departure, the victim interrupted: "I'm not going. I'm not going. They have given me three days' notice after so many years. It's a bloody disgrace."

Kenneth John Robinson was born at Ealing on April 26 1925 and educated at Ealing Grammar School. He had inherited his father's talent for the piano, and his first employment was playing for ENSA in the latter part of the Second World War.

At some stage he broke his hand – an accident, he claimed, which improved his talent for syncopation. Nevertheless after the war he eschewed music for journalism, and became the drama critic of the *Croydon Advertiser*. "All the actors in this play", he wrote of one performance, "were shot, poisoned or strangled one by one: it's a pity there are not more plays of this kind available to the public."

Robinson's editor was not amused, and the miscreant moved to *Architect and Building News*, and then became chief assistant editor on *Architects' Journal*. At the same time he was drama critic for the *Church of England Newspaper*.

Branching into new fields, he became chief promotions officer at the Council of Industrial Design, for which he first appeared on television. "Robinson," the director told him, "you are not paid to be funny."

He was always a strong family man, and in 1960 went

freelance so he could enjoy his children's early years. When he succeeded Robert Robinson as presenter of *Points of View* in the early 1960s he introduced his daughter to add her comments. Latterly Anne Robinson has taken over the programme; none of the Robinsons concerned are related.

For ITV Kenneth Robinson was involved with *Magic Box, About Anglia* and *Today* (with Eamonn Andrews). In the mid-1960s he wrote articles on architecture for *The Sunday Telegraph*.

He enjoyed himself in *The Worst of Kenneth Robinson*, a one-man show which he performed at the Mermaid in 1976, repeated three years later at the Westminster Theatre and also presented at the Queen Elizabeth Hall.

The entertainment was partly inspired by his friend Victor Borge. Robinson would turn aside from the keyboard to descant upon such subjects as the awfulness of London architecture or the illiteracy of bureaucrats.

Robinson was a regular contributor to *Punch*, the *Listener, Radio Times, What's On* and *Homes and Gardens*. He published *Not on Your Telly, Kenneth Robinson at Random, Startle the Weak, The Worst of Kenneth Robinson* and *On the Offensive*.

Kenneth Robinson married, in 1955, Mary Hargreaves; they had a son and a daughter.

March 28 1994

ALBERT GOLDMAN

ALBERT GOLDMAN, the American biographer, who has died aged 66, was both applauded and reviled for his lives of Elvis Presley and John Lennon.

Albert Goldman

An academic by background, Goldman spent three years researching his *Elvis* (1981) and he was clearly disgusted by his findings. With a cold eye he charted the pop idol's journey from mother-fixation through pederasty, voyeurism and orgies, to drug addiction, spectacular obesity and incontinence.

He followed this with *The Lives of John Lennon* (1988), from which Lennon emerged as similarly mad and damaged – a pervert, a drug addict, even a murderer.

Goldman's books annoyed many not so much because of the dirt they dished but because they ignored the obvious talents of Presley and Lennon and presented their celebrity as a mass delusion. Both books were also badly written and full of dubious critical assertions.

The fury they provoked caused their author to fear for his life. Goldman lived in Manhattan, in an apartment close to the Dakota Building, outside which Lennon had been assassinated. One day he claimed to have found a bullet-hole in the window at head level.

Goldman suspected the hand of Presley fans, but the New York Police Department was unimpressed. He was so frightened of repercussions from the Lennon book that he cancelled a promotional visit to London.

Goldman looked like Truman Capote and sounded like Bette Davis. He was not a modest man: "With the counter-culture", he declared, "I had found a great field that needed a great mind like mine to explore it."

Albert Goldman was born in 1927 at Mount Lebanon, Pennsylvania, and educated at Columbia University, New York. There he wrote a doctoral thesis on the 18th century writer Thomas De Quincey, to whose vice of opium addiction (which he himself had documented extensively) Goldman added that of plagiarism.

From 1952 he taught at Columbia, and later in that decade became music critic of the *New Leader*, writing about classical and jazz music. He discovered "the counter-culture" in the mid-1960s, when he coined a much quoted description of the Rolling Stones as "sado-homosexual-diabolic-sarcastic-nigger-evil".

In 1974 Goldman published his first biography, *Ladies and Gentlemen, Lenny Bruce*, which anticipated some of the sleaze of his later efforts in the genre.

At the time of his death Goldman was reported to be working on a life of Jim Morrison, the lead singer of the Doors.

He died of a heart attack in an airliner over the Atlantic after an argument concerning what he insisted was his right to have his seat "upgraded".

March 31 1994

INDEX